THE STRUCTURE OF A MODERN ECONOMY

Also by Kenneth E. Boulding

BEASTS, BALLADS AND BOULDINGISMS
BEYOND ECONOMICS
COLLECTED PAPERS: VOLUMES I–VI
CONFLICT AND DEFENSE
DISARMAMENT AND THE ECONOMY (*edited with Emile Benoit*)
ECODYNAMICS
ECONOMIC ANALYSIS
ECONOMIC IMPERIALISM (*edited with Tapan Mukerjee*)
ECONOMICS AS A SCIENCE
THE ECONOMICS OF HUMAN BETTERMENT (*editor*)
THE ECONOMICS OF PEACE
THE ECONOMY OF LOVE AND FEAR
EVOLUTIONARY ECONOMICS
HUMAN BETTERMENT
THE IMAGE
THE IMPACT OF THE SOCIAL SCIENCES
LINEAR PROGRAMMING AND THE THEORY OF THE FIRM (*edited with
    W. Allen Spivey*)
THE MEANING OF THE TWENTIETH CENTURY
THE OPTIMUM UTILIZATION OF KNOWLEDGE (*edited with Lawrence
    Senesh*)
THE ORGANIZATIONAL REVOLUTION
PEACE AND THE WAR INDUSTRY (*editor*)
A PREFACE TO GRANTS ECONOMICS
A PRIMER ON SOCIAL DYNAMICS
PRINCIPLES OF ECONOMIC POLICY
THE PROSPERING OF TRUTH
READINGS IN PRICE THEORY: VOLUME VI (*edited with George J. Stigler*)
A RECONSTRUCTION OF ECONOMICS
REDISTRIBUTION THROUGH THE FINANCIAL SYSTEM (*edited with
    Thomas F. Wilson*)
REDISTRIBUTION TO THE RICH AND THE POOR (*edited with Martin
    Pfaff*)
THE SKILLS OF THE ECONOMIST
THE SOCIAL SYSTEM OF THE PLANET EARTH (*with Elise Boulding and
    Guy M. Burgess*)
STABLE PEACE
THREE FACES OF POWER
TOWARDS A NEW ECONOMICS
TRANSFERS IN AN URBANIZED ECONOMY (*edited with Martin and Anita
    Pfaff*)
THE WORLD AS A TOTAL SYSTEM

The Structure of a Modern Economy

The United States, 1929–89

Kenneth E. Boulding
sometime Distinguished Professor of Economics, Emeritus
University of Colorado at Boulder

with the assistance of Meng Chi

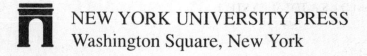

NEW YORK UNIVERSITY PRESS
Washington Square, New York

First published in the U.S.A. in 1993 by
NEW YORK UNIVERSITY PRESS
Washington Square
New York, N. Y. 10003

Reprinted 1994

Library of Congress Cataloging-in-Publication Data
Boulding, Kenneth Ewart, 1910–93
The structure of a modern economy : the United States, 1929–89 /
by Kenneth E. Boulding; with the assistance of Meng Chi.
p. cm.
Includes index.
ISBN 0–8147–1203–7
1. United States—Economic conditions—1918–1945. 2. United
States—Economic conditions—1945– 3. National income—United
States—Accounting. 4. Time-series analysis. I. Title.
HC106.B6883 1993
330.973'09—dc20 92–26913
CIP

Printed in Great Britain

Contents

List of Figures and Tables

Unless stated otherwise, all figures are for the United States and all dates are for 1929–89.

Figures

Tables

Abbreviations

COMER Committee on Monetary and Economic Reform
GATT   General Agreement on Tariffs and Trade
GCP   Gross Capacity Product
GNP   Gross National Product
GPDI   Gross Private Domestic Investment
ISEW   Index of Substainable Economic Welfare
MMMF   Money Market Mutual Fund
NCP   Net Capacity Product
NNP   Net National Product
NPDI   Net Private Domestic Investment
OPEC   Organisation of Petroleum Exporting Countries
PCE   Personal Consumption Expenditures
PIG   Profit and Interest Gap

Preface

Important aids to the development of human knowledge are careful records of the positions of a system over time, the study of which may reveal patterns amd relationships that otherwise would not be perceived. A classic example of this is the work carried out by Tycho Brahe (1546–1601) and Johann Kepler (1571–1630). For more than 20 years Tycho Brahe, a Danish astronomer supported by the Danish king, made the most careful records of the movement of the planets and the sun and moon that had ever been undertaken, and this without the aid of a telescope. He moved to Prague in 1597 and was joined by a young assistant from Germany, Johann Kepler, who later deduced from Tycho Brahe's records his three famous laws of planetary motion around the sun.

Something a little like the Brahe–Kepler process is happening in economics. Time series in economics go back at least as far as Sir William Petty (1623–87) for individual prices, which were used to a small extent by Adam Smith in *The Wealth of Nations*. It was not however until the development of national income statistics around 1929, largely under the inspiration of Simon Kuznets (1901–85), that what might be called the 'Brahe effect' of the continuous record over time of the major variables for an economic system as a whole became significant. We now have more than 60 years of national income statistics and their various components and supplements, such as figures on unemployment and the labour force, price levels, relative prices and so on. What might be called a 'Kepler effect', the use of these data to detect previously unrecognised relationships among economic variables, has lagged behind. The mathematisation of economics goes back, of course, to Cournot, Jevons and Walras in the 19th century, but the results have been disappointing, perhaps because of the 18th-century celestial mechanics type of mathematics that has generally been used. Deterministic dynamic mathematical models are often inappropriate to the structural and topological complexities of an economic system, and particularly to the instability of its fundamental parameters. If the planets had been moved by angels who didn't like astronomers, Keplerian and Newtonian celestial mechanics would have been quite inappropriate. Deterministic models are unsuitable for systems in which information is an essential element, as it is in the economic system, for information by its very definition has to be surprising. There is indeed a non-existence theorem about exact prediction in such systems. What we have to look for is persistent patterns in a world of changing parameters. To do this, a more topological analysis is needed rather than the numerical analysis which has hitherto dominated econometrics and statistics.

This book is a tentative step towards an interpretation of the record in terms of topological patterns represented by a variety of graphs, from which it is clear that 'regions of time' emerge, and that at the boundaries of these regions the system changes, something which does not happen in celestial mechanics. The conclusions which emerge are less secure than the conclusions derived from simple and deterministic systems. Nevertheless they can have evidence brought to bear on them which perhaps can at least expose some of the simplistic fallacies of more conventional economic theory.

The type of long-term topological analysis on which this book is based reveals some striking properties of the American economy which conventional economics and econometrics have tended to miss. One is the extraordinary nature of the disturbances to the economy produced by the Great Depression, the Second World War and the 'great disarmament' of 1945–7, followed by an almost equally surprising recovery and stability from the late 1940s onwards. Another striking property of the economy that emerges is the relative insignificance of the federal government, even in the period of the New Deal. The data also suggest the unexpected effects of governmental action. During the New Deal period after 1933, the great rise in the labour movement was accompanied by a sharp decline in the proportion of labour income going to labour, illustrating the principle that it is very dangerous to generalise about the macro economy from observations of the micro. A third striking phenomenon which emerges is the strong relationship between what I have called the 'profit–interest gap', as measured by the proportion of corporate profit to corporate profit plus interest as percentages of national income. This seems to be more closely related to the level of unemployment than any other characteristic of the system and has been completely neglected by mainstream economics. This relationship makes the erosion of profit by interest which we have seen since 1950 somewhat ominous.

This book is a product of some 20 years' work. It would never have been produced without a series of dedicated graduate assistants: Dr Guy M. Burgess, Dr Rich Ling, Dr Edward H. Lyell, Dr Dennis

Miller and Dr Jamel Zarrouk, to all of whom I owe a great debt of gratitude. I am particularly indebted to my latest assistant, Dr Meng Chi, without whose computer graphics skills this work would never have seen the light of day. I am also greatly indebted to my administrative assistant, Mrs Vivian Wilson, whose patient work and criticism have contributed a great deal to this volume.

There are some important aspects of the American economy that I have not been able to cover, partly because of the absence of data, especially in regard to capital structures, and partly because of insufficient time and resources. I am sensitive to the fact that the volume is incomplete. There is much more work to be done along this line of research and thinking. I hope, however, that this work will stimulate others to continue the processes which have produced it.

KENNETH E. BOULDING

Publishers' Note: After the text of this book had been passed for press, Kenneth E. Boulding died in Boulder, Colorado, on 19 March 1993 at the age of 83.

1 The Structure of an Economy

Any economy is a segment or subset of a larger system. The United States economy is a segment of the world economy, the world economy is a segment of the total system of Planet Earth. Any system, however large or however small, has two aspects involved in its description: one, its structure in space at a moment of time; the other, its structure in space and time. First we have to describe the system at a moment of time. This might be called a flashlight photograph or a single frame of a movie. The world globe provides a good example. The globe will show coastlines and oceans. It may also show national boundaries, mountains, plains, rivers, lakes and so on. Obviously what can be put on a globe a foot in diameter is a very small part of the reality of the world. Nevertheless it is a place to begin. Even on a small globe we can plot the density of the human population, the broad classification of the uses of land – forests, agriculture and so on – and perhaps give some indication of where the major industries are located. On a one-foot globe we obviously cannot plot the position of every one of the world's 5.2 billion human inhabitants. To do that we would have to have a globe about a mile high, on which each human being could be plotted as a point about one-thousandth of an inch in diameter, a house about one-tenth of an inch in diameter. With the aid of satellites we could probably do this on a flat map about one mile wide and two miles long. On this map we could probably plot just about every tree, although not every blade of grass, and certainly not every mosquito. In our minds, however, we can form some picture of the immensely complicated system that constitutes our world, with interacting and moving objects ranging from quarks to continents.

Suppose we now take our mental map of the world and try to form an image of the world economy. This would consist firstly of all human beings and valuable objects, most of these being human artifacts, but perhaps also things not made by humans, such as trees, beaches, mountains and animals. Economic value is a somewhat elusive concept. It includes all things upon which we can place a monetary (dollar) value and which would appear on balance sheets or

1

other accounts. On the other hand there are many things that do not appear in accounts but which have economic significance and can perhaps be given rough dollar values, such as wilderness areas, beautiful views, rivers and oceans, natural harbours and the human capital embodied in individual persons. There are also the things upon which are placed negative economic values, such as polluted air, streams, rivers and wells; garbage, sewage, toxic waste and weapons; perhaps even foul language and threats. An economy, then, is what mathematicians call a 'fuzzy set'. The boundary that divides what is in the economy from what is not may not always be clear, but this does not mean that it is not real or important.

A flashlight photograph or frame is not enough. All systems involve time as well as space and have to be thought of as patterns in space–time. The simplest way to think of them is as a movie, which is a succession of frames. In a frame, of course, nothing happens. Events and happenings consist of the difference between two or more successive frames. Events may be confined to a nanosecond or they may continue frame after frame for many frames. Some objects, such as protons, do not seem to change or change very, very rarely, except in location. All the objects with which the human race is familiar, however, are subject to constant change. A possible exception might be a diamond, but virtually everything with which we are familiar is born (produced), ages and dies (is consumed). There is a time before which it did not exist, and a later time after which it again does not exist. In between these two dates objects may first grow and then decay. This is the pattern of all living organisms and of most human artifacts, including clothing, houses, automobiles and even books. The question of how something new comes into the world is an interesting one and one that is not always easy to answer. Mountains come into existence through the movement and interaction of the earth's crustal plates. The Rockies and the Alps apparently have only been around for 70–100 million years. They have been eroded by wind, rain and snow, and the sediments resulting from the erosion have formed plains and deltas. Glaciers have dug out cavities that became valleys and mountain lakes.

It is only when we come to living organisms, however, that self-reproduction takes place, beginning with the extraordinary capacity of the DNA molecule to replicate itself and play a fundamental role in the synthesis of the various proteins that are essential to growth and survival. In a matter of hours cells are able to duplicate all their essential constituents and then divide into two identical halves, which then go on to grow and divide again. The DNA in fertilised seeds or eggs contains the 'blueprint' to reconstruct replicas of the organisms from which they came, but with individual characteristics that may have been inherited from either the male or the female parent. All production, whether of a plant from a seed or of a clay pot by a potter, involves the 'know-how' to direct energy of appropriate kinds and information to the selection, transportation and transformation of material into a particular phenotype – a tree, a bird, a cat or a human being – or into a house, a car or a clay pot. Human artifacts originate from human knowledge and know-how which can be passed on to others through the extraordinary capacity of the human race to transmit images from one mind to another through language and symbols, and this process lies behind every clay pot, painting, palace or any other product.

To come back to the economy, we must ask: what are the events that are characteristic of an economy? That is, what changes occur in the pattern or description of an economy between one period of time and the next? The economy shares the properties of virtually all systems in that it consists of objects which are produced, that is, born, which may change over their life, and which then die or are consumed. Economists have had an unfortunate tendency to think that objects die as soon as they are purchased by a household. This is clearly absurd. Household purchases are not the same thing as consumption. A household is just as full of capital (valuable objects) as is a factory or a shopping mall. Production as the creation of a new object however always involves the rearrangement of materials into a new form, which almost inevitably involves the disarrangement of materials in an old form. Flour has to be destroyed in order to be made into bread. Wheat has to be destroyed in order to grind it into flour. A certain amount of soil has to be destroyed in order to grow wheat. Rocks have to be destroyed in order to produce soil. What is destroyed in order to produce something else is often thought of by economists as a 'cost', and this is a concept which we will have to explore further.

An event which is peculiarly characteristic of an economy is exchange, or trade. This is a process of rearrangement of objects or assets among owners. If I buy a car for $10 000, at the beginning of the event I have $10 000 and the seller has the car. After the event I have the car and the seller has $10 000. Most exchanges, especially in more developed societies, have money as one of the things exchanged, although barter is not unknown and many exchanges involve a variety of objects as well as money. Thus when I buy a new car I may trade in my old car, worth say $6000, as well as pay $4000 in cash.

The exchange of promises and contracts is another very important aspect of an economy. A note or a bond is essentially a promise by the issuer to pay specific sums of money on specific dates in the future. A share of stock on the part of an issuer is a promise to pay indefinite sums of money at indefinite dates in the future depending on the enterprise's profits, which will be created and financed by spending the money raised by the sale of the stock. A futures contract is a promise to deliver certain quantities of commodities or financial instruments at some date in the future. A bank deposit of $1000 is a promise by a banker to pay to a depositor, or to anyone who is named on a cheque, any amount that the depositor requests up to $1000 (or even beyond this sum if there is an arrangement for an overdraft) at any date in the future. A cheque is a letter to the banker saying, 'Please pay to the person or institution named on this cheque the sum noted and deduct this sum from what you have promised to pay to me'. The person for whom the cheque has been written may then pay the cheque into his or her account in another bank. By endorsing it for deposit, the person named on the cheque in effect says 'Please pay this sum to my bank account instead of paying it in cash to me'. The second bank may present this to the first bank, saying 'Please pay me the $100'. If this is not offset by cheques drawn on the second bank by customers of the first, the first bank may give the second bank a cheque drawn on its account with the Federal Reserve Bank, and so on.

Cash or legal tender is a promise by all people who recognise the currency to give the owner something in exchange for it that is equal in value to the value of the cash. The willingness of people to do this may ultimately depend on the fact that the government that issued the money is willing to take it in payment of taxes, or will enforce its acceptance as legal tender for all debts, public or private. It is difficult to buy things with Russian rubles in the United States, simply because Russian rubles are legal tender only in Russia. It is clear that any economy involves a great amount of trust – a belief that promises will be fulfilled and so on – which is also an invisible but important part of a capital structure.

Another phenomenon common in economies is wages. A wage contract can be seen as a promise by an employer to an employee, saying 'If you will come and do what I tell you to do for a week or some other period of time, I will owe you a sum of money and pay it to you on a certain date'. If the worker accepts the contract, the worker in effect says 'I will do what you tell me to do', whether this be mowing a lawn, cleaning a house, baking bread, operating a machine, driving a truck or whatever is required.

Rent is another form of exchange, in which the renter says to the owner of an automobile, a tuxedo, a house, a farm or some acres of land, 'If you will let me use what you own for a given period, I will pay you so much money or its equivalent'. If the owner agrees, the renter is allowed the use of the property, usually subject to certain limitations or conditions such as its being returned in good condition, or that it should be used wisely and so on. The renter may or may not subrent the property to someone else, depending on the nature of the contract.

The existence of exchange and the vast variety of exchangeables means that there are many invisible aspects of the economy which are nevertheless very important. These include such things as trust, reputation, skills, knowledge and potential of all kinds. Organisational structures exist mainly in the minds of these who are in some way connected to them. They are often invisible, although evidence for them may exist in the form of constitutions, documents of incorporation or contracts. Organisations are part of the total picture, organisations such as families, firms, local and federal governments, states and foundations, as well as semi-public organisations such as water boards, school boards, churches, fraternal societies and so on. They all have the potential to change and all of them do change. They are born, they have a life history and sometimes they die.

All known systems, except perhaps the universe as a whole – and we cannot be sure of that – are open systems in the sense that they have things coming in and things going out. The earth is an open system with regard to solar energy, which comes in from the sun and is then radiated out from the earth. The earth is more of a closed system with regard to materials, but even here it receives occasional material in the form of meteorites and loses some atmospheric gases into space. It is very much an open system with regard to the information it receives from the universe, mostly in the form of light waves which are radiated back out as reflected light. Mankind now radiates information. Even with just our reflected light an astronomer on Mars could find out a lot about us, and we are now also surrounded by some 60 light-years of radio and television waves.

Changes in the environment of an open system can profoundly affect the system itself. If the sun warms up or cools off, for instance, the effect on the earth may be enormous. In an open system one always has to be sensitive to the nature of the environment of the system from which inputs come and to which outputs go. The world economy, like the earth, is an open system. A national economy like the United States economy is a subset of the world economy, and it is also very much an open system in that goods of all kinds are continually crossing its borders. International trade is an important aspect of border crossings, with exports going out and imports coming in, representing exchange. There is usually money of some sort coming in as payment for exports and money going out as payment for imports. Money and financial instruments also cross borders as foreign investment. Both exports and imports can be bought on credit or paid for with money borrowed by the purchaser, or even by the seller acquiring stock. Ownership can also cross borders: people buy assets in countries where they do not live. If a country has an export surplus, this usually means that its residents are acquiring more assets abroad than people abroad are acquiring from the exporting country. Of course, the value of these assets may be subject to change. Similarly if a country has an import surplus, this suggests that people abroad are acquiring more from within the country than people within the country are acquiring from abroad.

Imports and exports are not the only things to cross borders that may be significant for the economy. Organisational structures may also cross national lines, such as when a corporation within a particular country establishes enterprises outside it, or when an outside corporation starts enterprises within it. Information is also an important product that crosses national boundaries and this can sometimes produce profound changes, although unlike materials and energy information is not conserved. The information gained by the recipient is not lost by the sender.

A critical and by no means easy problem both in the description of an economy at a moment of time and in the description of its changes through time is identification of its significant parts, according to which it may be divided up and classified. The human population for instance may be divided by sex, age, years of formal education, nationality, net worth, net income, health and disease, skin or hair color, height and so on. None of these classifications can cover the great variety found in the human race, with its immense variety of knowledge, skill and potential. Each human being is an almost inconceivably complex structure, with perhaps as many brain cells as there are stars in the galaxy. We cannot hope to grasp the uniqueness of each of the 5.2 billion individuals. Classification is necessary, but it is always dangerous. We are always apt to miss significant differences and to emphasise differences which are not very significant. Race is a good example of a difference that is highly perceptible, but not very significant in terms of genetics, for the genetic differences within races are much larger than the genetic differences between them. The genes that create those differences, such as skin color, that are used to identify race are a very small proportion of the total genetic make-up of the human being. Genetically, gender differences are larger than racial differences, but even these are really quite small compared with the common features shared by all.

Economists are of course very fond of the 'measuring rod of money'. This is certainly convenient and it enables us to utilise single numbers, such as a price level or a gross national product (GNP) or a net worth, to ascertain the economic significance of very diverse aggregates of goods, services and events. The reality behind these aggregates, however, is an immensely complicated structure of very diverse parts, and it is a great mistake to take these aggregates as representing reality. Aggregates are useful and constitute important evidence, but they should never be mistaken for the truth. This is so even for such a simple aggregate as a human population. Two countries might have the same population in terms of numbers, and yet be extraordinarily different in terms of knowledge, skills, behaviour, ethnic diversity and so on.

Economists are also fond of measures of riches or poverty. There are a number of these. One, which is not much used but could well be the most significant, is the aggregate net worth of a population. Perhaps the most common is GNP, which we will look into later. We usually divide these measures by population to obtain a per capita measure, and this certainly gives a more vivid impression of what the measure means. Although it is very difficult to visualise the $5 trillion of a gross national product, if we divide this figure by 250 million people it comes to about $20 000 per head, which can be visualised very easily.

Yet two countries with the same GNP could be very different. One might devote a considerable proportion of its GNP to the military or to palaces and have it unequally distributed among the people, have a poor education system, and so on. The other might devote its GNP mainly to civilian uses, a more equal distribution and a good education system. One might be racked with internal conflict; the other, peaceable. One might be stagnating or getting poorer, the other might be getting richer. It is virtually impossible to devise a single measure of what might be called 'economic welfare' or, even more broadly, the 'goodness' of a society.

Another difficult question is: what is used to measure the value of the monetary unit itself in terms of purchasing power? We have a number of possible indexes for a single price level, and indeed for different price levels for different sectors of the economy and for different income classifications. Nevertheless it is virtually impossible for a price level index to take exact account of changes in the character and quality of what is purchased, that is the commodity mix. If we were asked what the price of a colour television set was in 1920, when such a commodity did not exist, the answer could only be that the price was infinite and the quantity zero. Unfortunately infinity multiplied by zero is any number we may care to write down. Difficulties arise because a price is a ratio of a quantity of money to the quantity of the commodity exchanged for it, and measuring the quantity of a commodity can be very difficult. In the case of simple raw materials – metals, grains, cotton and so on – this may not be too difficult, but even here the quality of each different commodity varies. When it comes to complex manufactured objects, though, it is extremely hard to say what is the quantity of a commodity. Is there twice as much automobile in an automobile costing $20 000 as there is in one costing $10 000? If so, all automobiles must be the same price! A particularly difficult example of this problem in the last three or four decades has been the extraordinary increase in the capacity of computers relative to their price. A simple solar-powered calculator costing just a few dollars today has the calculating capacity of a computer costing thousands of dollars 40 years ago. An attempt has indeed been made to correct national income statistics in the United States for sources of error of this kind. But such adjustments can only provide a very rough first approximation.

Economists, like the practitioners of any other academic discipline, have two major functions. One is to describe the phenomena of their particular field of interest. Geographers describe the spatial patterns of the earth. Anatomists describe the spatial patterns of the body. Ecologists describe the populations and interactions of an ecosystem.

Chemists describe the elements and their interaction to form compounds. Economists measure capital stocks and incomes, and the amounts of goods produced, consumed, transferred and distributed. There is however a second function, which is to explain and to understand. In geography and geology this involves studying plate tectonics as opposed to simple mapping and description. In biology it is carrying out research into how DNA organises the development of an entire organism from a single fertilised egg. In chemistry it is the understanding of how valency depends on the structure of atoms. In economics it is understanding the processes by which the overall economy changes. What is it, for instance, that produces inflation and depression? What is it that makes some countries and areas grow richer faster than others? What is it that makes some economies become more equal in the distribution of wealth and income and others less equal? It is the business of description to give us images of time and of space, and of the patterns that we have to try to understand. The process of understanding is very complex. Some of it involves simple thinking and theorising. Some of it involves various forms of testing, observation, recording and measuring.

Perhaps the purest form of thinking is mathematics. Arithmetic starts with simple counting – 1, 2, 3, 4, 5 and so on – where each number is one more than the previous one. Five, however, can be five of anything – apples, automobiles or people. It can be units of measurement like inches or feet, degrees of temperature, scores for an examination and so on. Yet concepts like addition, subtraction, multiplication and division apply to all numbers. Algebra is a generalised kind of arithmetic. X and Y can stand for any number. We develop propositions that are true no matter what the numbers are, such as the proposition that $(A + B)$ multiplied by itself is equal to A multiplied by itself, plus B multiplied by itself, plus two times A multiplied by B. That is, $(A + B)^2 = A^2 + 2AB + B^2$. Propositions of this kind do not require any empirical evidence. In this sense mathematics could be said to be the study of the obvious. We have to be careful here, though, because things that may be obvious in one environment may not be obvious in another. A good example is the famous axiom of Euclidean geometry, that if you take a straight line and a point not on the line, you can only draw one line through that point that is parallel to the first line. Any other line will intersect the first line at some point short of infinity. On a sphere, however, there is no way of drawing a line from the poles that will be parallel to the equator. When space–time is warped, there may be no such thing as a plane, so the geometry of the real world may turn out to be non-Euclidean, as it is in Einstein's theory. We may find similar propositions in algebra. Thus in ordinary algebra minus minus is plus. In social systems, not doing something bad may be very different from doing good.

Thought however, with or without mathematics, does enable us to perceive identities or truisms, propositions or relationships that cannot be otherwise. A good example is that the increase in anything is equal to the additions minus the subtractions, which I have sometimes frivolously called the 'bathtub theorem', the water in the bathtub being a good illustration of this. A somewhat broader proposition is that in a species reproduced sexually, only females of a particular age are able to produce offspring, and only a proportion of them may actually do so. A somewhat similar proposition in the economy is that only automobile plants will produce automobiles, and then only if they are not shut down. Physics is full of such truisms, like Ohm's Law which states that at constant temperature the electric current flowing between two points of a conductor is directly proportional to the potential difference and is inversely proportional to the resistance. In economics we have the proposition that in a closed economy with a fixed quantity of money (M), the sum total of all balances of payments has to be zero (for any individual account, the balance of payments is the quantity of money paid in minus the quantity of money paid out). Money is simply a cargo which shifts around among various holders.

Another proposition is that the total amount of money spent, that is transferred from one owner to another, in a closed economy in a given period is equal to the quantity of money multiplied by its velocity of circulation. The velocity of circulation (V) is the reciprocal of the average time that a dollar remains in the possession of one owner. The amount spent should be equal to the value of what is bought, which is the price (P) multiplied by the quantity (T). So we get the famous Fisher identity $MV = PT$.

A good deal of economic theory revolves around the proposition that in human behaviour everybody does what he or she thinks best at the time. This might almost be called a 'near identity', something that almost has to be true, but does not sufficiently define what actually happens. I describe the theory of maximising behaviour in economics as a set of mathematical variations on precisely this theme, that people always choose to do what they think best at the time. A critical empirical question is why people think some things are better than others, and what the learning process is that creates these preferences.

Measurement is an important aspect of an economy, although it is almost always an imperfect representation of complex systems. The 'measuring rod of money' is something that enables economists and accountants to reduce large, complex structures to single numbers which are significant in some overall process of evaluation. Accounting is a good example of this principle. A balance sheet starts off as a position statement, which is a list of assets and liabilities of many diverse kinds. By a variety of devices the accountant puts a dollar value on each of these items, which then can be added up and liabilities deducted from assets to obtain a 'bottom line' or a net worth.

Accountants also construct income statements that summarise the changes in the balance sheet over a given period. This provides gross addition to net worth if there is a profit, or gross subtraction if there is a loss. These statements again consist of very heterogeneous items, upon each of which a dollar value is placed. The accounting calculations of firms, non-profit organisations, individuals and governments can in turn be amalgamated to develop aggregates such as net national wealth (rarely, if ever, calculated) and the income aggregates – GNP, net national product, national income and so on – which are numbers purporting to measure aspects of the aggregate economic activity in an economy for a given period.

These numbers are by no means meaningless. They can provide a rough idea of the overall size of what are very heterogeneous aggregates, but we should never forget that the aggregates themselves and their innumerable component parts represent the reality, and that the various numbers which represent their total size are only one aspect of this reality. A somewhat parallel situation is found in measuring the size of a human body. We can measure a person's height and weight fairly easily, but these numbers do not represent the immense complexity of the body itself. They may indeed be misleading. An increase in weight, for instance, may reflect overall growth of the body in childhood. In adulthood it can represent increased muscle or increased fat. An increase in weight can either signify health or it can signify disease. Such measures of the economy as GNP are rather similar. An increase in GNP may go hand in hand with a genuine increase in economic welfare that reflects desirable and healthy pursuits. Or it may represent an expansion of the means of destruction in the military, a rise in crime and policing, the increased cost of pollution, the exhaustion of natural resources, absurd extravagances by the rich, diversions from education and learning into frivolous occupations, diversions from household production into production for a market and so on.

Another problem is that a unit of money does not always measure the same purchasing power, because of inflation and deflation. The statistics of the economy can be measured very roughly in constant dollars and adjusted for changes in price levels. On the other hand this cannot adequately take account of new commodities or changes in quality, so that what we mean by the overall quantity of 'real' production, consumption or accumulation in an economy is always subject to some doubt. Nevertheless the following chapters will attempt to show the patterns of the United States economy from 1929 to 1989 as revealed by official statistics, with the constant proviso that these patterns must be regarded as important evidence for the real events and not as exact and absolute truths.

This book uses very little in the way of conventional mathematics and statistics. This is not to deny the frequent usefulness of these tools. However they can easily distract attention from the real world, which is essentially topographical, consisting of shapes, sizes, patterns, structures, fittings and so on. To some extent numbers are a useful figment of the human imagination. The velocity of light, for instance, is any number we want to put on it, depending on our units of measurement. Conventional statistics likewise have the weakness that they tend to concentrate on averages, regressions, correlation coefficients and so on, which often reduce the complexity of the real world to misleading simplicity. We often learn more about complex systems by careful examination of their extreme positions than we do from studying their averages and correlations.

This book therefore concentrates on the structure of the economy, particularly in terms of proportional structures and time patterns. Of course without numbers these patterns could not be derived. Without deriving patterns, the numbers are meaningless. Without numbers to represent the latitude, longitude and altitude of a very large number of places on the earth's surface we could not derive an accurate map. But if all we had was a list of such numbers, they would be virtually meaningless. What this book tries to do is to translate the numbers of the economy into maps, especially time maps, particularly those which show the changes in the proportions of essential structures. Scatter diagrams give us much more information than regressions and correlation coefficients. What I have called 'time scatters', scatter diagrams in which the points are connected by arrows showing the sequence in time, can give us still more information. By such methods questions can be raised about the economy that more conventional methods of analysis do not raise, and yet which are of the utmost importance to both the understanding and the cure of possible economic ills.

2 Human Capital

The graphs in the following chapters show the patterns of change in the United States economy revealed by official statistics from (mostly) 1929 to 1989. They give us a picture of the economy over time that would have been impossible to produce earlier. I remember my old teacher, Professor Joseph Schumpeter, once saying, 'How nice economics was before anybody knew anything'. This was so even back in the 1930s. Herbert Hoover certainly had very little idea of what was going on around him. And Franklin Roosevelt was almost as ignorant, although much more successful. Now we do at least have a partial picture of what has gone on and what is going on. There are a good many deficiencies, but there is still enough information to make an important difference to our image of the world and, one hopes, to public policy. There was no Council of Economic Advisors or *Economic Report of the President* in 1929. What we now know about the economy may be very rough and incomplete, but it is a great improvement on the ignorance that prevailed prior to 1929.

We start with Figure 2.1, which shows the rise in the population of the United States. The population has risen very steadily and slightly more than doubled from 1929 to 1989, with an average growth rate of a little over one per cent per annum. Figure 2.2 shows the births, deaths and natural increase, that is births minus deaths, from 1910 onwards[1] in total numbers per annum. The First World War and its aftermath show up noticeably in the figures. The low number of births in 1919 reflects the fact that men were withdrawn from their families to join the armed forces. The higher number of births in 1920–21 reflects their return and demobilisation. The peak in deaths in 1918 represents a great influenza epidemic towards the end of the First World War, an epidemic which killed more people than did the war itself. The number of births shows a peak around 1921, a low in 1933, then a sharp rise until the late 1950s and early 1960s. The period from 1946 to about 1964 is sometimes called the 'baby boom'. There is a small trough during the Second World War, when many men were away, and a peak after the war, in 1947, when they had returned. There followed after 1964 what is sometimes known as the 'baby bust', a decline lasting until the early 1970s, but then the birth rate rose again, due in part to the fact that the members of the large

14

Figure 2.1   Total population of the US, 1929–89

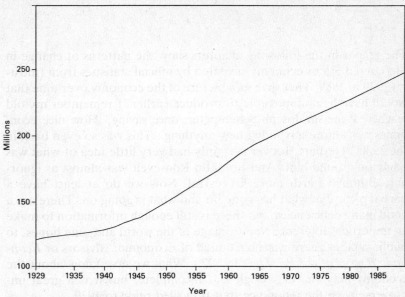

Source: *Economic Report of the President*, 1968, 1990.

Figure 2.2   Live births and deaths in the US, 1910–88

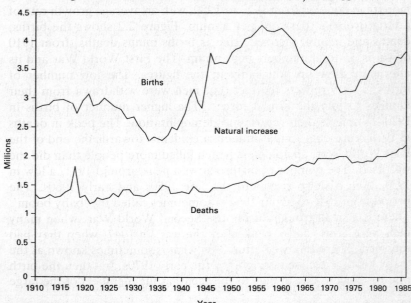

Sources: *Historical Statistics of the US: Colonial Times to 1970*; and *The World Almanac*, 1985, 1990

Figure 2.3   Total annual increase in population of the US, 1929–89

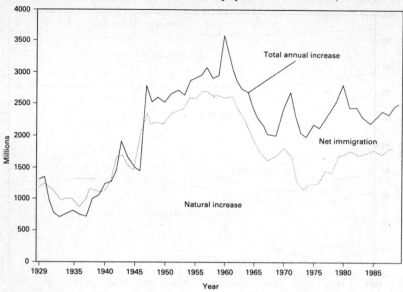

Sources: *Historical Statistics of the United States*; and *Economic Report of the President*, 1990.

generation of the 'baby boom' were themselves starting to have children.

Figure 2.3 shows how much of the increase in population is due to natural increase and net immigration. The decline in net immigration during the Great Depression of 1929–32 to a negative level (net emigration) in 1941–2, and in the Second World War up to 1945, is striking. There was a fairly steady rise from 1947 to 1971, and some decline from 1980. It should be emphasised that these figures are derived from other data, and may have substantial errors in the year-to-year estimates.

Figure 2.4 shows the population by age group, a significant aspect of the economy. From 1929 to the present there was more than a doubling of the older age group as a percentage of the total population. This group rose from 5.32 per cent of total population in 1929 to 12.23 per cent by 1987. We see the 'baby boom' in the bulge of under-five-year-olds and a later bulge of under-fifteen-year-olds from about 1950 to 1965. Figure 2.5 shows the proportion of the population aged between 20 and 64 and 16 and 64, representing the bulk of the labour force. This is compared with the total civilian labour force, plus the people in the armed forces. It is clear that the proportion of

Figure 2.4 Population by age group, US 1929–87

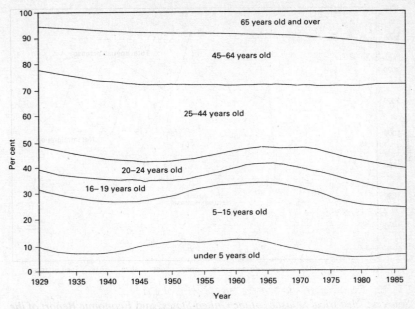

Source: *Economic Report of the President*, 1968, 1990.

the population in the labour force age group relates closely to the proportion actually in the labour force. Both rise from 1929 to about 1945, fall until about 1965, and rise again until about 1980, stabilising somewhat after 1980.

The somewhat larger proportion of the labour force age group in the labour force is largely accounted for by the striking increase in the proportion of women working outside the home. Figure 2.6 shows the proportion of the total population divided between the non-labour force, female employment, female unemployment, male unemployment and male employment. Unfortunately data does not seem to be available for the division between male and female workers before 1947. It is clear that the proportion of the population in the labour force has been increasing quite sharply since the early 1960s, mainly because of the rise in female employment. From about 1947 to the early 1960s there was a noticeable decline in the labour force as a proportion of the total population, reflecting mainly the change in age distribution (Figure 2.5). Figure 2.6 shows that from the early 1960s onwards the proportion of male employment was

Figure 2.5   Labour force and population of labour force age, US 1929–87

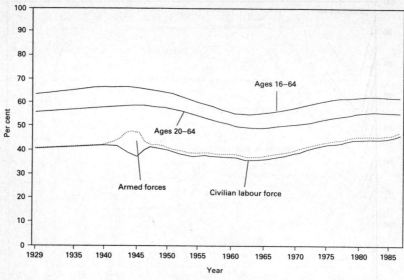

Source: *Economic Report of the President*, 1971, 1990.

Figure 2.6   Population in non-labour force, labour force and employment,
US 1929–89

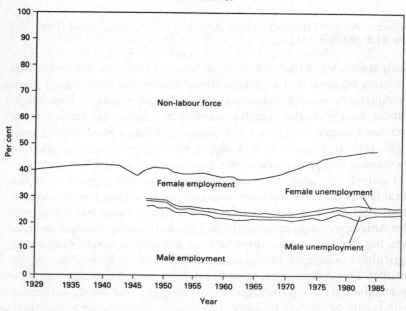

Source: *Economic Report of the President*, 1968, 1990.

Figure 2.7   Employment by sector, US 1929–89 (percentages)

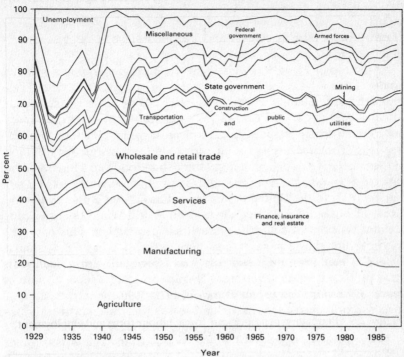

Year

Sources: Adapted from *Economic Report of the President*, 1968, 1990; and the *BLS Bulletin*, 1312–12.

fairly stable, while that of female employment increased sharply. This certainly suggests that a very profound change has been taking place in American society regarding the status of women. This might almost be called the 'gender revolution'. The total labour force increased from a little under 50 million in 1929 to about 120 million in 1989, reflecting not only a doubling of the population but also an increase in the proportion of the population in the labour force.

Figure 2.7 (a 'layer cake' diagramme)[2] shows the proportion of the total labour force in different occupations as well as unemployment from 1929–89. This gives a vivid picture of the structural changes in the American economy since 1929. One of the most striking changes was the decline in the proportion of the labour force working in agriculture, which fell from 21.1 per cent in 1929 to about 2.6 per cent in 1989. This reflects an extraordinary technological revolution, partly mechanical, partly biological (hybrid corn) and partly economic with regard to the size of farms and the rise of corporate agriculture.

As these figures represent the number of people actually working on the land, they exaggerate a little the decline of the agricultural industry as a whole, which ought to include the people who make the tractors, other farm machinery and so on that have made this extraordinary increase in productivity possible.

At the top of Figure 2.7 we see the unemployed proportion of the labour force – again a dramatic story. First came the Great Depression, with unemployment rising from 3.1 per cent of the labour force in 1929 to 24.7 per cent in 1933, one of the most extraordinary and disconcerting episodes in American economic history, and indeed the economic history of the entire capitalist world. We will look at the causes of this phenomenon later. Then followed what might be called a 'spontaneous recovery', a drop in unemployment to 14.2 per cent in 1937. In the United States legend has it that Hitler ended the Great Depression by starting the Second World War, but Americans certainly got out of half of it under their own steam. This recovery was interrupted by a short, rather sharp depression in 1938–9, almost wholly in manufacturing, and this was associated with a decline in gross private domestic investment (Figure 3.4) and a small decline in personal consumption expenditure. The shock of the introduction of social security taxes may have had something to do with this depression, although the relationship is not too clear.

Then of course the Second World War started. The armed forces went from 0.5 per cent (one two-hundredth) of the labour force in 1929 to 2.8 per cent in 1941 during in the pre-Pearl Harbor rearmament, when unemployment fell to 9.7 per cent. The armed forces represented 17.5 per cent of the labour force by 1945, and unemployment fell to 1.6 per cent. Then came the 'great disarmament', a remarkable episode in American history which somehow never touched the popular imagination. From 1945–6 the armed forces were reduced from 17.5 per cent to 5.7 per cent, and unemployment stood at 3.7 per cent. By 1950 the armed forces were down to 1.8 per cent. With the outbreak of the Korean War this figure had risen to 3.7 per cent by 1952, but it has declined pretty steadily since then, apart from a surprisingly small rise during the Vietnam War. The armed forces now represent 1.4 per cent of the labour force. As we shall see later, the total war industry, as it might be called, is a substantially larger proportion of the economy than the armed forces are of the labour force. This represents what might almost be called a dehumanisation of the armed forces, the development of nuclear weapons, elaborate equipment and so on. The war industry in 1989 was some 6 or 7 per cent of the total economy, while the armed forces were only 1.4 per cent of the labour force.

Another interesting change has been in civilian government. State government remained at between 5 and 6 per cent of the labour force between 1929 and 1948, with a small decline to 4.7 per cent during the Second World War. Between 1949 and 1975, however, it rose to 12.5 per cent, that is it approximately doubled in size. Since then it has reduced slightly. Civilian federal government was only 1.1 per cent of the labour force in 1929. It peaked in 1943 at 4.5 per cent, and has been declining slowly ever since, to about 2.4 per cent in 1989. The image of an expanding and overgrown federal government is completely belied by the statistics. It is state, not federal government, that has expanded, and even then not substantially so in the 1970s and 1980s.

Mine workers are a very small and declining proportion of the labour force, having gone from 2.2 per cent in 1929 to 0.6 per cent in 1989. Construction workers are a rather surprisingly small part of the labour force. Employment in construction declined very sharply during the Great Depression, from 3.1 per cent in 1929 to 1.6 per cent in 1933, recovering slowly to 3.6 per cent in 1942 and reducing sharply during the Second World War to 1.7 per cent in 1944. It had recovered to 3.5 per cent by 1948, and has hovered around 4 per cent since then. It is a fairly highly paid occupation. As a proportion of the national economy it is probably larger than indicated by the above figures, but data on this does not seem to be available. Employment in transportation and public utilities declined quite slowly over the whole period, from 7.9 per cent in 1929 to about 4.4 per cent in 1989.

The wholesale and retail trade (at 19.8 per cent) and services (at 19.9 per cent) are now the two largest employers of the United States labour force. The wholesale and retail trade actually overtook manufacturing around 1980. It employed 12.4 per cent of the labour force in 1929, dropping to 9.1 per cent in 1932 but rising fairly steadily ever since. Although its rate of increase did slow down somewhat in the 1970s and 1980s, its continued rise is a little surprising in light of technological improvements, especially in retailing with the growth of supermarkets and the introduction of electronic checkout counters, but perhaps the figures reflect the growth of shopping malls. The services sector, which includes education and medicine, provided the most spectacular growth in employment, going from only 5.5 per cent in 1933 to 20 per cent or more in 1989.

Manufacturing, which employed 21.6 per cent of the labour force in 1929 but only 13.5 per cent in 1932 has been by far the greatest contributor to unemployment. Employment in manufacturing had recovered to 19.9 per cent by 1937, fell to 17.2 per cent in the depression of 1938, rose to 27.3 per cent in 1943 during the Second World War, and stabilised at between 23 and 25 per cent until 1969 when it started its decline to about 15 per cent in 1989. Like the decline in agriculture, this certainly had something to do with the development of labour-saving technology, just as the rise in employment in services and in wholesaling and retailing probably had something to do with the relatively slow growth of labour-saving technology in these occupations, as well as with a shift in the structure of demand as incomes increased. Services tend to be demanded more by the richer than by the poorer. This is particularly true of education. Medicine is a difficult case, where evidence is not easy to collect. The development of drug treatments led to a massive decline in hospital care for the mentally ill, offset perhaps by increased technology and surgery, and undoubtedly influenced by the increasing number of elderly people.

Another striking change was the rise of the financial, insurance and real estate sectors, from 3 per cent of the labour force in 1929 to 5.4 per cent in 1989, all of this rise having taken place after 1950. If this is added to wholesaling and retailing, over a quarter of the labour force is now devoted to exchanging things, plus something under 4.4 per cent for transporting them, and only 18.3 per cent devoted to making and growing things. This dramatic change was mainly the result of the distribution of labour-saving technological devices. In agriculture, however, these labour-saving improvements have clearly reached their limit. It is not clear whether this is true in manufacturing. The release of labour from agriculture was an important element in the rise of per capita income by enabling the wide expansion of the proportion of labour in other sectors of the economy. This resource is no longer available. It looks as if labour release as a result of labour-saving technology will become a less important part of the economy from now on and as a result it will be much harder to continue the rise in per capita income that has been so striking since 1929.

Figure 2.8 shows the absolute numbers of employed and unemployed by sector. Agriculture is virtually the only sector of the United States economy in which there has been an absolute decline in the number of people employed. It is a tribute to the extraordinary mobility of Americans that this has been accomplished almost invisibly. It has inevitably been accomplished with a reward differential between agricultural and other forms of employment, for it is not

Figure 2.8   Employment by sector, US 1929–89 (16 years of age and over, thousands)

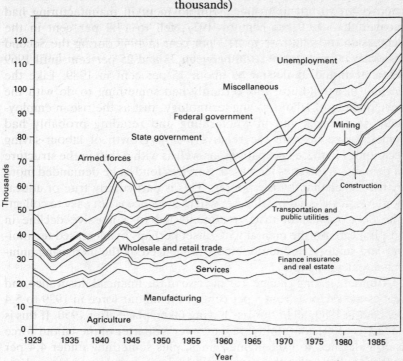

Note: 1929–46 Data includes those greater than or equal to 14 years old.

Sources: Adapted from *Economic Report of the President*, 1968, 1990; and the *BLS Bulletin*, 1312–12.

easy to avoid squeezing people out of a declining labour force. This differential has been modified somewhat by government subsidies to agriculture, but does not seem to have created severe social problems. There is some question as to whether the new technology in agriculture will always be sustainable. There are problems of soil erosion, pesticides and so on, but that perhaps is a matter for the future. There are also the social costs which may be incurred by the replacement of family farms by large corporate estates.

Another question that is difficult to resolve statistically is that of the effect which the shift in the proportion of the labour force in different occupations over the years has had on the average real wage, which, as we shall see later (Figure 3.6), has actually fallen somewhat since 1973 even though the proportion of national income going to labour has been fairly stable, mainly because of the increased proportion of women in the labour force. The relative decline in manufacturing and the relative expansion in services and the wholesale and retail trade may have contributed to these effects, as on the whole wages in manufacturing tend to be larger than in the other sectors of the economy.

3 Sizes and Proportional Structures of Total Output and Income

The rise in the labour force from about 50 million to over 120 million between 1929 and 1989 is certainly one indicator of the increase in the United States economy. The aggregate size of the economy is perhaps better measured by what the labour force – or perhaps we should say the whole population – has actually produced, consumed, accumulated or received as income. There are four standard aggregates in the national income statistics, and their history is shown in Figure 3.1. The most familiar of the aggregates is GNP. This is a concept which has been subject to some severe criticism.[1] It does not include household production, and since 1929 there has been a considerable shift from household production to market production, reflected for instance in the increase in the proportion of women in the labour force, and in some other changes, which would suggest that the GNP of earlier years may have been underestimated relative to the GNP of later years, so that some of the growth is illusory. The concept of GNP also identifies household purchases with household consumption. Many household purchases are durable goods which may be consumed over a long period of time, or may even appreciate like antique furniture or paintings. Household capital is almost completely neglected in the national accounts. There are not even any accurate estimates of its size, which could easily be greater than total industrial capital. If we compare what we are surrounded by at home with what we are surrounded by at work, the importance of household capital becomes very clear. Nevertheless it is probable that household capital increases along with an increase in real GNP, so that GNP can certainly be taken as an approximate indicator of a change in the total product, even though it may underestimate it.

Subtracting capital consumption allowances, with some capital consumption adjustment, from GNP gives the net national product (NNP). Capital consumption adjustment as a proportion of GNP has changed very little since 1929. It fell off sharply during the Second World War, rose a little after 1975, and is now falling (Figure 5.8).

Figure 3.1   Per capita national account index, US 1929–89 (1982 constant dollars)

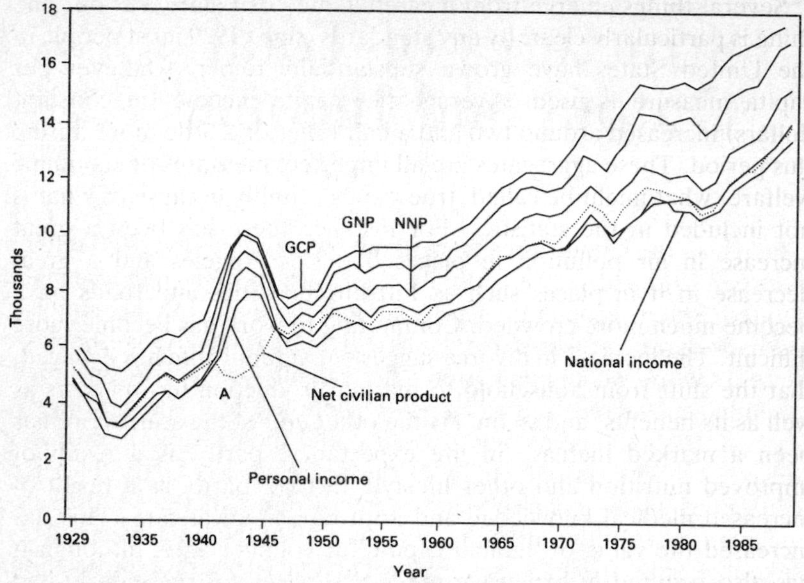

Source: *Economic Report of the President*, 1968, 1990.

NNP minus indirect business tax and non-tax liability, business transfer payments, the statistical discrepancy,[2] and current surplus of government enterprises, plus subsidies, is equal to national income. Of these items, the indirect business tax and non-tax liability is by far the largest. There is a further, even more arcane aggregate called 'personal income'.[3]

To these four I have added a fifth, which I have called the 'gross capacity product' (GCP). This is what GNP would have been if the unemployed had been producing at the average level of productivity. It could be argued that GCP could be somewhat exaggerated in that the unemployed, when employed, would probably be producing at lower than average productivity. On the other hand it is widely agreed that the official unemployment rate underestimates the level of unemployment and especially underestimates unemployment of part-time workers. One hopes that these two errors in opposite directions to some extent offset each other.

I have also added a sixth aggregate, which I have called the 'net civilian product' (NCP). This is NNP less expenditure on national defence. This is at least a rough measure of the ability of the average person to have a real income in terms of civilian goods.

Several things emerge from a careful study of Figure 3.1, but one thing is particularly clear: by any standards, since 1929 most people in the United States have grown substantially richer, whatever per capita measure is used. Average per capita income (in constant dollars) increased around two and a half times or a little more during this period. These aggregates are all imperfect measures of economic welfare, what might be called 'true riches', simply because of what is not included in the statistics. For instance there has been a great increase in air pollution in places like Los Angeles and a great decrease in it in places such as Pittsburgh. Cities and roads have become much more crowded. Commuting to work has become more difficult. The increase in divorce suggests that family life has decayed, that the shift from household to market production has its costs as well as its benefits, and so on. At the other end of the scale there has been a marked increase in life expectancy, partly as a result of improved nutrition and other lifestyle factors, partly as a result of increased medical knowledge and improved medical care. This has increased the value of 'human capital' at younger ages, although it has also resulted in expensive medical services for the elderly and incapacitated. The figures presented here must be taken as evidence rather than as absolute truth, but they are important evidence.

Looking at Figure 3.1 in more detail, during the Great Depression from 1929–33 all the indicators fell sharply. 'Real' per capita national income in 1933 was only 55 per cent of what it had been in 1929. Personal income did a little better, but was still only 66 per cent of what it had been in 1929. This suggests that the Great Depression produced not only 25 per cent unemployment, but also a sharp decline in productivity, even in that of those still employed. Then came a spontaneous recovery from 1933–7, followed by a great upsurge during the Second World War, peaking in 1943. This upsurge was in some sense fraudulent from the point of view of civilian welfare. If we deduct the expenditure on national defence from NNP we see that during the war NCP actually fell, as shown at point A in Figure 3.1 (years 1940–6). The dubious assumption is made in GNP, NNP and so on that the product of the war industry is equal to its cost. It is tempting to look at the Great Depression and the Second World War as *disturbances* in the long process of economic enrichment.

From 1950 onwards, as shown in Figure 3.1, there is a steady rise in all the per capita income measures, with occasional slight interruptions and very brief depressions, the most severe being in

Figure 3.2   Per capita real net product of the civilian labour force, US
· 1929–89

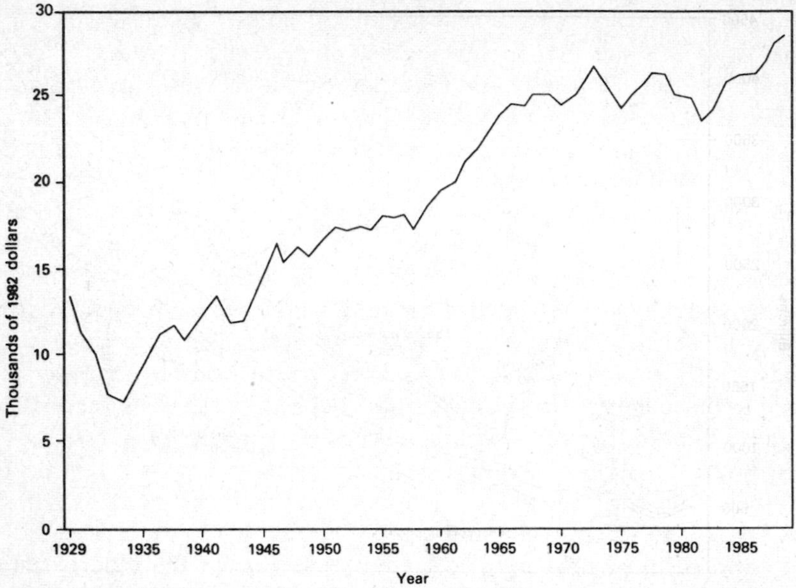

Source: *Economic Report of the President*, 1968, 1990.

1974 and 1981. A levelling off occurred in the late 1970s, but the
increase resumed after 1981. It is again tempting to look at the period
from 1950 to about 1973 as a kind of 'golden age' of steady enrichment, with the period after 1973 as a 'silver age' of rather slower and
less steady growth.

A very interesting question is: to what extent was this increase in
per capita real income a result of increased productivity, and to what
extent was it a result of an increased proportion of the population
being in the labour force? Figure 3.2 shows real NCP per capita of the
labour force, which provides a rough measure of the civilian productivity of the labour force (there is no measure of the productivity of
the war industry). It suggests that from about 1965 to about 1982
productivity increased very little, while as a proportion of the total
population the labour force increased quite substantially, due mainly
to the rise in the proportion of women, as we saw in Figure 2.5. From
1982 onwards the increase in per capita income may have been due
more to an increase in productivity than to a rise in the proportion of
the population in the labour force.

Figure 3.3 shows in absolute terms the major components of GCP

Figure 3.3   Major components of the gross capacity product, US 1929–89 (constant 1982 dollars)

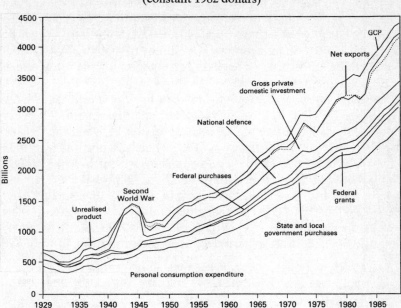

Sources: Adapted from *Economic Report of the President*, 1990; and the National Income and Product of the United States, 1929–82.

in real (1982) dollars. What happened to these components is more clearly seen in Figure 3.4, which shows them as a percentage or proportion of GCP. The first component (downward from the 100 per cent line at the top of the figure) is the unrealised product, which in effect represents the unemployment rate. This is measured by the distance between the 100 per cent line and the dotted line labelled Q. The vertical distance between line Q and the solid line R represents net exports when line Q is above line R, and represents net imports when line Q is below line R, as it was from 1943–5 and again from 1983 onwards. The distance between the base line, zero, and line Q represents the proportion of GNP in GCP. It is perhaps something of a convention that GNP is increased by net exports and diminished by net imports. But as we can see, net exports and imports are a very small proportion of the total economy, rarely going above 1 per cent. The peak of net exports at 4.9 per cent in 1947 represents to some extent the Marshall Plan – grants from the United States to Europe to aid reconstruction after the Second World War. This played a small but not insignificant role in the successful 'great disarmament' of 1947–48. The large net imports in the late 1980s mainly represent net foreign capital coming into the United States, just as net exports are a rough measure of net United States investment abroad. As can be seen, the United States economy was still overwhelmingly domestic, although the low figures for net exports or net imports may underestimate their qualitative impact.

The next layer in Figure 3.4, between lines R and S, shows the proportion of GCP in gross private domestic investment. The very close relationship during the Great Depression between the decline in gross private domestic investment to its near disappearance in 1933 (point B), and the enormous rise in unemployment is very striking. Similarly the initial recovery from the Great Depression was almost wholly a result of a rise in gross private domestic investment from 1933–7 (points B to C). The sharp depression of 1938 (point D) as well as the depressions of 1974 (point E) and 1982 (point F) are also largely associated with a sharp decline in the proportion of the GCP

Figure 3.4   Major components of the gross capacity product, US 1929–89

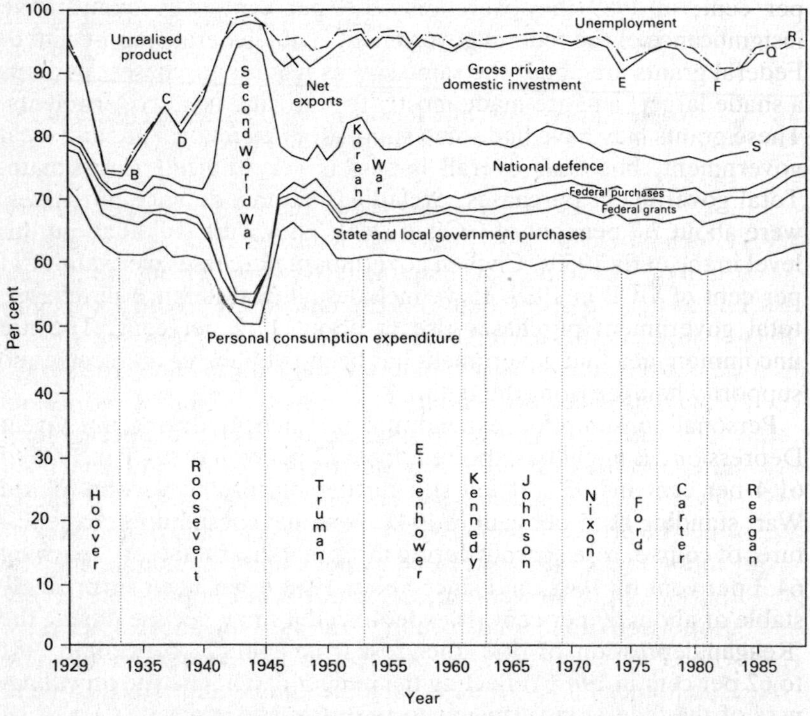

Sources: Adapted from *Economic Report of the President*, 1990; and the National Income and Product of the United States, 1929–82.

attributed to gross private domestic investment. The overall stability of this proportion from 1946 onwards is however striking.

The proportion of GCP in state and local government and in federal government civilian purchases is interesting. Many people do not recognise the overwhelming importance of state and local government, at least at the quantitative level of the economy, especially outside national defence. State and local government has grown somewhat, particularly after the late 1950s. It was 6.8 per cent of GCP in 1929, grew somewhat during the Great Depression, but fell sharply during the Second World War. By 1957 it was almost exactly where it had been in 1929. Then it started to rise throughout the 1950s and 1960s, reaching about 8.9 per cent by 1970. It fell a little in the late 1970s but had risen to 9.3 per cent by 1989. By contrast, what we might call federal civilian government, which was only 0.9 per cent of GCP in 1929, rose to about 3.7 or 3.8 per cent by 1938 under the New Deal. This was not very large quantitatively and had much less impact on employment than did gross private domestic investment. Federal civilian purchases declined sharply during the Second World War to 0.5 per cent in 1945. From 1945 they hovered around 2 per cent; in 1989 they were only 1.8 per cent. The quantitative insignificance of the federal government is not generally appreciated. Federal grants are about the same size as federal purchases, perhaps a shade larger, and are made mostly to state and local governments. These grants may have had some stimulatory effect on state and local government, but their overall impact is very difficult to estimate. Total government purchases, excluding national defence purchases, were about 7.7 per cent of GCP in 1929. They were still at about this level in the early 1950s. Civilian government purchases were about 11 per cent of GCP in 1989. If we include national defence purchases, total government purchases rise to about 17.2 per cent. The not uncommon idea that government has been gobbling us up receives no support whatever from the data.

Personal consumption expenditure fell sharply during the Great Depression, as might be expected, from 72 per cent of GCP in 1929 to 61.4 per cent in 1933. It fell still further during the Second World War, standing at 55 per cent in 1945. Personal consumption expenditure, of course, rose sharply during the 'great disarmament', reaching 64.3 per cent by 1948, and since about 1952 it has been surprisingly stable at about 60 per cent. It experienced a small decline during the 'Reagan depression' of 1981, then rose from about 58 per cent in 1981 to 62 per cent in 1987, reflecting the budget deficit and the unwillingness of the federal government to raise taxes to cover it.

In Figure 3.4 the tenure of different presidents is also shown and the transition from one president to another rarely seems to have had much effect on the structure of GCP. There was a sharp difference in GCP between the terms of office of Presidents Hoover and Roosevelt, mainly due to what may have been a mostly privately motivated revival in gross private domestic investment. The transition from Roosevelt to Truman just happened to coincide with the time that the Second World War was drawing to a close. The transition from Carter to Reagan is noteworthy for a rise in personal consumption expenditure as a proportion of GCP and also for a transition from net exports to net imports. This may also have been associated to some degree with the federal budget deficit. It is certainly very difficult to see very much difference in effect between Democrats and Republicans. However, and it may just be coincidental, the two largest depressions of the post-Second World War era were under the Republican presidents, Ford and Reagan.

Figure 3.5 shows the distribution of national income among types of income: corporate profits, net interest, rent, non-farm proprietors' income, farm proprietors' income and compensation to employees. The years of the Great Depression stand out very sharply, with profits becoming negative, and net interest almost doubling from 5.5 per cent in 1929 to 10.95 per cent in 1933. Farm proprietors' income and non-farm proprietors' income shrank much less. For the period 1932–3 it is almost true to say that anybody who hired anybody was either a philanthropist or a fool and was almost bound to lose by it. It is not surprising that unemployment reached 25 per cent; what is surprising is that it did not rise to 50 per cent and that the whole economy did not collapse. Perhaps the only answer to this is the force of habit, a desire to hold firms together in the hope of better times, which of course actually came. We can see the recovery, what might almost be called a 'spontaneous' recovery of profits, to about the 1929 level (11.33 per cent) by 1940 (11.06 per cent), peaking at 14.40 per cent in 1942 and then falling off somewhat during the rest of the Second World War to 10.85 per cent in 1943, undermining the great myth that war is good for business. The proportion of profits recovered by 1948, was fairly stable into the late 1960s at around 12 per cent, hovered around 10 per cent in the 1970s, then declined somewhat to 6.99 per cent in 1989, partly because of the rise in net interest.

The percentage of national income in net interest has a particularly interesting history. We have already noted its large rise during the Great Depression, mainly as a result of deflation. The United States financed its Second World War efforts at extraordinarily low rates of

Figure 3.5 National income by type of income, US 1929–89

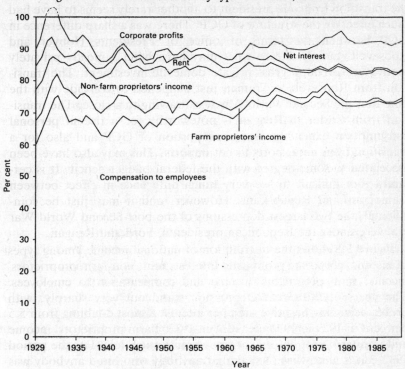

Sources: Adapted from *Economic Report of the President*, 1990; and the National Income and Product of the United States, 1929–82.

interest – under 2 per cent. Net interest income was actually only one per cent of national income in 1946, but rose steadily after that, peaking perhaps in 1982 at 10.81 per cent, and it has declined very little since. We shall explore the reasons for this later, but it is difficult not to regard it as a very ominous development. Interest, after all, is the reward of the passive capitalist, who does nothing more than decide who to lend money to. Profit is the reward of the active capitalist – the employer, the innovator, the person who really makes the decisions taken outside government, and who to a very large extent determines GNP. The United States does seem to be becoming a usurious society, though the reasons for this are by no means clear.

Rent is a rather curious item that has officially almost disappeared, largely because it has been redefined as interest. Non-farm proprietors' income has declined a little. It reached its maximum at 11.9 per cent in 1946 and since then has declined fairly steadily, though rather slowly, to somewhat less than 8 per cent in 1989. This represents the income of professionals – unincorporated business – and on the whole what might be called the small business sector of the economy. Farm proprietors' income peaked at 9.7 per cent in 1935 and has been shrinking fairly steadily ever since, to around 1 per cent in 1989. This again reflects the vast technological improvements in agricultural productivity we saw with the decline in the agricultural labour force.

By far the largest sector is compensation to employees – the proportion of national income going to labour. This includes pension contributions, and other fringe benefits and costs. The rise in the proportion of national income going to labour during the Great Depression was very striking, going from about 60 per cent in 1929 to 74.75 per cent in 1933. It is ironic that this proportion then experienced a fairly sharp decline, to about 62.67 per cent by 1942. This was the period of the New Deal, the Wagner Act, a dramatic rise in collective bargaining, and a great increase in labour union membership. Nevertheless the proportion of national income going to labour did fall sharply during this period, mainly because of a rise in profits. Hardly anything could illustrate better the difference between the 'micro' and the 'macro' in economics. Money wages certainly increased somewhat over the period, but this had very little to do with the rise in profits, as we shall see later.

Over the whole sixty-year period the proportion of national income going to labour increased quite noticeably, from about 60 per cent in 1929 to about 73 per cent in 1969, although the proportion going to labour has not increased perceptibly since 1969.[4] This perhaps again reflects the enormous rise in the proportion of national income going to interest. The failure of labour's share to rise since the late 1960s may have something to do with the increase in the proportion of the population in the labour force shown in Figure 2.7. The fact that this was mainly the result of a rise in female employment may also have something to do with the failure of the compensation to employees to rise. Female wages are almost universally less than those of males, even those in roughly the same occupation, partly because of discrimination, partly a matter of demand and supply.

There has also been a change in the number of hours worked. Figure 3.6 shows that while real compensation per hour rose pretty sharply from the late 1940s to the early 1970s, after which it changed

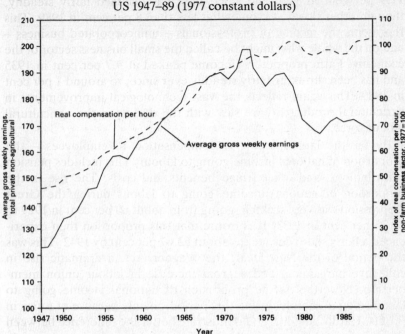

Figure 3.6   Average gross weekly earnings and real compensation per hour,
US 1947–89 (1977 constant dollars)

Source: Adapted from *Economic Report of the President*, February 1990.

little, average gross weekly earnings rose even more sharply until the early 1970s and then fell off quite sharply, all of this in constant dollars. Again this may be associated with the rise in the proportion of the population in the labour force, which prevented a fall in the proportion of national income going to labour but may also have contributed to a fall in real wages.

Another important aspect of the structure of the economy is the distribution of income among various income classes shown in Figure 3.7. From 1947 onwards two dramatic features of this graph show up immediately. One is the astonishing stability of proportional distribution – this is one of the most stable features of the United States economy and has hardly changed since 1947. The other is the inequality of the economy, with the lowest fifth of families getting less than 5 per cent of total income, the lowest two-fifths getting only about 13 per cent, the lowest three-fifths, about 16 per cent, the lowest four-fifths, a little less than 26 per cent, and the highest fifth getting over 40 per cent. The top five per cent of families get

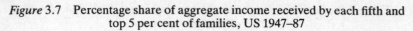

Figure 3.7 Percentage share of aggregate income received by each fifth and top 5 per cent of families, US 1947–87

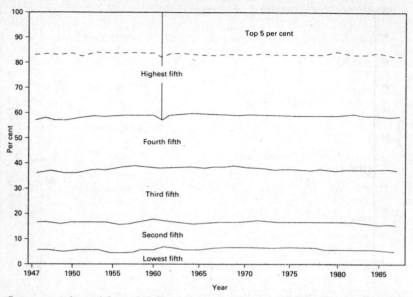

Sources: Adapted from US Bureau of the Census, Current Population Reports, Series P-60, no. 156, *Money Income of Households, Families and Persons in the US, 1985*; *World Almanac*, 1990.

something like 16 per cent. It is unfortunate that we do not have similar data for earlier years, as it would be interesting to see whether the New Deal of the 1930s, for instance, made any difference, and what impact was made by progressive income taxes. It could be argued that social institutions did not change very much after 1938 in spite of the disturbances of the Second World War and apart from the dramatic increase in the war industry, although this period did see the 'gender revolution' – the influx of women into the labour force – and fairly marked changes in the age composition of the population.

Perhaps even more striking is the income distribution shown in Figure 3.8. One is tempted to issue the warning that all labels may be misleading and within each income category there may be wide differences in personal adjustment. Poverty is a social concept as well as an economic one. My grandfather, who was a blacksmith and a Methodist lay preacher in a little town in the west of England, would certainly have been considered to be living well below the standard poverty line, living as he did in a tiny house with no 'modern conveni-

Figure 3.8   Families, distribution by total income, US 1947–88 (constant 1985 dollars)

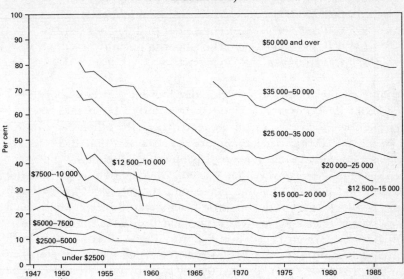

Sources: Adapted from US Bureau of the Census, Current Population Reports, Series P-60, no. 156, *Money Income of Households, Families and Persons in the US*, 1985, and no. 166, *Money Income and Poverty Status in the US*, 1988.

ences', not even running water, certainly no automobile and not even a bicycle. Yet he would have been insulted if anybody had called him poor. He was a man of great self respect. At the other end of the scale there are rich people who may be depraved, miserable and living wretched lives. This is not to say that economic quantities are meaningless, but we have to be sensitive to the wide differences within each class. One is tempted to name the eleven classes shown in Figure 3.8 to enable us to visualise a little better what the numbers mean:

Under $2500	The desperately poor
$2500–$5000	The lower poor
$5000–$7500	The middle poor
$7500–$10 000	The upper poor
$10 000–$12 500	'On the poverty line', as the official US poverty line tends to fall in the middle of this group.

$12 500–$15 000	The barely middle class
$15 000–$20 000	The lower middle class
$20 000–$25 000	The middle middle class
$25 000–$35 000	The upper middle class
$35 000–$50 000	The upper-upper middle class
$50 000 and over	The rich.

Striking changes took place in this distribution between about 1947 and about 1969. Poverty declined spectacularly. 'Desperate poverty' declined by about 75 per cent, poverty below the official level more than halved. Going back to Figure 3.7, we see that this was accomplished with virtually no redistribution of income. What happened is that almost everybody became twice as rich. Both national income and personal income per capita roughly doubled between 1929 and 1969. They rose very little from then until 1982, after which they started to rise again. It is ironic that President Johnson's 'War On Poverty', which began in 1964, was followed soon after by a virtual cessation of the decline in poverty which had been going on for the previous 20 years or so. Poverty actually rose after 1973. The reasons for this are by no means clear, but the rise in the proportion of national income going to interest, the decline in the proportion of taxes paid by richer groups, the slowdown in the increase in productivity, the rise of the drug culture, and the increased number of women in the labour force, may all have had some impact.

Poverty levels may be very different between different groups in the population. It is not surprising that blacks, Hispanics and women have higher poverty levels than white males. A little over half of the families headed by black females are living in poverty. A little over a quarter of the families headed by white females are in poverty. What is somewhat surprising is that the distribution of total income by fifths in black families is not very different from that of white families, and the distribution in different regions of the country is also very similar, as Table 3.1 shows for 1987. I know of no theory that explains this extraordinary stability of the proportional distribution of income over time, space and race or cultural groups. It is one of the most striking phenomena to emerge from an examination of the numerical data, yet there seems to be no theory that would explain it.

Table 3.1   Income distribution by population fifths, families, 1988

| | Per cent distribution of total income | | | | | |
	Lowest fifth	Second fifth	Third fifth	Fourth fifth	Highest fifth	Top 5%
Race						
Total	4.6	10.7	16.7	24.0	44.0	17.2
White	5.1	11.1	16.8	23.7	43.3	17.0
Black & other	(NA)	(NA)	(NA)	(NA)	(NA)	(NA)
Black	3.3	8.5	15.0	25.1	47.9	17.7
Region						
Northeast	4.8	11.1	16.9	24.0	43.3	16.5
Midwest	5.0	11.4	17.3	24.0	42.4	16.5
South	4.3	10.2	16.3	24.2	44.7	17.4
West	4.8	10.7	16.5	23.5	44.5	18.1

Note: NA = not available.

Source: *The World Almanac and Book of Facts*, 1991, p. 561.

4 Money and Prices

A very important property of any economy over time is the degree to which it has experienced inflation or deflation of prices, including money wages. Any monetary unit like the dollar is subject to fluctuations in its general purchasing power because of changes in money prices. We try to measure these fluctuations by constructing a price level index or a price deflator (or inflator), of which there are many varieties. There is some dispute among economists that has never quite been resolved as to what the ideal price index should be. One index is calculated by estimating how much money it would take to buy a 'market basket' of relevant commodities, corresponding more or less to the relative quantities that are produced or consumed. Other measures have been proposed, but this seems to be the simplest and perhaps the most meaningful. A difficulty arises, however, when deciding which market basket is significant when the relative quantities of commodities actually purchased change over time. The price level index will be different if we take the market basket at the beginning or at the end of the period. When there is a change in the quality of commodities, and when new commodities appear, the task of defining a price level in an exact form becomes virtually impossible and we have to be content with rough measures (Chapter 1). These indexes however are better than nothing. Different sectors of the economy may require different measures of price levels as they constitute significantly different market baskets. The sixty-year history of some of these measures is shown in Figure 4.1 (for GNP), Figure 4.2 (for personal consumption expenditure and gross private domestic investment) and Figure 4.3 (for exports, imports and government purchases of goods and services). In all of these there was sharp deflation during the Great Depression: about 25 per cent for GNP, personal consumption and gross private domestic investment; nearly 50 per cent for exports and imports; and only 12 per cent for government purchases (summarised in Table 4.1).

Since then there has been almost continuous inflation, which from 1929 to the present has served to increase the price level of GNP by 7.8 times, that of personal consumption expenditure 6.7 times, gross private domestic investment 9.9 times, government expenditure 12.8 times, exports 5.8 times and imports 7.2 times. These differences

Figure 4.1   Implicit price deflator (1), US 1929–89

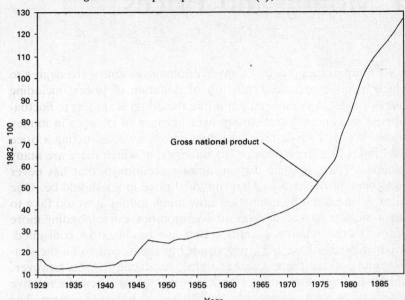

Source: *Economic Report of the President*, 1968, 1990.

Figure 4.2   Implicit price deflators (2), US 1929–89

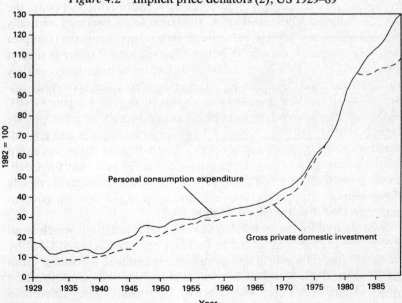

Source: *Economic Report of the President*, 1968, 1990.

Figure 4.3   Implicit price deflators (3), US 1929–89

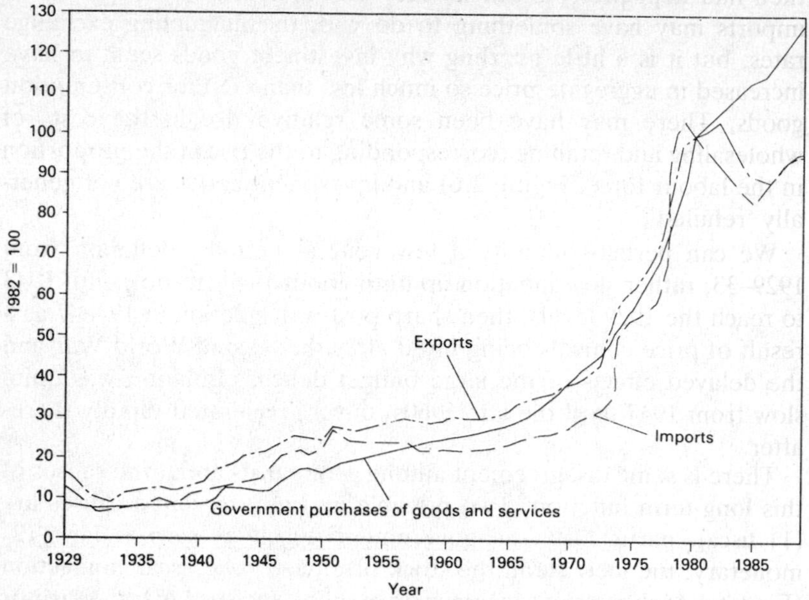

Source: Economic Report of the President, 1968, 1990.

Table 4.1   Price deflators in the Great Depression, 1929–33

Year	GNP	Personal Consumption Expenditure	Gross Private Domestic Investment	Exports	Imports	Government Purchases of Goods & Services
1929	100.0	100.0	100.0	100.0	100.0	100.0
1933	76.8	76.6	74.7	55.9	51.4	88.0

reflect significant changes in the relative price structure of the total economy.

If we take the period of lowest price level (1933) as our base, inflation becomes even more dramatic: nine-fold for personal consumption expenditure and fourteen-fold for exports and imports. One curious thing shown by the figures is that after 1980 the inflation figures for gross private domestic investment and for exports and imports were much less than for the other aggregates, which until then had kept pretty much in line. The divergence of exports and imports may have something to do with the fluctuating exchange rates, but it is a little puzzling why investment goods seem to have increased in aggregate price so much less than GNP or consumption goods. There may have been some relative rise in the costs of wholesaling and retailing (corresponding to the rise in the proportion in the labour force, Figure 2.6) and investment goods are not generally 'retailed'.

We can perhaps identify a few general periods: deflation from 1929–33, rather slow inflation up until about 1940 (it took until 1943 to reach the 1929 level), then sharp post-war inflation in 1946–7 as a result of price controls being lifted after the Second World War and the delayed effects of the large budget deficits. Inflation was quite slow from 1947 until the late 1960s, but it accelerated rapidly thereafter.

There is some disagreement among economists about the causes of this long-term inflation. Two possible and not unrelated causes are (1) fiscal, particularly the government deficit or surplus, and (2) monetary, the increase in the stock of money. The fiscal connection (Figure 4.4) shows the consumer price index and the federal deficit or surplus. We see that the deficit of the Second World War may have produced a delayed inflation after the war, partly because of price controls and also perhaps because of a diminished velocity in the circulation of money during the war. People held onto their cash because there was not much to spend it on. No private automobiles were produced for over three years! The period from about 1946 to the early 1970s on the whole was a period of balanced budgets, with very little cumulative budget surplus or deficit. Then from the 1970s onwards the restraints on budget deficits seem to have disappeared. How long this will continue is difficult to say. Proposals for reducing the deficit, like the Gramm–Rudman Act, may remain hopes rather than become realities if military expenditure continues near the present level and if resistance to tax increases remains. The hope that military expenditure will decrease in the light of the remarkable events of 1989 and the end of the Cold War now seems frustrated by the events of 1990 in the Middle East.

The quantity theory of money, always a favourite of economists, that price levels are closely related to the total stock of money, is well supported in a general way by the data presented here. Irving Fisher's more sophisticated version of the quantity theory, as noted in Chapter 1, is expressed in the famous identity, $MV = PT$, or $P = MV/T$,

Figure 4.4   Federal government deficit or surplus vs consumer price index,
US 1929–89

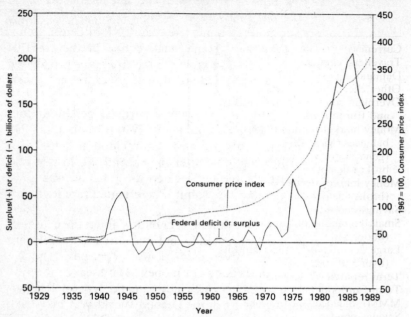

Source: Adapted from *Economic Report of the President*, February 1987.

where M is the quantity of money, V is the velocity of circulation, P is
the price level, and T the volume of all transactions. This rests on
the identity that in exchange equal values are exchanged. MV then is
the total amount of money given in exchange over a period and PT is
the value of goods or whatever MV is exchanged for. There may be
some problems here in terms of profiṭ and surplus value, but we will
ignore these for the time being.

One problem is that a quantity of money is not easy to define.
There are a great variety of assets having different degrees of liquid-
ity. It is not even easy to define liquidity. *The Economic Report of the
President* distinguishes seventeen kinds of liquid assets, as shown in
Table 4.2. In the last 30 years there have been extraordinary changes
in the kinds and relative proportions of these different liquid assets.
Six of them did not even exist in 1959. *The Economic Report* dis-
tinguishes four major categories, M1, M2, M3 and L, all defined in
Table 4.2, which are listed in order of their general liquidity,
although they are rather arbitrary aggregations.

Table 4.2   United States liquid assets (in billions of dollars)

	1959	1989	Increase 1989/1959
Currency	28.8	221.9	7.70
Travellers' cheques	0.4	7.4	18.50
Demand deposits	110.8	279.7	2.52
Other checkable deposits	0.0	285.7	
Overnight repurchase agreements and Eurodollars	0.0	77.4	
Money market mutual fund balances (MMMF) (general-purpose and broker-dealer)	0.0	312.4	
Money market deposit accounts (broker-dealer)	0.0	483.7	
Savings deposits	146.4	409.0	2.79
Small denomination time deposits (under $100 000)	11.4	1142.3	100.20
Large denomination time deposits (over $100 000)	1.2	558.3	465.25
Term repurchase agreements	0.0	96.9	
Term Eurodollars	0.7	81.1	115.86
MMMF balances, institutions	0.0	102.3	
Savings bonds	46.1	117.5	2.55
Short-term treasury securities	38.6	330.3	8.56
Bankers acceptances	0.6	41.2	68.66
Commercial paper	3.6	347.9	96.64
M1	140.0	794.7	5.68
M2	297.8	3219.5	10.81
M3	299.7	4058.1	13.54
L	388.6	4895.0	12.59

The braces in the table group:
- Currency, Travellers' cheques, Demand deposits, Other checkable deposits → **M1**
- ...through Small denomination time deposits → **M2**
- Money market deposit accounts onward → **M3**

Source: *Economic Report of the President*, 1991.

The significance of the changes to the liquid assets over the last 30 years is brought out in Figure 4.5, showing the purchasing power in terms of the GNP index of the five major categories. It is significant that the stocks of currency and M1, which most closely resemble what most people think of as money, have maintained a remarkably constant purchasing power, suggesting that a rise in the price level is very closely connected with the stock of what might almost be called 'real money'. This is shown in Figures 4.6 and 4.7, which show currency and M1 against the price level. The relationship is very striking in both cases. In the 1980s currency per capita rose a little faster than

Figure 4.5   Purchasing power* of the various forms of liquid assets, US
1959–89

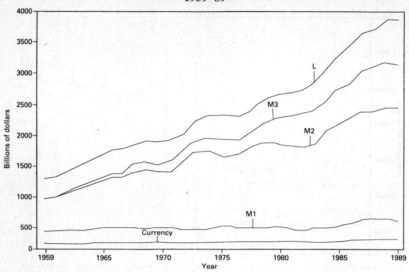

* Liquid assets/GNP deflator

Source: *Economic Report of the President*, 1990.

Figure 4.6   Average currency held per capita, US 1929–89

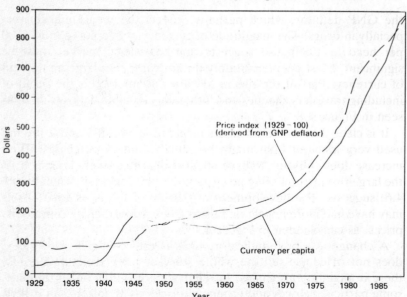

Source: *Economic Report of the President*, 1968, 1990.

Figure 4.7 Per capita currency plus demand deposits, and GNP deflators, US 1929–89

Sources: Federal Reserve Bulletin: *Measure of Money Stock Components*, 1929–87; *Economic Report of the President*, 1989.

the GNP deflator, which perhaps reflects the illegal market, especially in drugs. The magnitude of currency per capita (almost $900 per head in 1989) also suggests that the illegal market must be significant. Most people certainly do not carry that large an amount of currency. Part of the rise in M1 after about 1959 is the result of including travellers cheques and 'other checquable deposits' in it, as seen in Figure 4.8.

It is clear that the liquid assets included in M2, M3 and L are not used very much in what might be called ordinary purchases. Their increase does not seem to have affected the price level very much, as the large rise in purchasing power of the total stocks (shown in Figure 4.6) suggests. The development of these new forms of liquid assets may have had more impact on raising stock prices than on commodity prices, as can be seen in Figure 4.13.

A change in a price indicator, such as the consumer price index, does not of course tell the whole story of price structure because there is a continuous change in relative prices going on all the time, some particular prices and groups of prices rising faster than others.

Figure 4.8   Components of M1, US 1929–89

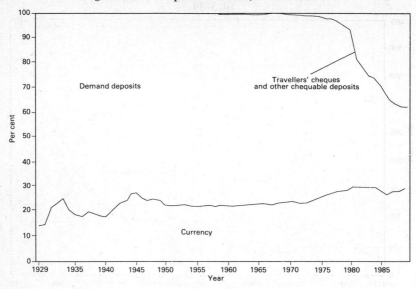

Source: *Economic Report of the President*, 1968, 1990.

Figures 4.9, 4.10, 4.11 and 4.12 illustrate some of these changes in a broad way as it is very difficult to portray the total structure of the prices of millions of commodities that constitute the United States and the world economies. We also run into the difficulty, noted earlier, that the quality and type of commodities change all the time. An automobile today is not the same as an automobile in 1929. Computers have changed enormously and there have been considerable changes in fabrics and clothing, in kinds of buildings, in household furnishings and equipment and so on. Many of today's commodities did not exist in 1929. These new commodities, such as television sets and electronic computers, plastics and pharmaceuticals, many fertilisers and so on, cannot really be put into long-term price levels. Nevertheless there are also many commodities that have not changed very much, so the price indexes do have some meaning. On the whole, as we can see from the figures, the prices of particular groups of commodities do tend to go along with the general price level, especially when there is a rise as large as the one since 1929. In a sense all this represents a change in the value of the purchasing power of the dollar. But the purchasing power of the dollar depends to some degree on what is being purchased; it is not an absolute figure.

Figure 4.9   Consumer price indexes: all items, rent and residential, US
1913–89

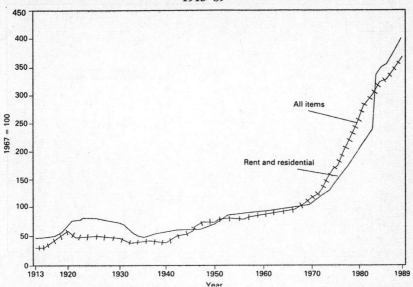

Sources: *Handbook of Labor Statistics*, June 1987; *CPI Detailed Report*,
January 1990.

In Figure 4.9 we see that prices of rent and residential purchases
were above the general price level from 1913–46, were about the
same from 1947–67, then were below again from 1968–83 and above
after 1983. These movements may reflect changes in interest rates,
especially in the 1980s. There are of course quite large regional
differences in housing prices. Regions with rapidly increasing populations, such as California, Washington DC, Florida and so on, have
higher rents and housing costs, whereas places with diminishing
populations tend to have lower rents and housing costs.

Figure 4.10 shows that food and clothing prices diverged little from
each other until 1972, when clothing continually became cheaper.
This is a little surprising. It may have been due to the technical
improvements in productivity in the clothing industry that began
somewhat earlier than 1970 with the development of chemical fibres
such as nylon and dacron. It may also have been due to the industry
shifting to low-wage areas around the world. The data does not seem
to provide information on this.

Figure 4.11 shows that prices of durables and non-durables did not
change very much relative to commodities in general. Durables have
become a little cheaper over the years.

Figure 4.10   Consumer price indexes: food, clothing and upkeep, US 1913–89

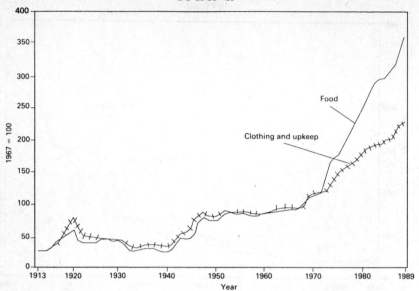

Sources: *Handbook of Labor Statistics*, June 1987; *CPI Detailed Report*, January 1990.

Figure 4.11   Consumer price indexes: commodities, durables and non-durables, US 1935–88

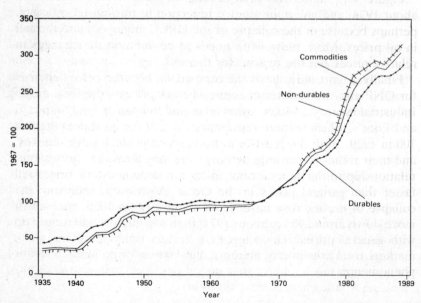

Sources: *Handbook of Labor Statistics*, June 1987; *CPI Detailed Report*, January 1990.

Figure 4.12   Consumer price indexes: transportation and medical care, US
1935–89

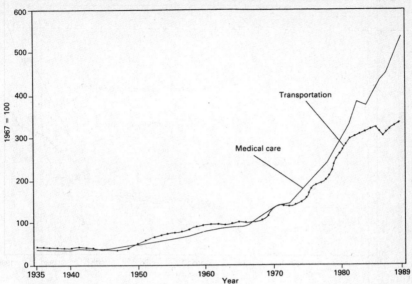

Sources: *Handbook of Labor Statistics*, June 1987; *CPI Detailed Report*,
January 1990.

Figure 4.12 shows the skyrocketing of medical care costs since
about 1974, and a certain relative reduction in transportation casts,
perhaps because of the collapse of the OPEC monopoly and the fall
in oil prices. Much more work needs to be done on the changes in
relative prices and the reasons for them.

Finally, Figure 4.13 shows the comparison between price deflators
for GNP and two indexes of common stock prices – the Dow Jones
Industrial Average, which covers 30 major companies, and Standard
and Poor's, which is more representative. All the indicators start at
100 in 1929. Both the short-term fluctuations in stock price indexes,
and their rather loose, although over the long term very noticeable,
relationship to the general price index are striking. Stock prices fell
faster than general prices in the Great Depression, reflecting the
collapse of profits, rose faster from about 1950 to 1965, rose much
more slowly from 1965 to about 1977, then rose rapidly and caught up
with general prices. This suggests a certain isolation of the stock
markets from commodity markets, but I know of no studies of this
phenomenon.

Figure 4.13   Common stock price indexes, US 1929–86

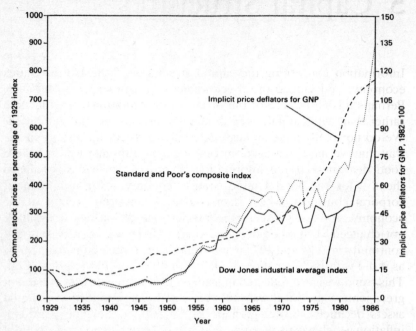

Source: Adapted from *Economic Report of the President*, February 1987.

5 Capital Structures

Information concerning the capital structures of the United States economy, and indeed of all economies, is surprisingly inadequate. Perhaps this is because of the obsession of economists with income rather than with capital, even though the two are intimately related. We do not really have an aggregate balance sheet for society in the way that we have aggregate income figures, although we do have a good deal of scattered information. Figure 5.1 provides a balance sheet – for the total United States economy – for non-financial corporate business, which is of course an important sector of the economy. As can be seen, the proportions of various items have not changed very much over the years. There was a surprising discontinuity in 1974 and 1975 in consumer and trade credits, coinciding as it did with the formation of OPEC and the rise in the price of oil. This trend was also reflected in trade debt. Foreign direct investment grew somewhat, but it was still very small. The proportion of liquid assets declined a little, perhaps as a result of the long period of inflation which gave a negative real rate of return to holding stocks of non-interest-bearing money. Structures, plant and equipment grew but the general change was not large. On the liability side, mortgages declined, loans increased, net worth as a proportion of total assets (roughly two-thirds of the total, one third being liabilities) declined a little in the 1980s but not spectacularly so. Foreign direct investment in the United States grew a little from 1978–88, to the point where it was about equal to United States investment abroad. But both were quite small, less than 5 per cent of total assets. The United States is still an overwhelmingly domestic economy in terms of its capital structure, although as we shall see later exports and imports grew quite substantially over the period in question. However they were still a small proportion of the total.

Figure 5.2 shows the balance sheets of the household sector from 1945 onwards. Here again the overall picture is one of great stability. Household net worth declined from about 95 per cent of total assets in 1945 to about 85 per cent in 1989 with the relative increase in mortgages and consumer credit, although consumer credit was a surprisingly small part of the total.

On the asset side, equity and non-corporate business declined a

Figure 5.1   Balance sheets for the US economy: non-financial corporate business, 1945–88

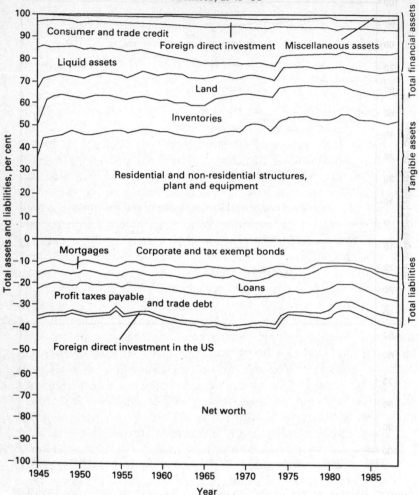

Sources: Balance sheets for the US economy for 1946–85, 1949–88, Board of Governors of the Federal Reserve System, April 1986, April 1989.

little, reflecting a slight increase in the corporate sector, but what is really surprising was the sharp decline in corporate equity from 1973–5, corresponding to the discontinuity in that period in the corporate balance sheets. This can hardly be blamed on OPEC and the oil crisis, nor on any stock market crash. Currency and deposits increased somewhat. It is a little surprising to find that they were larger than consumer durables in view of houses being full of furni-

Figure 5.2   Balance sheets of the household sector, US 1945–88

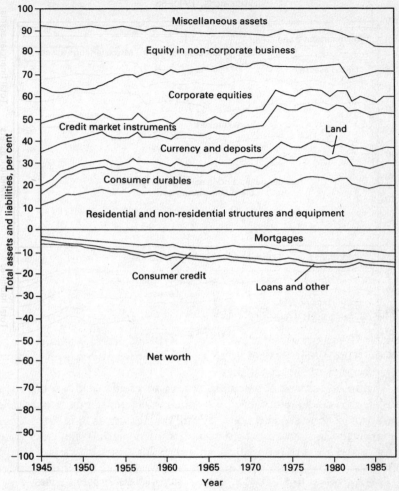

Source: Balance sheets for the US economy for 1945–82, 1949–88, Board of Governors of the Federal Reserve System, October 1983, April 1989.

ture and garages full of cars. One would have expected that for the average household the value of its consumer durables would have greatly exceeded its money holdings, even though the average cash holding edged towards $1000, perhaps partly because of the illegal drug trade. The rise in residential and non-residential structures and equipment is not surprising. If we offset this with the rise in mortgages, it looks as if the net worth of owning a house, that is the value of a house minus the outstanding mortgage, did not change all that

Figure 5.3   Consumer credit outstanding as percentage of GCP, US 1929–89

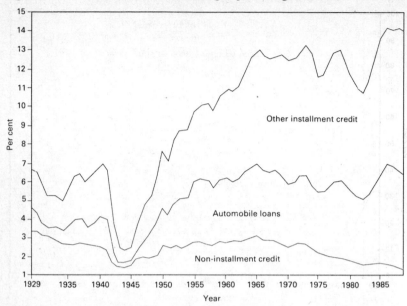

Source: *Economic Report of the President*, 1968, 1990.

much. Consumer credit grew, but it was still surprisingly small in view of the increased use of credit cards. It is difficult not to wonder about the accuracy of these statistics.

Figure 5.3 shows outstanding consumer credit, divided between instalment credit/automobile and non-installment credit from 1929 onwards. The sharp shrinkage during the Second World War is not unexpected in view of the combination of rising incomes and price controls. The explosion of consumer credit from 2.39 per cent of GCP in 1944 to 13 per cent in 1965, and its relative stability (subject to two or three cycles) since then is very striking. The troughs of the credit cycle in 1975–6 and 1981–2 correspond quite closely with peak levels of unemployment, noticeable even in 1959.

Figure 5.4 shows mortgage debt outstanding as a percentage of GCP. Here again we see a steady rise from about 1945 to 1965, after which it flattened out, with small cycles roughly corresponding to the unemployment cycle. There was a sharp rise after 1981.

Figure 5.5 shows outstanding mortgages by type of property, again showing surprisingly little change in the proportions, especially after 1950. A large proportion of mortgages were for single-family houses. I would have expected a larger proportion in multi-family properties

Figure 5.4 Mortgage debt outstanding as percentage of GCP, US 1939–89

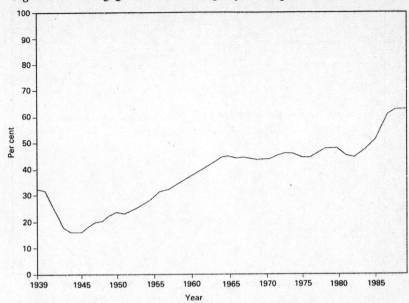

Source: Adapted from the *Economic Report of the President*, 1963, 1990.

Figure 5.5 Mortgage debt outstanding by type of property, US 1939–89

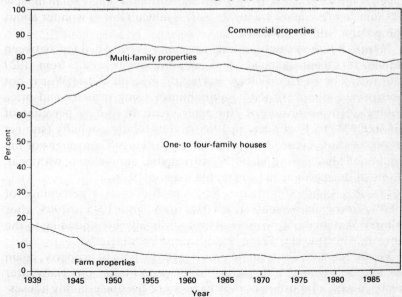

Source: *Economic Report of the President*, 1968, 1990.

Figure 5.6   Mortgage debt outstanding by holder, US 1939–89

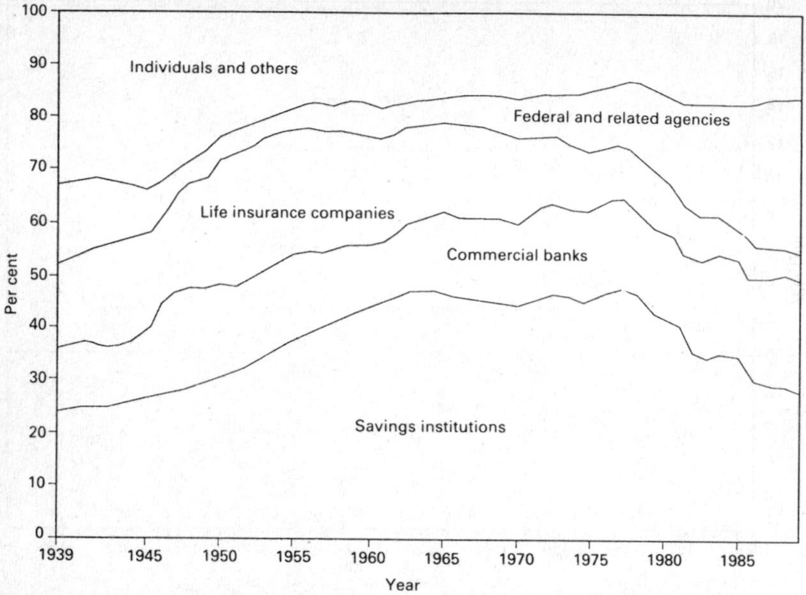

Source: *Economic Report of the President*, 1968, 1990.

in the age of condominiums. Residential mortgages were around 75 per cent compared with 25 per cent for commercial and farm properties, which illustrates the importance of household capital.

Figure 5.6 shows the proportion of outstanding mortgage debt by holder. Here the changes are quite substantial. Savings institutions expanded up until about 1965 and then contracted sharply after 1975, reflecting perhaps their increasing financial difficulties. Commercial banks were pretty stable. Life insurance companies declined from about 1970. Federal-related agencies expanded greatly from the late 1960s, an indication perhaps of the increasing difficulties of the savings and loan institutions. The proportion of mortgages going to individuals shrank substantially over the whole period, especially in the earlier years.

It is virtually impossible to get data on the total capital stock of the United States, but an important clue to this is net private domestic investment. This is shown in Figure 5.7. Net private domestic investment should be roughly equivalent to the increase in the capital stock of businesses in any particular year. We can see the devastating effects of the Great Depression on net private domestic investment, which fell sharply to about minus 8 per cent of GCP. We can also see

Figure 5.7 Private domestic investment as percentage of GCP, US 1929–89

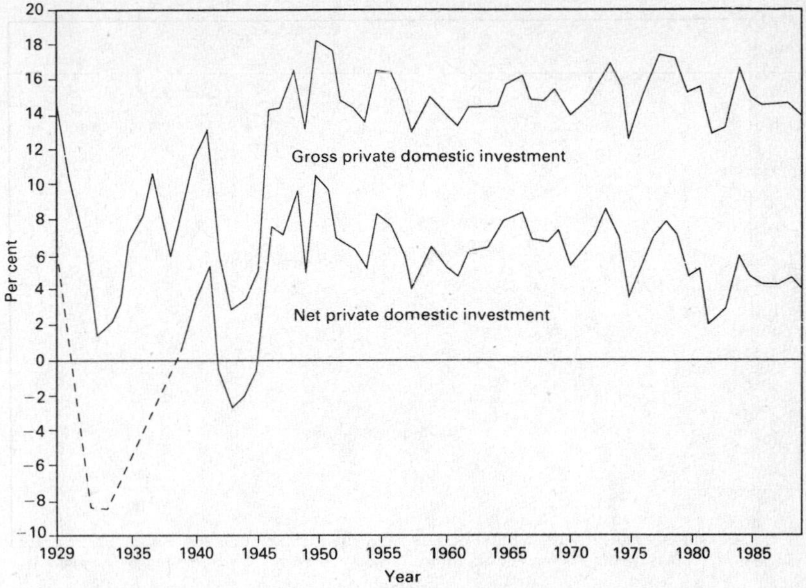

Source: *Economic Report of the President*, 1968, 1990.

the subsequent recovery up until 1940, which was the major factor in the spontaneous recovery from the Great Depression. During the Second World War net private domestic investment again became negative. The bulge in the national income figures during the war, as we saw in Chapter 3, was rather fraudulent as the civilian economy was actually running down. After the 'great disarmament' net private domestic investment started up again, reaching a peak in 1950 at about 10 per cent of GCP, after which it declined slowly and irregularly, reaching levels as low as 3.1 per cent in 1975 and 1.83 per cent in 1982, before recovering substantially. The cycles of net private domestic investment of course correspond very closely with the cycles in gross private domestic investment. The differences are the rather arbitrary figures for capital depreciation. The troughs in both gross private and net private domestic investment again correspond very closely with the peaks of unemployment – in 1932, 1948–9, 1953, 1957, 1960, 1970, 1973 and 1980–1.

Figure 5.8 shows capital consumption (gross minus net private domestic investment) as a percentage of GCP. This is almost inevitably a very rough figure. The trough in 1945 certainly reflects a decline in total capital during the Great Depression and the war. The

Figure 5.8   Capital consumption as percentage of GCP, US 1929–89

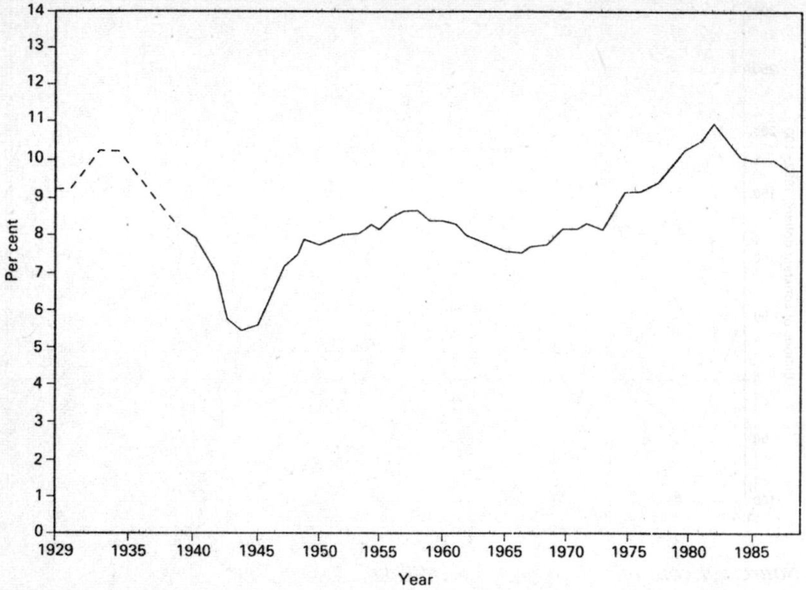

Source: *Economic Report of the President*, 1968, 1990.

recovery by the late 1950s reflects an increase in capital as a result of net private domestic investment during this period. The slight trough in the 1960s is a little puzzling, but a sharp rise began in 1973 and peaked at a higher level than previously, perhaps reflecting increasing recognition that capital stock had been growing. We would normally expect an increase in capital stock to be followed by a rise in the amount of depreciation.

Figure 5.9 shows real net private domestic investment in absolute figures (in 1982 dollars). These figures, by cumulating them year after year, provide at least a rough indicator of the increase in real capital in the United States since 1929, shown in Figure 5.10. As we do not have any figure for 1929 we cannot ascertain the absolute figures. And of course this cannot show increases in household capital, but if these rose fairly proportionately to each other then the figure that we have for net private domestic investment is at least suggestive of what happened to total capital. The second line in the figure shows the increase in real GNP from 1929. The parallel path of the two lines is very striking. Also the divergence after about 1975 suggests that the advance in human knowledge and technology played an increasing

Figure 5.9   Real net private domestic investment, US 1929–89

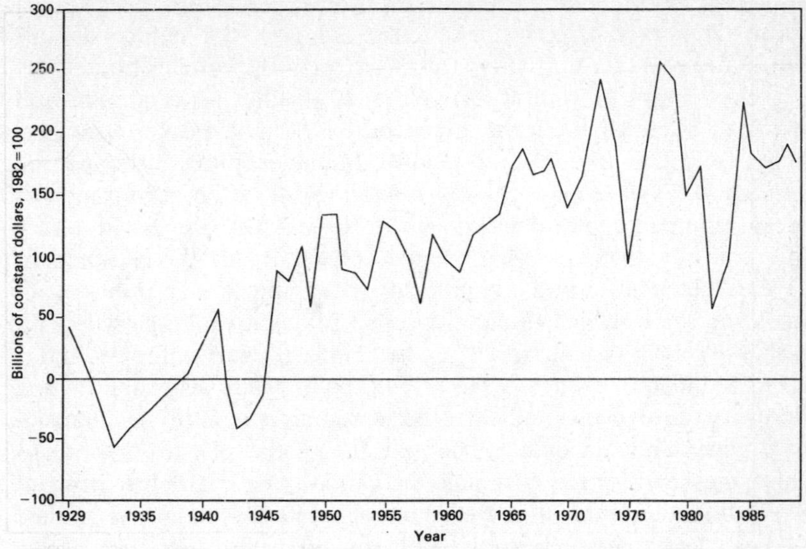

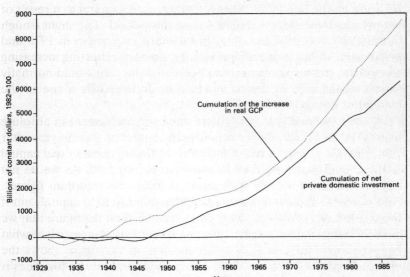

Source: *Economic Report of the President*, 1968, 1990.

Figure 5.10   Increase in real capital, US 1929–89

Source: *Economic Report of the President*, 1968, 1990.

role from that time. Somewhat contradictorily this went hand in hand with a certain decline in the rise in productivity, as we saw earlier. These figures perhaps are more suggestive of the defects in our information system than they are of any positive conclusion.

The structure of capital has two very distinct aspects: real and financial. 'Real' capital is the total stock of valuable goods in society, which of course should also include human capital, although the distinction between physical and human capital is an important one because human capital participates in the market process in a very different way from physical capital, especially in the absence of slavery. Financial capital consists of stocks and bonds, debts of all kinds and so on, which essentially represent claims on the ownership of the value of physical capital. These claims are very complex, and it is often difficult to know exactly who owns what, especially when there are insolvencies. Ideally the total net value of all financial instruments should equal the total value of the physical capital to which they correspond, although we cannot rule out debts incurred by persons when increasing their human capital in minds and bodies, such as when students borrow to pay for their education.

The value of capital, whether of real capital or of stocks and bonds, depends both on expected income from profits or interest (which represents a gross increase in net worth over the period of time in which income is calculated), and also on the rate of interest or rate of discount at which future incomes are discounted.[1] The situation is made much more complex by the existence of bonds of different maturities or different types of stock, such as preferred stock as well as ordinary stock. There is however a well organised and active market in financial instruments of all kinds – in the stock markets and in the bond markets – which follows the principles of all markets that the relative price structure of these financial instruments tends to move towards that at which people in the market are willing to hold what is there to be held, including money in all its forms. This is the theory of market equilibrium. These markets are often subject to strong fluctuations because a change in people's expectations of the future affects their willingness to hold what is there to be held. These expectations of the future themselves have several aspects. One is expected future payments in terms of dividends or interest. This will ultimately depend on the increase in the net worth of businesses and individuals who hold real capital. The other is the uncertainty involved in these expectations, upon which the rate at which future returns are going to be discounted largely depends, uncertain prospects being discounted at a higher rate than more certain prospects.

The situation is further complicated by the fact that changes in the relative price of these instruments is also a form of profit or loss, either potential if the capital continues to be held, or realised if it is sold. Money in all its different forms is part of this financial market and there is a great deal of exchange among different forms of money and liquidity as well as among stocks and bonds. Money is itself a kind of non-interest-bearing 'bond' as it represents a promise to exchange something in the future. A $50 bill is implicitly a promise on the part of all who sell things for dollars to sell its owner $50 worth of something on demand. Even legal tender derives a good deal of its value from the fact that the government that legalises it has to accept it in payment of taxes, which transaction amounts to a diminution of the debt of the person paying the taxes.

The situation is still further complicated by the fact that rates of return on old debt are determined by the price which these obligations fetch in the market, together with the expected price at which they may be sold later on. One of the reasons why inflation is so popular is that it reduces the burden of old debt on society. Most debt is contracted in terms of 'current dollars'. If inflation is widely anticipated however, these contracts may be changed into 'real dollars', that is current dollars multiplied by the amount of inflation. Inflation then has very little effect on the debt burden. There may however be legal obstacles to 'real dollars' contracts.

Interest and profit rates, as we have seen earlier and will see again later, play a very important role in determining the overall character of the economy. These have fluctuated a great deal since 1929 and are indeed one of the most changeable elements of the United States economy.

Returning to Figure 3.5 – national income by type of income – we see the 'gobbling' up of profit by interest in 1932–3 and the erosion of profit by interest from the mid-1960s. A very important question that is surprisingly difficult to answer is the extent to which this erosion of profits by interest, which was disastrous in the Great Depression and was noticeable in the 1980s, was a result of changes in the rate of profit and the rate of interest, or of changes in the proportion of stock to bond financing.

Figure 5.11, a 'time scatter'[2] relating the Federal Reserve Bank discount rate to the proportion of national income going to interest, at least throws some light on the relationship with regard to interest. The relationship between interest and different types of lending is

Figure 5.11   Interest rate vs interest as percentage of national income, US
1929–89

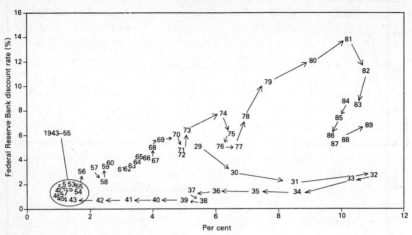

Source: *Economic Report of the President*, 1968, 1990.

quite a difficult one and the data on it are not easy to obtain. We do
have data however on the Federal Reserve Bank discount rate, which
is very closely related to the rate of interest charged by banks.

Figure 5.11 shows how extraordinarily low real interest rates were
in the 1930s and 1940s. From 1938–47 the Federal Reserve discount
rate was 1 per cent. The Second World War budget deficit was
financed at a rate of interest so low that it did not become much of a
burden in the future. The interest rate started to rise fairly steadily
after 1947, with small declines in 1970–2 and from 1974–6, peaking at
13.42 per cent in 1981. However since then it has fallen fairly sharply
but without changing very much the proportion of national income
going to net interest, perhaps because of the volume of old debt. This
dramatic rise in interest rates is a puzzling phenomenon. Whether the
Federal Reserve System helped to create it and led it, or whether it
merely followed something that was happening anyway, is not easy to
determine, but it is certainly a very ominous aspect of the United
States economy today. It is strange that John Maynard Keynes predicted what he called the 'euthanasia of the rentier'[3] and thought that
rates of interest would continue to fall in the years following the
Second World War, with continued accumulation of capital. Why he
was so wrong still remains something of a mystery.

The relationship between nominal rates of interest and 'real rates'

Figure 5.12   Real rate of return and interest rate, US 1929–89

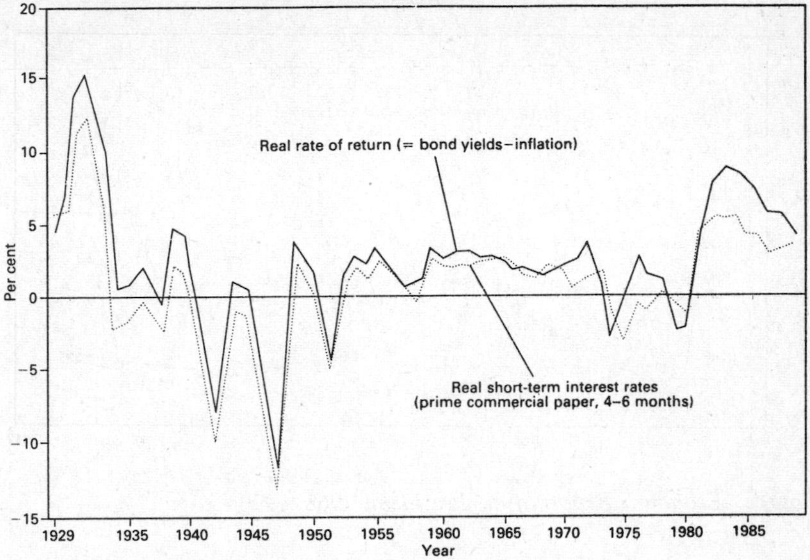

Source: *Economic Report of the President*, 1968, 1990.

and the rate of inflation depends very much on the time period of the note or bond (see Figure 5.12). For a short-term loan, say for one year, the real rate of interest is roughly the nominal rate multiplied by the annual rate of inflation. If the loan is $100 at 10 per cent, $110 is paid back one year later. If the price level goes from, say, 100 to 104 during the year, the $110 at the end of the year is only worth $110 divided by $104 times 100, which is $105.76, which means that the real rate of interest would be 5.76 per cent per annum instead of the 10 per cent nominal rate. Suppose however that we have a ten-year bond at 10 per cent (a bond which pays $100 every year for nine years and then $110). To find the real rate of return we would have to find the value in dollars for the first year and payments of all succeeding years and calculate the real rate of return from that.

Another aspect of the capital structure that may have some significance is the structure of business inventories. Figure 5.13 shows the distribution of manufacturers' total inventories between materials and supplies, work in process and finished durable and non-durable goods. The proportions are remarkably stable, roughly one-third for each category. There was a slight increase in work in process, at the expense of materials and supplies. Every production process involves

Figure 5.13   Components of manufacturers' inventories by stage of process,
US 1953–89

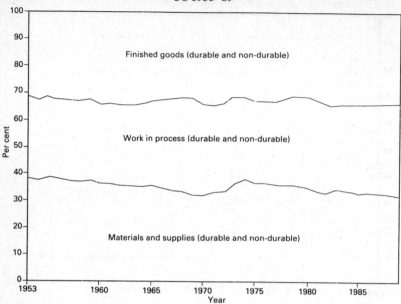

Source: *Economic Report of the President*, 1990.

the collection and transportation of some form of raw material, either from mines, from agriculture or from forests. These materials are processed into partly finished goods (work in process) and end up as stock in the hands of the producers of finished goods. Not much information is available on the time that it takes to complete this process, which Austrian economists call the 'period of production'. If the 'pipelines' become empty (this happened not infrequently in centrally-planned economies) the whole process is seriously hampered. This very rarely seems to be a problem in market societies, although it is not wholly clear why. Sometimes there are markets along the way in the production process for raw materials, for half-finished goods or for parts, and if these are active markets shortages will be reflected very rapidly in price increases, which will encourage supply and relieve the scarcity. Similarly, surplus accumulation will lower prices and lead to a reduction in the output of too plentiful articles. The remarkable stability of these proportions over the years suggests that these processes seem to work very well. There is a little evidence that the oil crisis of 1973 led to some accumulation of

Figure 5.14   Components of manufacturers' inventories by durability of goods, US 1953–89

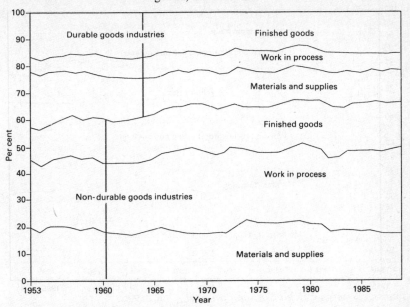

Source: *Economic Report of the President*, 1990.

materials and supplies, both at some expense to work in process and to stocks of finished goods, but this effect was really very small.

Figure 5.14 shows the same division between durable and non-durable goods industries. Again the stability in their relationship is striking. There was a small shift from non-durable goods into durable goods in the late 1960s as a result of a slight increase in the proportion of work in process in non-durable goods industries, but the overall effect was not very significant.

Figure 5.15 shows the distribution of business inventories between manufacturing, wholesalers and retailers. Again the proportions were quite stable, with a small but noticeable decline in manufacturing inventories after 1970, especially after about 1981, and a corresponding expansion in the wholesale and retail trade, which perhaps reflects the increase in the proportion of the labour force in wholesaling and retailing we saw in Figure 2.6.

Figure 5.16 shows the proportions of sales of the manufacturing, wholesale and retail trades. Their sales were strikingly parallel, although with a few slight differences. As we shall see later, there is

Figure 5.15   Inventories of manufacturing and trade, US 1948–89

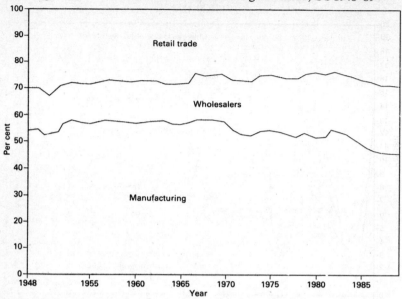

Source: *Economic Report of the President*, 1968, 1990.

Figure 5.16   Sales by manufacturing and trade, US 1948–89

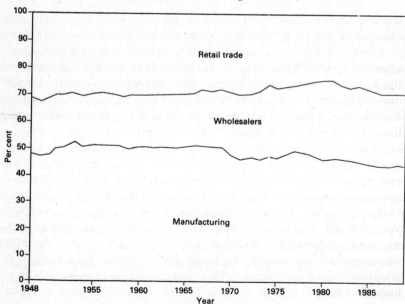

Source: *Economic Report of the President*, 1968, 1990.

Figure 5.17   Gross private domestic investment as percentage of GCP, US
1929–89

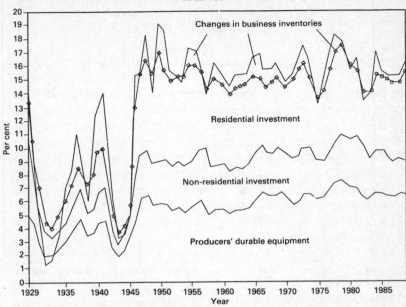

Source: *Economic Report of the President*, 1968, 1990.

some evidence that inventories affect employment levels, but this
effect does not seem to be very large.

Another interesting example of proportional stability, particularly
after the Second World War, is illustrated in Figure 5.17 which shows
the components of gross private domestic investment (producers'
durable equipment, non-residential structures, residential investment
and changes in business inventories, which are occasionally negative). In the age of disturbance (from about 1929 to about 1948), we
see how in the Great Depression the decline in business inventories
was a very important contributor to the overall decline in gross
private domestic investment. We see how the decline in residential
investment and in non-residential structures contributed considerably
to the decline in gross private domestic investment during the Second
World War. From about 1948 onwards, however, the proportions
were remarkably stable. There was some cyclical fluctuation, and this
was especially noticeable in producers' durable equipment. The
possible relationship between the above and unemployment will be
looked at later.

6 The Role of Government

The role of government in the United States economy has two major aspects: (1) quantitative – taxes collected, borrowing, government expenditure, purchases, sales and so on, and (2) qualitative – the laws and regulations which affect economic behaviour. There is even a subtle psychological aspect of trust, respect, hope for the future and so on, which government can create or destroy as the case may be. The impact of regulation and deregulation is something that cannot be estimated from simple statistics. The transition from one president to the next (Figure 3.4) seems to make surprisingly little difference to the quantitative aspects of the economy, with perhaps two exceptions: the transition from Hoover to Roosevelt in 1933, which marked the beginning of the 'New Deal' and an increase in gross private domestic investment, which brought the United States part of the way out of the Great Depression; and the transition from Carter to Reagan in 1980, which seems to have stimulated a steady rise in personal consumption expenditure as a proportion of the economy.

The quantitative role of government in the economy is illustrated in Figure 6.1. This shows total government expenditure as a percentage of GCP split up into national defence, federal purchases, state and local purchases, all government transfers and federal grants. The fluctuations both in the total and in its components were very large over the period of the study. Total government payments went from 8.3 per cent of the economy (GCP) in 1929 to 45.3 per cent in 1944, and were about 20 per cent thereafter. National defence expenditure of course experienced very large fluctuations, going from 0.5 per cent of the economy in 1929 to 40.9 per cent in 1944 (the Second World War). It stood at 4.1 per cent in 1947 (the 'great disarmament') and 12.8 per cent in 1953 (the Korean War), after which it on the whole declined, with just a small upsurge to 8.6 per cent in 1967 during the Vietnam War. Then in the Carter–Reagan rearmament, national defence expenditure went from 4.5 per cent in 1978 to 6.1 per cent in 1987, before declining to 5.5 per cent in 1989.

Federal civilian purchases, which were only 0.9 per cent of GCP in 1929, rose to 3.8 per cent during the Great Depression and its aftermath in 1938, then fell to 0.5 per cent in 1945. In 1989 however they stood at about 2 per cent. State and local government purchases,

Figure 6.1   Government expenditure by components as percentage of GCP, US 1929–89

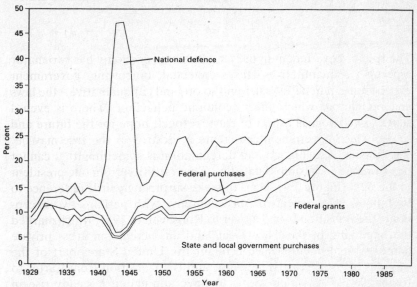

Source: *Economic Report of the President*, 1968, 1990.

on the other hand, have always been much larger than federal purchases. These stood at 6.8 per cent in 1929, rose to 8.6 per cent in 1932 during the Great Depression, declined to 3.1 per cent in 1944 during the Second World War, and rose fairly steadily thereafter, reaching about 9.3 per cent in 1989. As noted earlier, it is curious that there seems to be a myth in the United States of a gigantic and ever-increasing federal government, when in fact total government has remained a remarkably stable proportion of the economy (about 20 per cent) since 1960. It is twice as large as it was in 1929, but still the main increase has been in state and local government, not in federal, although federal grants to state and local governments have played a part in this. Another very striking phenomenon was a dramatic increase in government transfers to individuals, particularly at the federal government level. Total transfers went from about 1.4 per cent of the economy in 1929 to over 11 per cent in 1989.

Figure 6.2 shows federal outlays by function, each as a percentage of the total outlay. This includes both government purchases, which are part of GNP, and government transfers, which are not included in GNP but appear rather as personal income. The Second World War

Figure 6.2   Federal outlays by function, US, fiscal years 1940–91

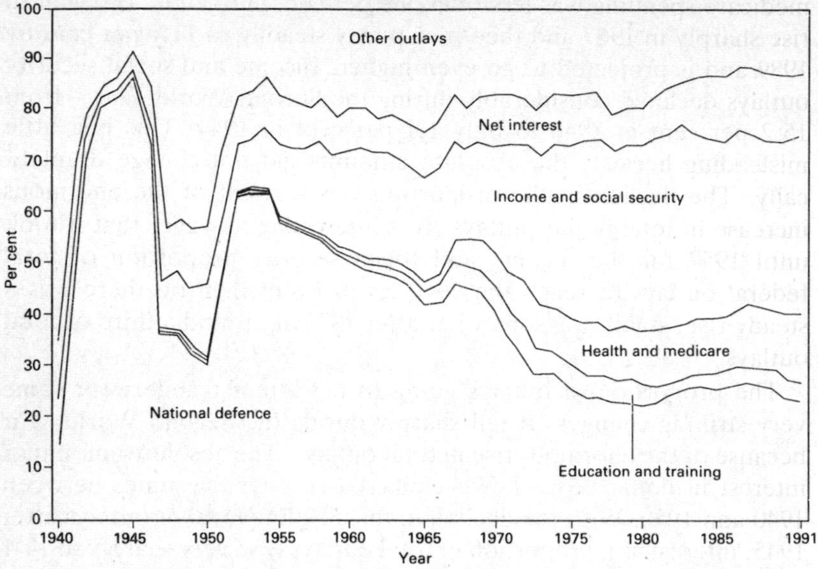

Source: *Economic Report of the President*, 1990.

shows up very dramatically, as does the 'great disarmament' which followed it. National defence was only 15.7 per cent of total government expenditure in 1940, rising to 85.7 per cent in 1945 and falling to 35.4 per cent in 1947 and 30.4 per cent in 1950. The Korean War pushed national defence expenditure up to 65.8 per cent by 1954, and this was followed by what might be called a 'slow disarmament', which reduced spending to 27.2 per cent by 1980. There was a small rise during the Vietnam War, which had a surprisingly minor effect economically, although its qualitative effect was much larger. National defence's proportion rose from 41.9 per cent in 1965 to 46 per cent by 1967, then reduced to 35.9 per cent in 1971. After reaching its lowest point in 1980, there was some climb during the Reagan rearmament – to 28.1 per cent in 1987 – but by 1990 it stood at 24.8 per cent.

Education and training, which accounted for one per cent or less of total spending from 1940–60, had of course declined very sharply during the Second World War. From 1960 onwards it rose pretty steadily to 6 per cent in 1979, followed by a rather sharp decline during the Reagan years to 3.2 per cent in 1989. Likewise health and medicare spending was less than one per cent until 1961. It began to rise sharply in 1967 and then rose pretty steadily to 11.7 per cent by 1989 and is projected to go even higher. Income and social security outlays declined considerably during the Second World War – from 15.2 per cent in 1940 to only 1.1 per cent in 1944. This is a little misleading because the absolute amounts did not change dramatically. The decline in the proportion was a result of the enormous increase in total dollar outlays. It is interesting however that it took until 1957 for the income and social security proportion of total federal outlays to reach the 1940 level. From then on there was a steady rise, stabilising somewhat after 1975 at around a third of total outlays.

The proportion of outlays going to net interest underwent some very striking changes. It fell sharply during the Second World War because of the enormous rise in total outlays. The absolute amount of interest in dollar terms however increased over five times between 1940 and 1950. With the decline in the absolute level of outlays after 1945, interest as a proportion of total outlays rose very sharply to 14.1 per cent in 1948, reflecting of course the budget deficits of the Second World War. After 1952 net interest remained at a fairly stable 8.6 per cent and was still only 8.9 per cent in 1980. Then it climbed very noticeably to 14.8 per cent in 1989, largely as a result of the budget deficits of these years and the high interest rates. The principal statistical victim of the Second World War seems to have been 'other outlays', mostly involving civilian government, which fell very sharply from 56.9 per cent in 1940 to 8.9 per cent in 1945. They recovered to 44.3 per cent in 1950 and have tended to decline slowly ever since, reaching 11.5 per cent in 1990. The principal victim of the 'Reagan Rearmament' (1980–8) seems to have been education and training.

Figure 6.3 shows federal receipts by source as a proportion of total receipts. What is striking here is the relative stability of the proportion from individual income taxes, at least after 1950, at about 45 per cent, although in 1940 it was only 16 per cent. Since 1950 the proportion of combined social insurance taxes and contributions and corporate income taxes has been pretty stable. Corporate income taxes declined from a maximum of 38.2 per cent in 1943 to only 6.2 per cent in 1983, after which they rose to 10.5 per cent in 1989. On the other hand, social insurance taxes and contributions, which were low during the war, increased fairly steadily from 10.7 per cent in 1950 to 36.3 per cent in 1989. This corresponds roughly, of course, to the

Figure 6.3   Federal receipts by source, US, fiscal years 1940–91

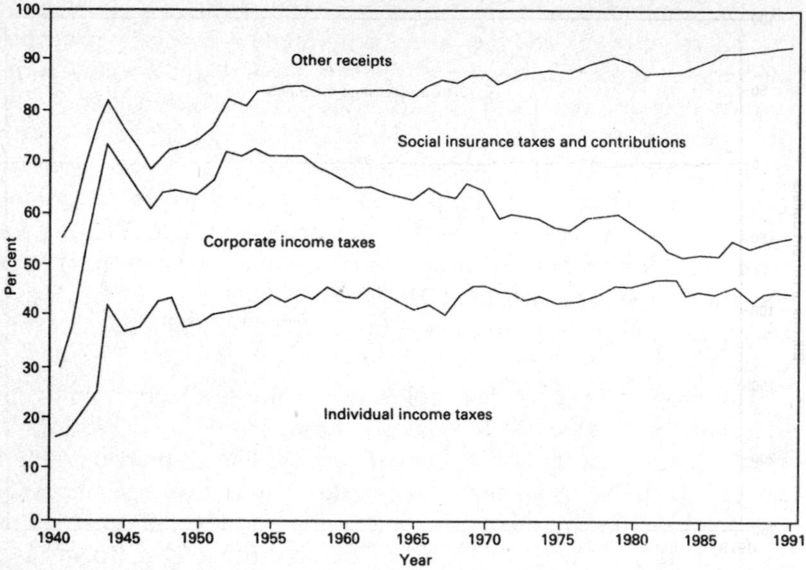

Source: *Economic Report of the President*, 1990.

increase in income and in social security outlays from 10.9 per cent in 1950 to 32.3 per cent in 1989.

Figure 6.4 shows the government budget surplus and deficit for federal, state and local governments in current dollars, and Figure 6.5 in constant 1982 dollars. In these terms the deficit of the Second World War briefly looms very large. From 1945 onward the federal budget was on the whole balanced until the late 1960s. The last year with a surplus was 1969. After that deficits were continuous, reaching a maximum of $180.7 billion (in 1982 dollars) in 1986. This was to some extent offset by state and local government surpluses. The cumulative deficit for 1942–5 was $1439.6 billion in 1982 dollars, or $1361.1 billion if state and local surpluses of $78.5 billion are deducted. The cumulative federal deficit in 1982 dollars from 1970–89 was $1835.8 billion, or $1161.5 billion when state and local surpluses of $674.3 billion are deducted. The four years in which the United States participated in the Second World War produced real deficits of the same order of magnitude as the 20 years from 1970. As mentioned earlier, the deficit of the Second World War was financed at interest rates of 2 to 3 per cent or less, whereas the deficits of the years since 1970 have been financed at an average rate of 8 to 9 per

Figure 6.4   Government budget surplus/deficit, US 1929–89

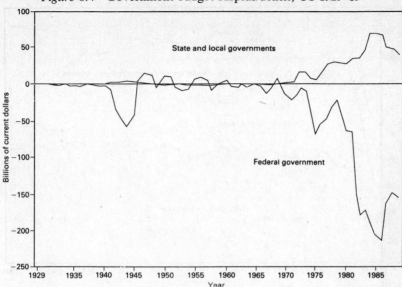

Source: *Economic Report of the President*, 1968, 1990.

Figure 6.5   Government budget surplus/deficit, US 1929–89

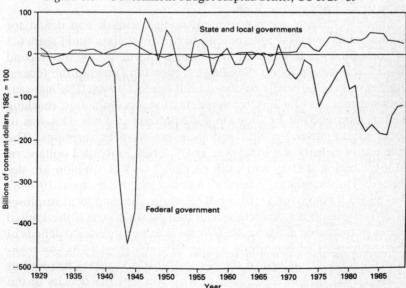

Source: *Economic Report of the President*, 1968, 1990.

Figure 6.6   State and local government revenue by source, selected fiscal
years, US 1927–88

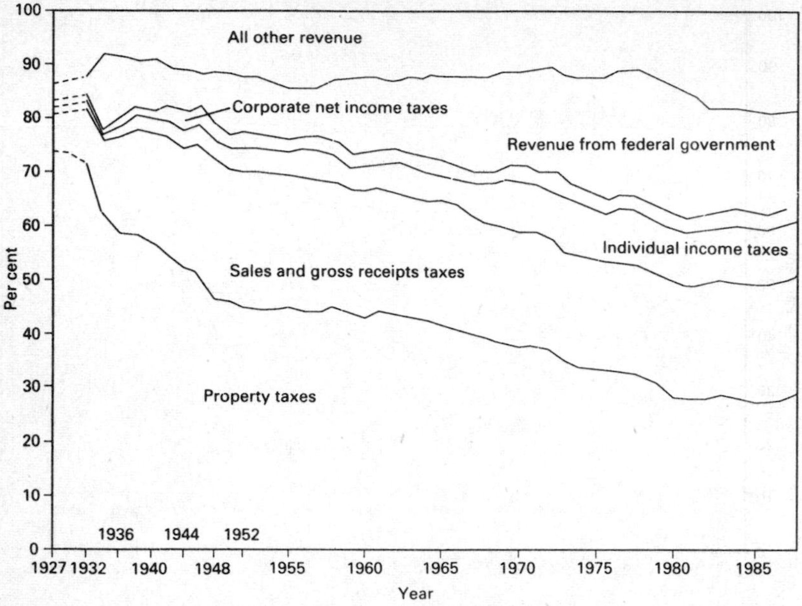

Source: *Economic Report of the President*, 1968, 1990.

cent. It is clear that the deficit alone cannot be held responsible for
the rise in interest rates. The Federal Reserve discount rate rose from
1 per cent in 1947 to 13.42 per cent in 1981, falling to 6.93 per cent in
1989 as Figure 5.11 shows. This is a puzzling phenomenon. Clearly
something happened to the bond market over these 50 years, indicat-
ing a decreased willingness on the part of the public to hold bonds,
thus lowering their price and raising interest rates. The problem
becomes even more puzzling if we look at total government (federal
and state) deficits for these two periods as a proportion of total GCP
– from 1942–5 this was 26.14 per cent and from 1970–89 it was
1.7 per cent.

Figure 6.6 shows state and local government revenue from different sources as a proportion of the total. The most dramatic change
was the decline in property taxes, offset in part by an increase in
individual income taxes and revenue from the federal government.
The revenue from the federal government is especially interesting, as
it does represent a certain effort on the part of the federal government to increase the responsibility of state and local governments but

Figure 6.7   State and local government expenditure by function, US, fiscal
years 1927–88

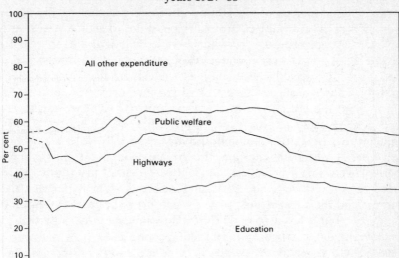

Source: *Economic Report of the President*, 1968, 1990.

also to influence their decisions, as some of this revenue is in the form
of matching grants. It is not altogether clear why property taxes seem
to be so politically unpopular as property owners do not usually
constitute a majority of the voters. Property taxes however are frequently passed on to renters in the form of higher rents, so it is fairly
difficult to estimate their real incidence.

Figure 6.7 shows state and local expenditures as a proportion of the
total. Again there are no dramatic changes. The proportion devoted
to highways has been declining since the mid-1960s, perhaps because
most of the major highways have now been built and focus has shifted
to maintenance. Education also peaked out somewhat in the 1960s
and thereafter declined slowly, in spite of – or perhaps even because
of – the fact that there seems to be very wide dissatisfaction with the
education system. There may be something of a trap here: dissatisfaction with the system leads to a reduction in support for it, which in
turn leads to greater dissatisfaction. Public welfare, which expanded
very substantially during the Great Depression, declined somewhat
during the 1950s and 1960s. From the late 1960s it again expanded,

reflecting perhaps some increase in the level of unemployment and perhaps also an increase in households headed by females.

The indirect impact of the United States government on the economy is very difficult, indeed almost impossible, to estimate with any accuracy, simply because of what I have called the 'echo effect'. Every act of government produces changes in the behaviour of those most directly affected; these changes affect the behaviour of others and this causes changed behaviour in yet further people, and so on throughout the economy. However we must do what we can to try and analyse these effects, even though the overall impact is very difficult to estimate. In the United States especially, it is not easy to tell where government ends and the private economy begins as numbers of what might be called 'quasi-governmental' institutions have been set up. Of these the Federal Reserve System is perhaps the largest and most significant. It was created by the legal system and Congress, but it has a good deal of independence in its activities.

Government has two major functions: one is to plan budgets – receipts and expenditure – which provide most of the direct impacts on the economy. The other is to create laws and agencies to deal with violations of laws, which form the basis of most of the indirect effects. The main object of laws is to define illegal behaviour and distinguish it from legal behaviour, and to establish a system of penalties – fines or imprisonment, or even capital punishment – which are administered by courts of law. The main object of these penalties is presumably to deter people from breaking the law. The dramatic rise in the number of people in prison, especially since 1970, suggests that this deterrence is not very effective. Of every 100 000 people, 99 were imprisoned in 1929, 118 in 1960, 98 in 1970, 139 in 1980, 245 in 1988 and 285 in 1989. The United States now has the largest proportion of its population in prison of any developed society.[1] The direct economic impact of the system of penalties is in a sense the redistribution of net worth from the convicted violator to the government itself, whether this is through fines or through imprisonment. Imprisonment however turns the criminal (for the duration of the sentence) into a kind of slave of the government, although a non-saleable and rather inefficient one. The net cost of this to government is substantial – and increasing – and can only be justified by the benefits of deterrence. Conscription into the military is analogous to temporary governmental, non-market slavery. In both cases the economic evaluation of the benefits of deterrence are virtually impossible to calculate.

We can distinguish a number of different forms of illegal activity as defined by government. First, illegal activity can be devoted to the formation of illegal forms of organisation. Here the anti-trust laws are brought into play in an attempt to prevent the formation of monopolies. In the case of what are called 'natural monopolies', where the advantages of scale of organisation are so large that the cost of having a number of competitive organisations is too high, the answer is sometimes government ownership, as with the post office, and sometimes government regulation of prices, as in the case of public utilities. Crime gangs and the mafia might also be regarded as illegal organisations, although these are usually dealt with by the prosecution of individual members.

Second, another form of legal intervention is the definition of illegal exchanges, for which either the purchaser or the seller, or both depending on the circumstances, may be responsible. Examples would be the minimum wage, legislated in 1938 and approved by the Supreme Court in 1941; and price and wage controls, which were effected during the Second World War and again under President Nixon in 1971. Another possible example would be the Robinson–Patman Act of 1936, which prohibited firms from offering low prices aimed at destroying competition.

Third, a government may render illegal certain commodities or products, such as drugs. Also fitting into this category is the control of pollution, that is regulations covering the production of negative commodities such as sulphur dioxide from power plants, or oil spills. There may also be regulation of the nature and quality of goods sold, such as seat belts and children's safety seats in automobiles.

Fourth, a somewhat related system of laws defines the illegality of certain methods of production, such as workmen's compensation laws that regulate occupational hazards. Fifth, there may be illegal communications, such as lies in advertising, the use of inside information in stock and commodity markets, the libelling of competitors and so on. The prosecutions that took place in 1990 of offenders in the stock market provide a good example of this.

Sixth, there may be illegal failures – sins of omission, that is failure to do something that should have been done, such as registering for a draft or sending in an income tax return. Finally there may be illegal movement of goods or people across boundaries; for instance smuggling and violated quotas in the case of commodities, immigration restrictions in the case of people.

If we look at the long-term movements of some of these aspects of government over the 60 years we can detect a number of different

Figure 6.8   Tariff indexes, US 1929–87

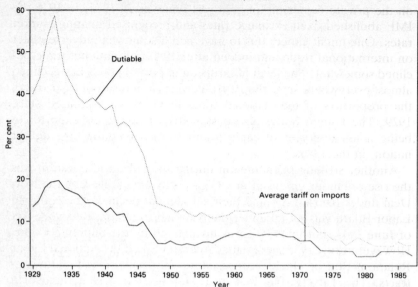

Sources: *Historical Statistics of the US*; *Statistical Abstract of the US*, 1990.

patterns. First, there has been a striking movement from protection towards free or at least freer international trade, as Figure 6.8 shows. Tariff collections as a percentage of the total value of dutiable goods fell from nearly 60 per cent in 1932 to 3 per cent in 1989. The Smoot–Hawley Tariff of 1930, which was passed in spite of the protests of a thousand economists, may have played some role in deepening the Great Depression, although it is very difficult to judge what actual impact it had. Since the Second World War especially, the General Agreement on Tariffs and Trade (GATT) has lowered tariffs almost everywhere and is at least one factor behind the tremendous expansion in international trade, which increased about six times between 1950 and 1980 (Figure 7.5). Figure 6.8 shows the dramatic reduction of the level of tariffs in the United States, as measured by the tariff charge as a percentage of the total value of imports (dutiable and total).

Related to the free trade movement was the abandonment of the gold standard and the move towards free exchange rates, which was to an extent governed by the International Monetary Fund (IMF). President Roosevelt took the United States off the gold standard in April 1933, which meant that the government was no longer offering to buy and sell gold at approximately a fixed price. The prohibition on the private ownership of gold was removed in 1974. In 1976 the IMF abolished fixed exchange rates and recognised floating market rates. One might expect this to have had a somewhat adverse effect on international trade and indeed after 1980 international trade declined somewhat. The level of tariffs on imported goods has declined almost everywhere since the 1930s. Perhaps as a result of freer trade, the proportion of international trade in GCP has increased since 1929. The United States also passed from being a net exporter to being a net importer of capital, and from a creditor to a debtor nation, in the 1980s.

Another striking phenomenon during the period in question was the rise of labour unions after 1933 – partly encouraged by the New Deal under Roosevelt – and their subsequent decline. The National Labor Board was set up under the National Industrial Recovery Act of June 1933, but in 1935 it was invalidated by the Supreme Court. However in July 1935 the Wagner Act established the National Labor Relations Board, which encouraged union formation and union contracts. The Taft–Hartley Act of 1937 represented something of a reversal of policy and led to increased government control over strikes. The proportion of the labour force belonging to unions rose very sharply in the 1930s (11.6 per cent in 1930, 35.5 per cent in 1945), but thereafter declined slowly to 16.4 per cent in 1989.[2] Along with some discouragement of unions, however, there was a marked increase in legislation aimed at preventing discrimination in employment, either by race or by gender. Martin Luther King played a charismatic role in this process from about 1956 until his assassination in 1968. The Civil Rights Bill of April 1968 was a landmark in the anti-discrimination movement.

Another movement that has made its presence felt, especially since the 1960s, has been the environmental protection movement, the effectiveness of which the National Environmental Policy Act of January 1970 bears witness. The Air Quality Act of 1990 in the long term may perhaps have even more dramatic effects.

A further example is the regulation of stock and commodity markets and banking, dating from the United States Security Act of 1933. The regulation of airlines until recently provided another example. However under President Reagan there was a move towards deregulation, and this may have had a hand in bringing about the savings and loan crisis of the late 1980s. The state has also intervened in housing and housing loans, beginning again with the New Deal and tapering off somewhat as the decades went on.

Intervention in agriculture, especially with regard to prices, is particularly striking. The establishment of the Federal Farm Board goes back even to Herbert Hoover in 1929. An attempt to prevent a fall in the relative price of major agricultural products had some success, but it did not prevent the dramatic decline in the agricultural labour force shown in Figure 2.7. In this area too there has been a long and slow reduction in government intervention, but it is still fairly extensive.

Along with the increased government intervention associated with the New Deal there was one very striking move in the opposite direction: the repeal of prohibition in December 1933, which of course led to the rise of a substantial liquor industry and some increase in cirrhosis of the liver.

A final, perhaps rather irregular, pattern has been a shift in monetary policy, especially that of the Federal Reserve System. There is little doubt that the Federal Reserve Board exacerbated the Great Depression by not preventing deflation and perhaps even accentuating it after 1932. In subsequent years monetarism became very popular, inspired in part by Milton Friedman,[3] and the Federal Reserve tended to adopt as its objective the control of inflation. The fact that the United States has experienced roughly tenfold inflation since 1933 suggests that this has not been very effective. Indeed it is not easy to find any regular or even rational pattern in the decisions of the Federal Reserve Board. In 1980 and 1981 it certainly created a sharp, brief depression and a spectacular rise in interest rates. To its credit, it did intervene somewhat after the stock market crash of 1987, which had remarkably little impact on the economy as a whole, suggesting perhaps that the stock exchange has become a rather isolated casino which does not have much to do with the general investment decisions of the business community. What the Federal Reserve Board was not able to do was to prevent the rise in interest rates from the late 1940s into the early 1980s, which has certainly contributed to the slow rise in poverty since the mid-1970s and the failure of wages to rise since 1970. It is ironic indeed, as noted earlier, that the 'War on Poverty' declared by President Johnson in 1964 actually first brought about a slowdown in the fall in poverty that had been taking place since 1950 and then an eventual rise in poverty (Figure 3.8).

This very brief account cannot encompass the complexities of the period being studied here. The record is mixed, although on the whole one is tempted to give the United States economy, particularly after about 1945, at least a 'B'. Americans did get richer, poverty was reduced, at least in the first 30 years, and inflation has not done much harm to the economy as a whole and it is certainly manageable. There has not been a repeat of the Great Depression, although there have been two small ones. But the United States is laying up trouble for the future with the rising debt burden and its apparent inability to manage the federal budget. Political ideology seems to have played a fairly small role in all of this. In many ways Reagan, for all his conservative talk, was a very Keynesian and almost radical president, and it is becoming increasingly difficult to distinguish Democrats from Republicans.

The role of government in what can certainly be described as a noticeable success in terms of current incomes is still a little obscure. One suspects that economic success has been due far more to the individual energies, imagination and risk-taking of millions of civilians, who on the whole see government as a bit of a nuisance but something that can be lived with. Perhaps this reflects the view of an economist rather than of a political scientist. But at least the evidence suggests that the importance of government can easily be overrated.

7 The World Economic Environment

The United States, like all other countries, lives in a world environment of international trade, with imports and exports, investments, grants and migrations that cross national boundaries. There is also a world environment of international political and military relations, with diplomacy, treaties, trade agreements, war industries, threats and occasionally wars.

The world is now divided into over 160 independent nations, with a number of other units that have some degree of independence. National boundaries are an important source for the information system. Information is collected at immigration stations, customs houses and so on. At national boundaries tariffs, quotas, immigration restrictions and so on are imposed, which represent certain obstacles to the free flow of commodities or persons. Occasionally even information is blocked, although in these days of radio and television it is difficult to interrupt except by jamming the airwaves. International trade is generally defined as the flow of commodities across national boundaries. Commodities crossing from the inside to the outside of a country are defined as its exports; commodities crossing from outside to inside are its imports, so any commodity that crosses a national boundary is an export of one nation and an import of another. Therefore for the world as a whole exports and imports should be equal. For any one country however, imports can exceed exports (an import surplus), or exports can exceed imports (an export surplus).

Also crossing international borders are money ownership, debts, property rights and so on. Every country has its own currency, which is only valid for ordinary purchases inside that country. There is therefore a large foreign exchange market in which these currencies are exchanged one for another. Foreign investment is a complex process whereby property in one country may be created, as in for instance the building of factories, buildings and so on, with the purchasing power coming in from other countries. In this respect, if a country has an export surplus it is an indication that it is investing abroad; if it has an import surplus this suggests that other countries are investing in it. Financial transactions on the whole involve the

84

circulation of assets among owners, and some of these assets will cross national boundaries.

International trade cannot be considered a thing in itself. It is really a sample of the total volume of exchange that happens to cross national boundaries. If the world were a single country, of course, there would be no international trade, but the overall pattern of trade might not be very different, although it is true that the existence of national boundaries distorts the total pattern of trade through such things as foreign exchange rates, tariffs and quotas.

Migration can be thought of as a transfer of human capital from one country to another. Some migrants are refugees seeking political freedom and asylum. Others are motivated more by economic considerations, believing that the human capital of their minds and bodies will be better valued in the country to which they migrate than it was in the country from whence they came, just as capitalists who invest abroad do so because they think the rate of return abroad will be higher than if they invest at home. There should be some tendency therefore for both foreign investment and migration to diminish the differences among wage rates and rates of profit and interest in different parts of the world. This effect can however be easily overshadowed by offsetting movements in domestic economies.

The United States now has about 5 per cent or a little less of the total world population. This is a somewhat smaller percentage than in 1929. The population of the United States has doubled since that time and the world population has more than doubled. In terms of GNP however, the United States had something like 27 per cent of the gross world product in 1988. At the time of writing the world product figures for 1929 were not available, but the percentage held by the United States in terms of gross world product has probably not changed very greatly. In 1988 it was about 33 per cent of the sum of the GNP of the rich countries.

Figure 7.1, a 'geographical scatter' diagram, shows the relationship between trade per capita and GNP per capita, trade being defined as the average of imports and exports for 1985. The relationship between the two is remarkably close and almost logarithmically linear, that is a given percentage increase in one is accompanied by a constant proportional percentage increase in the other. The richer the country per capita, the more trade per capita, which is not surprising. The former communist countries are something of an exception, with most of them having less trade per capita than their GNP per capita would suggest. It is a little surprising that the United

Figure 7.1   Trade per capita vs GNP per capita for 114 countries, 1985, (US dollars)

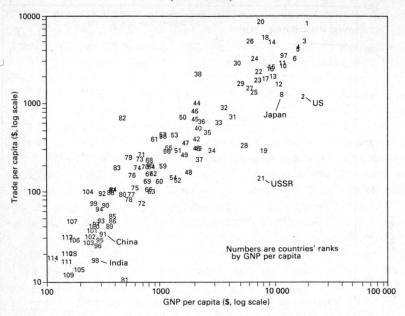

Note: See pp. 000–0 Appendix for complete list of countries

Sources: World Bank, *World Development Report*, 1987; *Information Please Almanac*, 1988; International Monetary Fund, *Direction of Trade Annual*, 1987.

States has about the smallest trade per capita of the rich countries, just $1160 compared with a GNP per capita of $16 690 in 1985. This may in part reflect the large population of the United States, as countries with a large population would be expected to have less international trade per capita than countries with small populations. If all fifty states of the United States became independent nations (assuming no trade restrictions), what is now interstate trade would become international trade, and the total volume of international trade of the area would increase very substantially. But the relationship is by no means clear. Countries with large populations, such as the United States, Japan, the former USSR, China and India, show a tendency toward lower per capita trade (appearing on the lower side of the scatter in Figure 7.1), but the effect is not large.

Figure 7.2 shows the relative shares of trade measured by the

Figure 7.2   Relative shares of world trade, average of exports and imports, 1960–86

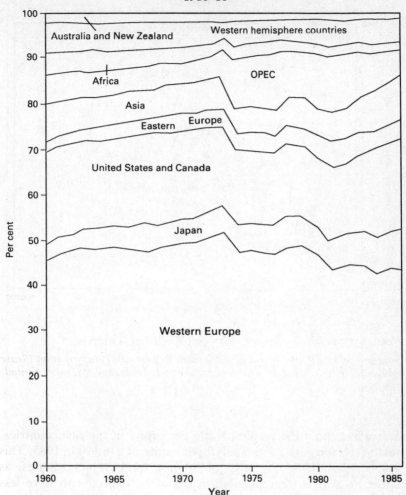

Note: Asia, Africa, and western hemisphere countries are exclusive of OPEC countries.

Source: Adapted from International Monetary Fund, Direction of Trade, Annuals 1960–4, 1963–7, 1974–80, 1987.

average of imports and exports by major regions since 1960. Figure 7.3 shows the same relative shares by exports and Figure 7.4 by imports. The changes are not great, except for the OPEC (the Organization of Petroleum-Exporting Countries) episode in 1973, which

Figure 7.3   Relative shares of world trade: exports by major regions, 1960–86

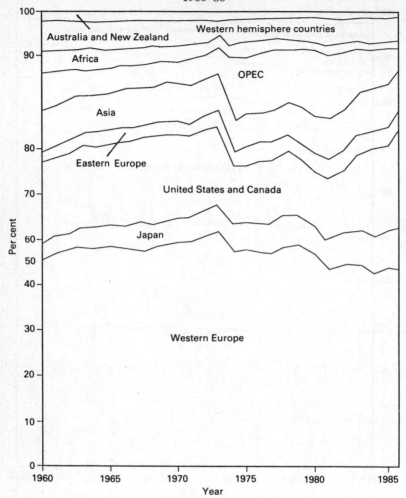

Note: Asia, Africa, and western hemisphere countries are exclusive of OPEC countries.

Source: Adapted from International Monetary Fund, Direction of Trade, Annuals 1960–4, 1963–7, 1974–80, 1987.

led to the newly-rich OPEC countries developing export surpluses and external investments. We can see that the United States, Canada, Japan and Western Europe account for between 60 and 70 per cent of the total, with Western Europe taking about 45 per cent. A

Figure 7.4   Relative shares of world trade: imports by major regions, 1960–86

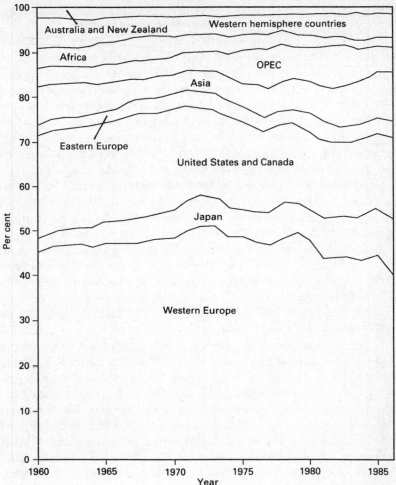

Note: Asia, Africa, and western hemisphere countries are exclusive of OPEC countries.

Source: Adapted from International Monetary Fund, Direction of Trade, Annuals 1960–4, 1963–7, 1974–80, 1987.

considerable part of this is of course in trade between the Western European countries. If Western Europe were a single country, as it may soon become, its trade would probably look very much like that of the United States and Canada. Japan's proportion of world trade has approximately doubled since about 1960, but Figure 7.1 shows that trade per capita in Japan is about the same as it is in the United States. The idea that Japan is 'conquering' world trade is something of an illusion.

The impact of OPEC was very striking, especially in 1973–4, although its decline in the 1980s back to the pre-OPEC proportion was equally striking and suggests the ultimate instability of cartels. The increase in 1973–4 of course represents an increase in oil prices rather than in quantities traded, as a result of the monopolistic power of OPEC. This monopolistic power was however very short lived and by 1986 had virtually disappeared. It is significant, and perhaps ominous, that the proportions of world trade held by Latin America and Africa have both been declining and together they now only account for about 7 per cent of the total. Asia, excluding Japan, has increased a little, but this may be due mainly to the efforts of Singapore, Hong Kong, Taiwan and South Korea. Eastern Europe increased its share from 1960–75, but has not shown much of an increase since then. It will be interesting to see what will result from the great changes of 1989–90. The United States and Canada have increased their share somewhat. The domination of the world economy by the temperate zones, especially the northern temperate zone, is illustrated dramatically in these figures, and there seems to be no sign of this diminishing.

The above changes in the proportion of world trade were accompanied by a spectacular increase in the total volume of trade after the Second World War, as shown in Figure 7.5. We can see a noticeable decline in world trade during both world wars, a collapse during the Great Depression and a spectacular increase between 1945 and about 1980, when the volume of international trade increased about six times in real terms. The causes of this are not altogether clear. Part of the reason was the development of GATT, which led to a substantial diminution of tariff charges around the world. Another factor was the change in the technology of sea transport and seaports that is sometimes called the 'container revolution', with large containers being transferred from ships to land by big cranes, which are highly labour saving compared with longshoremen loading and unloading cargo on their shoulders and in hand carts.

Turning now to the United States, Figure 7.6 shows exports, imports and net exports from 1929 onwards as a percentage of GCP. The collapse during the Great Depression is very noticeable, and not surprisingly the shrinkage of exports during the Second World War

Figure 7.5   World trade total: average of imports and exports, 1865–1987

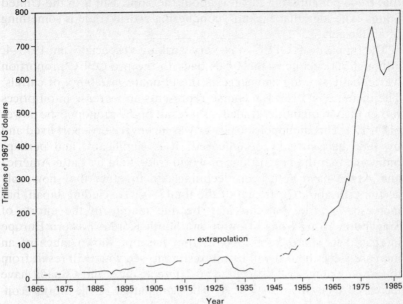

Sources: For data from 1868 to 1938, W. S. Wytinsky and E. S. Wytinsky, *World Commerce and Governments: Trends and Outlook* (New York: The Twentieth Century Fund, 1955) pp. 38–9; for data from 1938 to 1978, various issues of UN Monthly Statistics and UN Yearbooks; for data from 1979 to 1987, 1987 International Trade Statistics Yearbooks. The Bureau of Labor Statistics wholesale price index was used to adjust to 1967 constant US dollars.

produced a short period of net imports. The surge in exports in the late 1940s had a lot to do with the Marshall Plan for rebuilding Western Europe. As late as the early 1970s, imports and exports as a proportion of GNP and GCP did not differ much from what they had been in 1929. There then followed a sharp upsurge in both imports and exports, which more than doubled between 1968 and 1981. After that exports declined somewhat, but imports continued to increase, leading to a net import figure of unprecedented size, reaching 2.58 per cent of GCP by 1987 but falling to 0.92 per cent in 1989.

An important aspect of the international trade situation is the structure of foreign exchange rates. Fluctuation of these rates has increased very markedly, especially since the early 1970s. In the days of the gold standard the exchange rates between those countries using it were very stable. Fluctuations were limited to the 'gold points'.

Figure 7.6   Exports and imports as percentage of GCP, US 1929–89

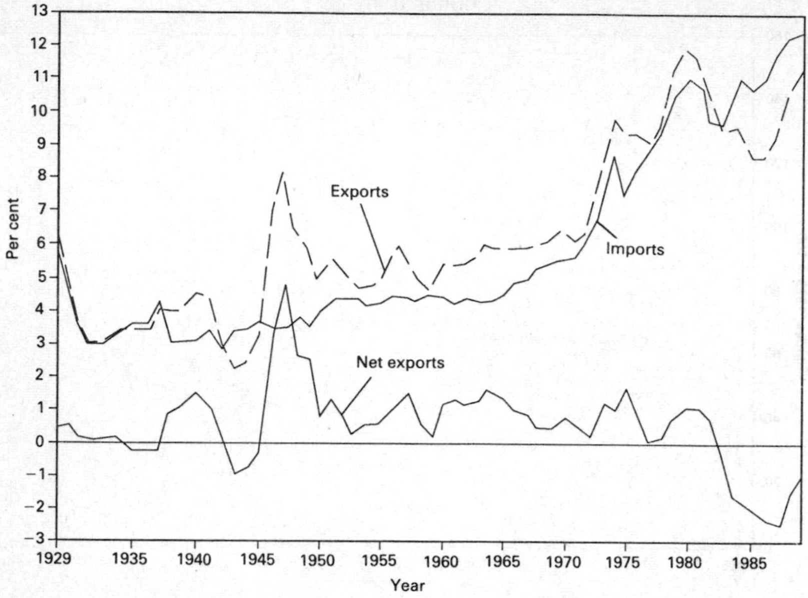

Source: *Economic Report of the President*, 1968, 1990.

Since the Second World War there has been an increasingly free market in foreign exchange, with a considerable increase in the occurrence of fluctuations. For the dollar this is illustrated in Figure 7.7, which shows the fluctuations of the dollar against two other major currencies, the German mark and the Japanese yen. Here both fluctuation and overall decline are striking. One dollar bought 362 Japanese yen in 1967 but only 128 in 1988. It bought 3.98 marks in 1967 but only 1.75 in 1988.

Fluctuating exchange rates are a real handicap to international trade. It is not surprising that the total value of international trade has declined somewhat since 1980. It is a little surprising that this did not happen earlier as large fluctuations in foreign exchange rates actually began in the early 1970s. The shifting value of the dollar in terms of foreign currencies and the change from net exports to net imports are not unrelated, but it is difficult to say which caused what. The foreign exchange market contains a certain element of speculative fluctuation. The trade balance (net imports or net exports) is not

Figure 7.7   Foreign exchange rates of US dollars, currency units per US dollar, 1967–89

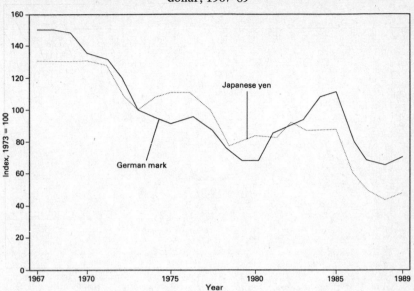

Source: *Economic Report of the President*, 1990.

unrelated to budget deficits, relative interest rates and foreign investment in the United States.

Perhaps one of the biggest of the post-war crises was the formation of OPEC and the dramatic rise in the price of oil in 1973, and the proportionately less dramatic increase around 1980. The rise in the price of oil is shown in Figure 7.8, going from $1.30 per barrel in 1970 to $10.72 by 1975 and $33.47 in 1982, from which level it has been declining. This of course was the result of the power of monopoly exercised by OPEC from 1973–82.

Figure 7.9 shows the result of this remarkable change in terms of the percentage of oil imported by the United States from different sources. The proportion from the OPEC countries rose from a little under 50 per cent in 1973 to almost 70 per cent by 1978 before declining sharply to a little under 40 per cent by 1983, after which it rose to about 50 per cent in 1989. This whole experience is a remarkable tribute to the powers of substitutability and the weakness of monopoly. In the United States the panic over petroleum shortages

Figure 7.8   World petroleum wholesale price, Libya (Es Sidra), 1960–87

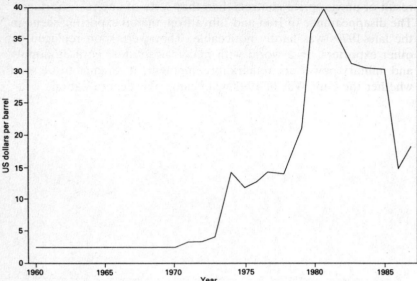

Source: IMF, *International Financial Statistics Yearbook*, 1988.

Figure 7.9   Crude oil and petroleum product imports, US 1973–89

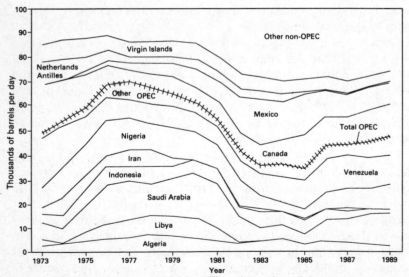

Source: US Department of Energy, *Monthly Energy Review*, November, 1983, 1989.

and the long lines at the filling stations in 1973 were much more the result of unwise price controls than they were of any real shortages. The disappearance of Iran and Libya from the oil exporting scene in the late 1970s was hardly noticeable. They were soon replaced by other exporters. In a world with many substitutes, both monopoly and military power are remarkably impotent. It remains to be seen whether the Gulf War of 1991 will change this generalisation.

8 Towards Understanding and Control

We should now have some image in our minds of the patterns and behaviour of the United States economy since 1929, at least in terms of its major components. We still lack a good deal of detail, partly because of deficiencies in the official statistics, but also because the details are more than any mind can manage. We cannot possibly have knowledge of the economic history of every one of the 300 million or so Americans who have lived during this period. It would be even more difficult to visualise the households, firms and other organisations that have existed, and still less could we visualise all the commodities that have been produced and consumed during this period. Nevertheless we do have some image of the aggregates and at least a rough idea of some significant proportions of the economy.

These images however are not adequate. It is not enough to have an image of what is and what has been. We crave an understanding of how and why things happened the way they did. Understanding comes from the asking of important questions to which at least some kind of answers can be found. We seem to be particularly interested in things that are perceived to have gone wrong, that is in the diseases of the economy. We are interested in identifying these and asking why they occur, and also how they might be cured. This is a problem of control. Underlying the history of the economy are certain decisions which could have been different. We are interested in trying to identify which decisions, or lack of decisions, may have caused the changes that we perceive as adverse and pathological. One of the purposes of understanding is to learn how to improve the processes of control and cure. The more we understand the immense complexities of the human body, the more effective are the health sciences and the healing professions in curing disease. Similarly we hope that the better we understand the economy, the more likely are the economic 'doctors' – legislators, executives, regulatory agencies such as the Federal Reserve System and advisory agencies such as the Council of Economic Advisors and the Office of Technology Assessment – to be able to cure what is perceived as economic disease.

The problem of economic health of course differs from that of the health of the human body, although there are some parallels. Both are subject to certain self-correcting injuries or diseases. In the body a cut heals and stomach aches and head colds pass away. In the economy such disasters as earthquakes, tornadoes or fires will usually be followed by rebuilding, and also to some extent by the reconstruction of damaged human lives. There are even parallels between mental depression and economic depression. Both are characterised by unemployment. In the case of the mind there is an inability to activate the potential for productivity and enjoyment; in the economy there is an inability to realise the productive potential of the unemployed.

There are also illnesses of the body which do not cure themselves and have to be cured, if possible, by diets, drugs, operations and even psychoanalysis. Likewise in the economy there may be illnesses which can only be cured by injecting or removing money or other assets, by laws and regulations, or even just by cheering people up, as President Franklin Roosevelt seems to have done in his 'fireside chats'. Growth is a tricky problem here. There is a tendency among economists to regard economic growth almost as an absolute value, and the faster it grows the better. In the case of the body, growth is a sign of health up to maturity, after which any increase in weight is usually fat. On the other hand growth can continue in the form of learning, even into old age. Just when economic growth is fat – or even cancer – and when it is healthy is not always easy to tell.

Understanding almost always begins with thinking. 'Pure' thinking however, unless modified by some kind of testing, can easily lead to erroneous images. Testing involves a choice among alternative images, and unless we have these alternatives, and unless in some sense at least one 'good', or reasonably true, image is found among these alternatives, testing will not necessarily eliminate error. Thinking, as noted in Chapter 1, involves the perception of identities and near-identities, relationships and patterns that almost have to be true. Testing however always involves a choice among plausible but uncertain images.

In complex systems the relationship between cause and effect often becomes very difficult to identify. If A sometimes causes B and sometimes does not, as so often seems to be the case not only in social systems but even in biological systems, causality becomes probabilistic. When a change in A causes a change in B, the change in B causes a further change in A, which causes a further change in B and so on, we have a positive-feedback system, where simple cause and effect relationships disintegrate. Where a system of negative feedback operates, should equilibrium be disturbed dynamic processes come into play to restore it; here the disturbances can be said to 'cause' a return to equilibrium. We see this phenomenon, as noted above, in the recovery from catastrophes: after the Germans destroyed Warsaw in the Second World War, the Poles rebuilt the medieval city almost exactly as it had been before. A firm that is sustaining losses may change its management or its policies so that profits may be restored. Economists have a very firm belief that the relative price structure has certain equilibrium properties, that if the actual structure of relative prices deviates from some equilibrium position, whether in the short term in the market or in the longer term when production and consumption are taken into account, prices that are too 'high', that is above equilibrium, will fall; prices that are too 'low', that is below equilibrium, will rise.

All equilibria however, whether in the price system, in a pond or on a prairie, are essentially temporary. The parameters which determine them are constantly changing in the evolutionary process. By constant change of parameters evolution destroys all equilibria. An interesting question however is whether the evolutionary process may itself have some property of equilibrium, in the sense that if change is proceeding 'too quickly' it may slow down; if it is proceeding 'too slowly' it may speed up. In a society that is exhibiting sustained development, such as Japan or the United States, an interruption in the developmental process, for example a war or a depression, is frequently followed by more rapid development, so that the average rate of development over long periods may be remarkably stable. There can however be important exceptions to this rule.

Returning to the United States economy, how do we distinguish what is pathological and how do we identify possible cures? The roughly tenfold inflation experienced from 1929 can certainly be regarded as unaesthetic, even if it has not caused much damage to the economy. What might be called the 'proximate causes' seem to be fairly clear. There were two periods of substantial federal budget deficits (during the Second World War and in the 1970s and 1980s) and these were not unrelated to increases in the money stock, however we define money, and in turn these increases were not unrelated to increases in price levels. Whether there is a deep underlying unwillingness to do those things that have to be done if inflation is to be kept down is a question that certainly goes beyond economics.

The two periods of substantial inflation may well have been rather different in this regard. The first period was during the Second World War (somewhat postponed by price and wage controls and a fall in the velocity of the circulation of money). Inflation almost always accompanies war. It is perhaps accepted as part of 'war suffering'. It is accepted politically as a cost of pursuing a war that is perceived, even if not as 'just', at least as inevitable. The second period of major inflation, following the late 1960s, can perhaps be explained in part by the 'cold war' and the arms race with the Soviet Union, but this hardly seems large enough to account for the unwillingness to raise taxes to balance the budget. There may be an almost unconscious factor here, in that inflation is one way of diminishing the burden of interest on old debts. This suggests that debtors have more political influence than creditors. In the Reagan administration there was also a theory of 'supply-side economics',[1] that lowering tax rates would raise incomes sufficiently to raise the amount of taxes collected to the point where the budget was balanced. This expectation was *not* fulfilled.

The rise in the burden of interest, which is very striking in spite of the inflation, is something which could also be regarded as a pathological element in the economy, but it is one which surprisingly few people seem to be worried about.[2] Net interest, as we saw in Figure 5.10, went from one per cent of the national income in 1946 to 10.81 per cent in 1989. This phenomenon deserves much more attention than has hitherto been paid to it. As we will see, the rise in net interest during the Great Depression of 1929–33 was catastrophic. The long-term rise from 1950 onwards had a much milder impact but it may well have been in part responsible for the slow increase in poverty since the 1970s, for income from interest is much more likely to go to the middle and upper income groups, although there does not seem to be any data on this. The rise in interest has somewhat diminished eroding profit, although not to the extent that it did during the Great Depression, and this may have something to do with the slowdown in productivity, especially during the late 1960s and 1970s, as shown in Figure 3.2. From 1982–7 the proportion of national income in net interest declined somewhat, but it rose again from 1987–9, as can be seen in Figure 5.10. It is interesting that the decline in interest rates seems to have been accompanied by a recovery in the rate of increase in productivity.

Largely because of the inadequacy of the data on capital structures, it is not easy to identify the extent to which the rise in the proportion of national income going to interest has been the result of a rise in

Figure 8.1 Federal Reserve discount rates vs prime rates, US 1939-89

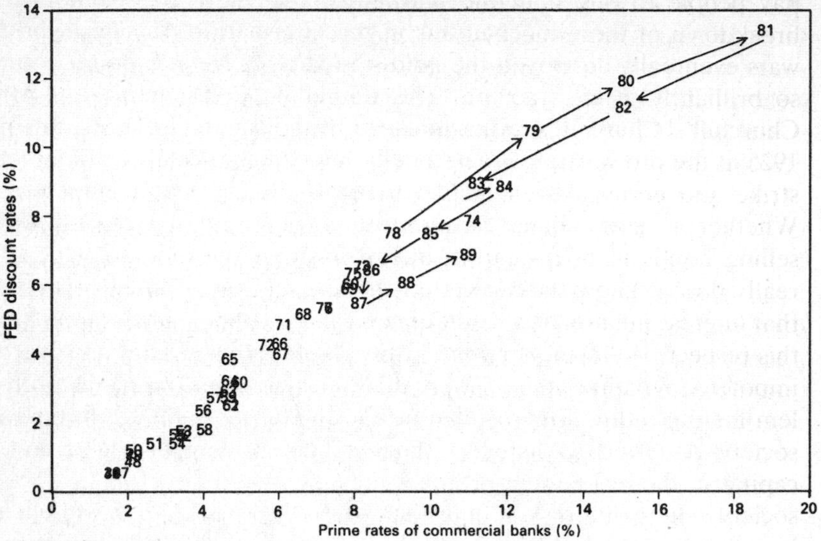

Source: Economic Report of the President, 1968, 1990.

interest rates themselves or a rise in the proportion of financing done by debts and bonds rather than by stocks. Figure 5.10 does however suggest that the rise in the rate of interest has been the major factor, except possibly in the 1980s. As mentioned earlier, the rise in interest rates did not start properly until the late 1940s, so the Second World War and the subsequent budget deficit and increase in the national debt cannot be blamed for this rise. How far it was a result of deliberate policy on the part of the Federal Reserve System and how far it was simply a market phenomenon with people unwilling to hold bonds, so that their price fell, thus raising the rate of interest on them, is something I have not been able to determine. Figure 8.1 shows that there is a very close relationship between the Federal Reserve discount rate and the rate at which money can be borrowed from banks, but which causes what is difficult to say. They may both simply reflect an underlying condition of the market.

Under the gold standard central banks were able to stabilise the price of gold within very narrow limits by offering to buy and sell gold for currency at fixed buying and selling prices, which were set closely together. This was only possible, of course, as long as the economy reacted to a decline in the gold stock of the central banks by bringing the price of gold in the market down to the point where it began to pay people to buy it in the market and sell it to the bank. The breakdown of these mechanisms in the aftermath of the two world wars eventually destroyed the gold standard, as Keynes pointed out so brilliantly in his tract on 'The Economic Consequences of Mr Churchill'.[3] Churchill's return to use of the gold standard in Britain in 1925 at the pre-war rate created deflation, which produced a general strike and perhaps even helped to initiate the Great Depression. Whether a central bank can control interest rates by buying and selling bonds in open-market operations is a question to which I really do not know the answer. If the answer is 'yes', then it is true that interest-inflation is a result of central banks being incompetent in this respect. If the answer is 'no', this suggests that central banks are impotent. Whatever the answer, this clearly remains a serious problem for the future. Interest can in a very real sense be a burden on society. As noted in Chapter 3, the recipient of interest is the inactive capitalist, the recipient of profits is the active capitalist. In a usurious society where interest gobbles up profit, as seems to have been happening in the last decade or so, there is a grave danger of economic stagnation or collapse.

This brings us to the question of unemployment and, of course, to the Great Depression. There is no question that this was a deeply pathological experience, not only for the United States but for the entire capitalist world. It had a good deal to do with the rise of Hitler, the Holocaust and the Second World War. Up until 1933 the vote for Hitler's party in Germany was closely related to the level of German unemployment, which was even higher than it was in the United States in 1932 and 1933. Much of the trouble in the world seems to arise from the fact that some people achieve power because they give the wrong answers, which turn out to be disastrous, to questions that others are not answering at all. Hitler was perhaps the most spectacular example of this principle. The recent collapse of Marxism suggests that Marx and Lenin also gave a good many wrong answers, which makes it all the more important that we should find the right answers to the right questions.

To gain some understanding of the Great Depression we must look at how the economy changed, especially in its proportions, between 1929 and 1933. Looking again at the proportions of the total labour force shown in Figure 2.6, we see that unemployment rose from 3.1 per cent in 1929 to 24.7 per cent in 1933. The biggest decline was in manufacturing, from 21.6 per cent of the labour force in 1929 to 14.3 per cent in

1933. Federal, state and local government, plus the armed forces, remained more or less stable as a proportion of the labour force during those years, amounting to 6.7 per cent in 1929 and 6.6 per cent in 1933. Construction – a rather small proportion of the labour force – fell very sharply from 3.1 per cent in 1929 to 1.6 per cent[4] in 1933. All the other categories fell somewhat. Manufacturing and the wholesale and retail trade together accounted for about half of the total decline in employment. What we see then is an overall decline in employment in the private sector, with no offsetting increase in government.

Some insight into why this happened is provided by Figure 3.4, which shows the major components of GCP. Here we see a spectacular collapse of gross private domestic investment, from 15.6 per cent in 1929 to 1.3 per cent in 1932 and 2.1 per cent in 1933. In those years net private investment was negative, as we saw in Figure 5.9. Household consumption expenditure likewise fell from 72 per cent of GCP in 1929 to 61.4 per cent in 1933. Government purchases expanded a little, but nothing like the amount that would have been required to offset the collapse of gross private domestic investment and the sharp decline in personal consumption expenditure.

Looking a little further for the explanation of these extraordinary changes, we saw in Figure 3.5 that corporate profits as a proportion of national income fell from 11.33 per cent in 1929 to −3.81 per cent in 1932 and −3.79 per cent in 1933. Net interest rose from 5.55 per cent in 1929 to 10.95 per cent in 1932 and 10.35 per cent in 1933. Compensation to employees rose from 60.33 per cent in 1929 to 74.75 per cent in 1933. Clearly the disappearance of corporate profits, due mainly to the rise in the proportion of national income going to wages, coupled with the almost doubling of the proportion of national income going to net interest, was primarily responsible for the high unemployment. We must go back for a moment to 'thinking'. As shown in Chapter 3, when an employer hires an employee, the employer sacrifices the interest that could have been gained on the money now going to wages in the hope of making a profit on the product made by the employee. In a situation like that of 1932 and 1933 it is almost literally true that anybody who hired anybody was bound to lose by it. The reason why unemployment did not rise to 50 per cent and the whole economy collapse was probably due to habit, the desire to hold firms together, and perhaps also irrational expectations. If the situation in 1932 and 1933 had continued into 1934, the whole economy might well have collapsed. As it was, in 1934 profits became positive (2.28 per cent), the proportion of net interest declined a little and unemployment started to fall.

In looking for an explanation of these extraordinary changes, the first thing we tend to look at is the money stock (see Figures 4.5 to 4.8). Between 1929 and 1933 demand deposits at commercial banks fell from $22.81 billion to $15.04 billion, reflecting a massive collapse of the banking system. Currency actually increased somewhat from $3.56 billion to $4.78 billion, but what is usually called 'old' M1, the sum of currency and demand deposits, fell from $26.37 billion to $19.82 billion. If we look at national income, this almost halved in current dollars on a per capita basis, from $5012 in 1929 to $2754 in 1933 (in 1982 dollars). About half of this decline may be attributed to deflation – the decline in money prices – and the other half to a decline in output.

Between 1929 and 1933 there must have been an enormous redistribution of income and of net worth that has not been recorded, although some of it can be deduced. Among capitalists there was a great redistribution away from debtors towards creditors, and away from those who owned stocks towards those who owned bonds, notes and other forms of debt, the holders of which in those days were called 'bloated bondholders'. There was likewise a very large redistribution within the working class, away from those who were unemployed towards those who were employed. It is very hard to obtain good data on money wages, real wages or transfers to the unemployed over this period. Certainly part of the problem of the Great Depression was that the deflation was very unevenly spread around the economy. We could say roughly that in agriculture money income nearly halved, because while output kept up prices about halved. In manufacturing, as far as we can tell, money wages only fell by something like 25 per cent and employment fell by 36 per cent. And of course output also fell sharply. It looks as if there was a shift in the stock of money out of businesses into households, as households reduced their expenditure in view of the uncertainties of the period.

It is very difficult to separate out all these causal effects, but it is at least a reasonable hypothesis to say that if deflation had been spread equally over the economy, with most prices and wages falling by about the same proportion, the results would not have been so disastrous. The change in the distribution of money would then have been more neutral. As it is, it seems that there cannot even be inflation, especially inflation that is not anticipated, without considerable redistribution away from old debtors towards profit makers, and the redistribution under deflation seems to be even more drastic. This may perhaps happen partly because even when labour is unorganised it is easier to raise money wages than it is to lower them. Lowering money wages is perceived as a hostile act on the part of the employer; raising them is perceived as a more benevolent act, although in the macro economy things might look very different.

It is indeed ironic that during the Great Depression, when one would have thought that large numbers of people seeking work would have given employers great bargaining power, the proportion of national income going to wages rose very sharply. However from 1933 to about 1943, with the New Deal, the Wagner Act, the great rise in the labour movement and a tremendous increase in collective bargaining, the proportion of national income going to labour fell sharply, from 72 per cent to about 62 per cent, net interest fell from 10.41 per cent to 1.59 per cent, and profits recovered.

At the micro level, the impact of inflation and deflation on profits can be understood when it is recognised that profit is derived from buying something at a particular time and selling it later at a higher price. When all prices are rising this is very easy to do; when all prices are falling it is almost impossible. Deflation therefore always shifts income from profit into interest. It is less clear why in 1929–33 it shifted income from profit to wages. Ironically the sharp fall in the percentage of national income going to wages, from 75.13 per cent in 1933 to 62.63 in 1942, may have been accentuated by the rise of the labour movement and collective bargaining. In an inflationary period with labour shortages, collective bargaining *delays* the rise in money wages, for negotiations take time. In the unorganised labour market with a labour shortage, employers raise wages more quickly.

The existing data enable us to take a look at the problem of unemployment and its possible causes since 1929. We can begin perhaps, as noted earlier, with a theoretical proposition at the micro level: when hiring somebody an employer sacrifices the interest that could have been made on the money going to wages in the hope of making a profit on the product of the work. The work may consist of alleviating depreciation and decay, such as that carried out by janitors. It may involve transforming one substance into another that has a higher value, such as raw iron into automobiles, or wheat into flour. It may involve selling things, disposing of business inventory for more money than otherwise would have been obtained. All these involve operations in which the increase in the 'gross worth' of the business is expected to be greater than wages and other costs, which represent a subtraction from the gross worth, so that the net worth increases, the increase being profits.

It follows that we should expect two things to be relevant to the number of workers employed. The first is the gap between profit and

Figure 8.2   Corporate profit/(profit + interest) vs unemployment rate, US
1929–44

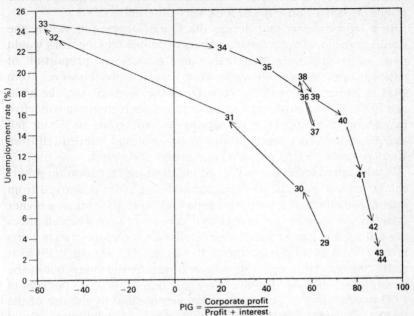

PIG = $\dfrac{\text{Corporate profit}}{\text{Profit + interest}}$

Source: Economic Report of the President, 1988.

interest, or between expected profit and interest. Unless this gap exists, that is unless the expected rate of profit is higher than the potential rate of interest, say on the purchase of bonds, the employer will lose by employing somebody, as indeed happened in 1932 and 1933. The way for people with capital to get rich between 1929 and 1933 was to sell all they had in 1929 and hold onto the money, with which they could then in 1933 buy almost twice as much as they could have in 1929. It would have been even better to lend it out at interest, provided that the debts were honoured.

It is difficult to obtain sufficiently aggregated data on profit and interest rates. A reasonable measure of the gap between profit and interest is the ratio of profit as a proportion of national income to profit plus interest as a proportion of national income. I am tempted to call this the 'profit-interest gap', or PIG. Figures 8.2, 8.3 and 8.4 are time scatters showing the profit–interest gap and the unemployment rate for different periods. The Great Depression is shown very dramatically in Figure 8.2, with the collapse from 1929–33 when profits became negative, and the recovery from 1933–44. There was a curious interlude in the small depression of 1938, but the general pattern is very clear.

Figure 8.3   Corporate profit/(profits + interest) vs unemployment rate, US
1944–61

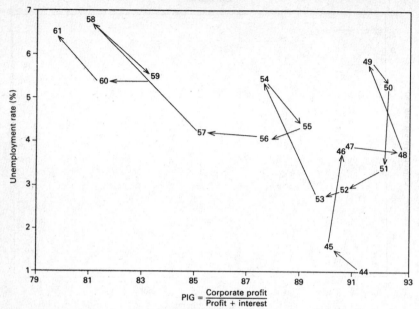

$$PIG = \frac{\text{Corporate profit}}{\text{Profit + interest}}$$

Source: *Economic Report of the President*, 1988.

Figure 8.3 shows the same time scatter from 1944–61. The picture is confused from about 1945–53, perhaps because of adjustments following the Second World War and then the Korean War, which again increased national defence expenditure. From 1953–61, however, the general trend is very clear. We see something that almost looks like a conventional business cycle from 1954–6, and from 1958–60.

Figure 8.4 shows the time scatter for 1961–87. The decline in unemployment from 1961–8, with little change to the PIG ratio, is somewhat related to the rise in national defence purchases with the start of the Vietnam War. From 1969–82 the relationship is very clear. It was interrupted by what looks like three business cycles, from 1970–3, from 1974–9 and, perhaps related to a decline in interest rates, from 1983–7, which was not closely reflected in the proportion of national income going to interest, as we see in Figure 5.10.

A second possible causal factor in unemployment is excess business inventories. If inventories pile up, firms may experience a shortage of cash that can only be replenished by the sale of inventories, or by bank loans. If storage facilities are not adequate, or if the increase in inventories diminishes cash holdings, an increase in inventory beyond a

Figure 8.4   Corporate profit/(profit + interest) vs unemployment rate, US 1961–87

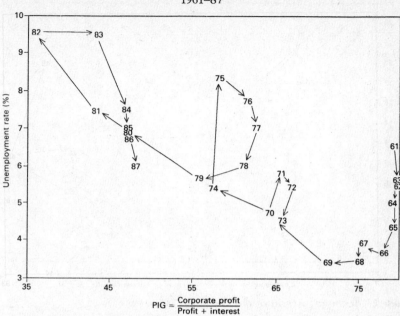

$$PIG = \frac{Corporate\ profit}{Profit + interest}$$

Source: Economic Report of the President, 1988

certain point will create a crisis, the easiest reaction to which is to lay off people 'down the line' so that the production of finished goods diminishes. The statistical evidence here is not as convincing as it is in the case of the profit–interest gap, but it is still noticeable.

In Figures 8.5 and 8.6 we have a time scatter of the change in business inventories from one year to the next as a proportion of GCP plotted against the unemployment rate. The Great Depression again shows up very clearly. From 1929–32 businesses reduced their inventories, in spite of the fact that less was being sold to households, mainly by not employing people to produce finished goods. From 1932–41, again with the curious depression of 1938, a rise in business inventories is associated with a decline in unemployment. From 1941 onwards however, the relationship largely disappears. From 1951–68 it reappears at intervals, for instance with rising unemployment from 1953–54, from 1957–8 and from 1960–1; and with falling unemployment from 1961–2 and from 1964–6.

In Figure 8.7, from 1969–85 the relationship is again intermittent but noticeable for some years (for instance from 1969–70, from 1971–5 or even 1978, from 1979–80 and from 1981–4). In other

Figure 8.5   Business inventories vs the unemployment rate, US 1929–51

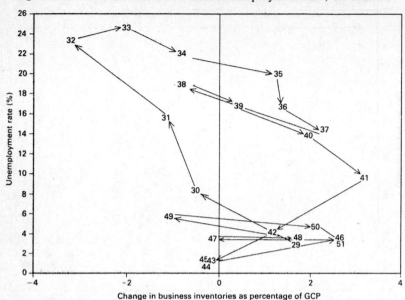

Change in business inventories as percentage of GCP

Source: *Economic Report of the President*, 1967, 1988.

Figure 8.6   Business inventories vs the unemployment rate, US 1951–68

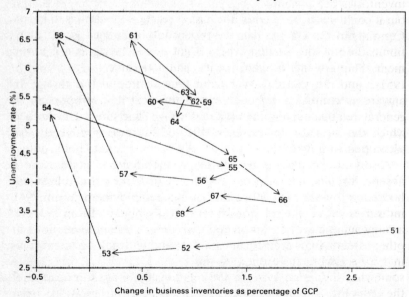

Change in business inventories as percentage of GCP

Source: *Economic Report of the President*, 1967, 1988.

Figure 8.7   Business inventories vs the unemployment rate, 1968–87

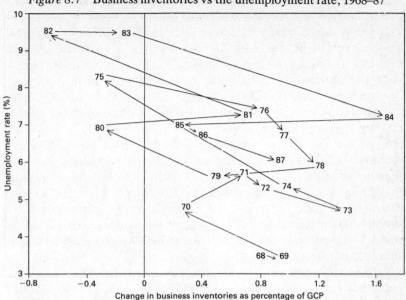

Source: *Economic Report of the President*, 1967, 1988.

periods the movement goes the other way. It is clear that business inventories are a significant element in the unemployment picture, but it could easily be overshadowed by other forces and other causes. Certainly from 1941–51 it was overshadowed by the enormous disruption caused by the Second World War and the subsequent disarmament. Similarly we see the impact made by the Korean War from 1951–3 and the Vietnam War from 1966–8. The picture from 1968 onward is confusing although, apart from a few exceptions, the general relationship is clear. Of the 60 years there are only 14 in which the direction of change is 'wrong', and eight of these were associated with wars.

A serious deficiency in the United States information system is the absence of adequate information on balance sheets, for instance of household by income groups and of businesses and corporations by industries. Not enough is known for instance about how money shifts around among its holders in the economy, and the same goes for other assets. An interesting question is why the stock market collapse in 1929 seems to have initiated the Great Depression, whereas the somewhat similar collapse of 1987 had virtually no impact at all on the economy. This is a question to which existing information systems provide no answer. Certainly much more is known about the United

States economy than was known in 1929, but there are still very frustrating gaps and there is still much left to be done.

One unresolved question in economic theory, for which the evidence presented in this book at least suggests a tentative answer, relates to the theory of macrodistribution, that is, what really determines the distribution of national income between profit, interest, rent and labour income. The evidence presented in Figure 3.5, particularly during the Great Depression when profits became negative, certainly suggests that the conventional answers to this question in terms of the marginal productivity of the factors of production are seriously inadequate. According to this theory we would have to explain the extraordinary situation of 1932 and 1933 by supposing that during that period capital became fantastically plentiful, so that its marginal reward in terms of profit was negative, and that labour became extraordinarily scarce, so that wages and the proportion of national income going to labour rose. Anything more absurd than this could hardly be imagined!

An alternative theory, which I have called the 'K theory',[5] is propounded rather sketchily by John Maynard Keynes in *A Treatise on Money*,[6] by Kalecki in his famous remark, apparently part of the Cambridge oral tradition, that 'capitalists get what they spend and workers spend what they get', to some extent in Nicholas Kaldor's models,[7] in my book, *A Reconstruction of Economics*,[8] and in my paper on 'Economic Theory: The Reconstruction Reconstructed'.[9]

The critical question here is why both unemployment and profits seem to be so closely related to the proportion of GCP devoted to gross private domestic investment, and also to inflation and deflation. There is no simple equilibrium model to describe this relationship, simply because the processes that created the Great Depression, and even some of the smaller ones, were essentially positive–feedback processes, which do not lead to equilibrium but to some kind of turnaround in the process itself. Thus from 1929–33 an initial fall in profits seems to have led to a fall in gross private domestic investment, leading to a further fall in profits, a further fall in investment and so on. After 1933 a rise in profits led to a rise in investment, which in turn led to a further rise in profits, a further rise in investment and so on. We could certainly argue that since the late 1940s the United States has had something that looks much more like an equilibrium system, but the relationship between gross private domestic investment and profits is still very noticeable. There are important questions here that still remain unanswered.

9 What of the Future?

We now have a fairly clear picture of the structure of the United States economy since 1929, even if the brushstrokes are broad and important details are missing. We certainly have a much more accurate and detailed picture than we have for the 60 years before 1929. The question arises therefore of whether this picture of the United States economy gives any insights into its possible future. We have no experience of the future. Our images of it can only be derived from our images of the past, but it is on images of the future that all our decisions depend. We cannot make decisions about the past, although we can improve our images of it. It is the decisions that we make now that are going to affect the future, and if these are unrealistic they are likely to make the future worse than it otherwise might have been. Our images of the future are more likely to be realistic if our images of the past are accurate and if we become skilled in the art of deducing our images of the future from our images of the past. Images of the past will be the more accurate the more accurate and well sampled the records, and also the better we are able to interpret and understand these records in terms of perceived patterns, relationships, necessary connections and structures that are likely to go forward into the future. The following methods are suggested for making this transition from our image of the past to our image of the future:

First, *projections* into the future from past patterns and parameters are apt to be the most accurate images of the future. A very good example is to be found in celestial mechanics, where we can project the position of the planets and other objects in the solar system with great accuracy, simply because we now have very accurate past records and these records reveal that there are certain stable parameters of the system, such as the gravitational constant. We are fairly certain about the orbits, velocities and accelerations of the planets, and we can predict eclipses and phenomena of that kind with remarkable exactitude, mainly perhaps because the sun is very large and the planets are far enough away from each other so that they do not interact very much. There have been recent suggestions that the mechanics of the solar system might at certain points break down into chaos, and we certainly are not completely sure about the early

111

history of the solar system, but within the span of modern astronomy the parameters have been remarkably stable.

The future size of populations of humans or any other species can be projected if parameters like birth, death and migration rates are constant for all age groups. One thing we can be sure about the future is that anyone who is alive now will either be a year older or dead at this time next year, and if the death rates of each age group are constant we know how many women of childbearing age there will be at this time next year. Then if the birth rates are constant for each age group, we can predict the overall birth rate. In fact these rates are not constant. Also, migration rates are difficult to predict, so population projections have a noticeable margin of error, though they are still worth doing. The 'baby boom' after the Second World War came as a great surprise! The fact that the United States population doubled from 1929–1989 does not necessarily mean that it is going to double from 1990–2050. Because the birth, death and migration rates are different for different sections of the population we can also make tentative projections about the proportionate composition of the population.

If the parameters of a system change at a constant rate or even at a constant rate of change, we can still make projections that are non-linear through differential or difference equations. A stable rate of change in parameters however is very rare. The parameters of social systems are much more likely to change suddenly and rather unpredictably, so that models derived from projections and trends have to be treated with a great deal of suspicion. Projections are wonderful for celestial mechanics; in social systems they are of doubtful validity. The problem with econometrics is that it has been far too obsessed with the projection model and has been insufficiently aware of the peculiarities of social systems. It has been accused, indeed, of trying to find the celestial mechanics of non-existent universes.

An interesting question with regard to social systems and economies is whether we can perceive certain constants in the dynamics of the system, such as economic development with its tendency to raise per capita income over time. These constants may have temporary interruptions such as depressions and wars, as occurred during the first two decades of the 60 years we have studied. The rise in per capita income in the United States from 1929–89 gives a long-term linear growth at a fairly constant rate, interrupted by the Great Depression and the Second World War, and also perhaps by a slowdown in productivity in the 1970s. Japan is an even more interesting case, where the Second World War resulted in tremendous destruction of the economy, and yet in a little over a generation it recovered to about where it would have been if it had grown at its pre-war rate without interruption. There also seem to have been long periods in the history of many societies where the rate of economic development has been extremely low, or even zero or negative, and has then accelerated. Japan again is a good example after 1870.

One thing we can be fairly sure about is that no system can grow forever. Any system will have limits to growth and the world economy may be faced with this during the next century as populations are continuing to increase on an essentially limited resource base. It would certainly be surprising, therefore, if even in the United States per capita real income were to continue to increase from 1989 to 2049 at the rate it did from 1929 to 1989.

There is a phenomenon that might be called the 'exhaustion of change' – patterns which have caused change in the past may themselves change. Thus in the United States there is now very little possibility of a release of labour from agriculture, as there was in 1929. There is also not much possibility of an increase in the proportion of women in the labour force, as there was in 1950. What cannot be predicted is the rise in human knowledge and skill, for we cannot know the potential of the human mind.

Second, another very important source of knowledge of the future is knowledge of the existence of *plans*, together with some image of the probability of their being carried out. Again, the growth of a body from the 'plan' in a single fertilised egg is a good example. My own fertilised egg knew how to produce a male *Homo sapiens* with pale skin, originally black hair, blue eyes, and certain intellectual capacities. It certainly did not have a plan to produce a hippopotamus. The plan in a fertilised egg may, of course, not be realised fully because of early death, malnutrition, various life experiences and so on. My fertilised egg certainly had a potential for my learning one or more languages. If however I had grown up in a Chinese family my native language would have been Chinese; growing up in an English-speaking family the language was English. Economies have similar potentials and these may or may not be realised depending on the culture of a country, its institutions, learning processes, political structures and so on. It seems highly probable that the Russian economy would be healthier today if Lenin had had a somewhat different view of the world or had not come to power.

Budgets, architects' plans and promises to pay – such as bonds –

are all guides to the future. We may estimate the practicality of plans by the abilities of the planners and their determination to carry the plans out. As the poet Robert Burns said, 'The best laid schemes o' mice and men Gang aft a-gley',[1] and corporation plans and those of planned economies are not exempt from this principle. There are those who believe that the future is predetermined, but the evidence for this is meager. While there is little doubt that this book was in the potential of the universe, whether it was founded in the 'big bang' or not, the universe and its origin had the potential for a very large number of different possible universes and evolution seems to be dominated by the time at which highly improbable events happen. The future is, therefore always highly indeterministic.

Third, our image of *parallels* from the past could be important guides to the future. Preludes may tell us something about a play, an opera, a performance or a symphony. The question 'what does this remind you of?' is sometimes helpful in thinking about the future. We have a very strong conviction that a baby boy will grow up into a man and will age unless there is premature death, but there may be some exceptions even to this rule. Shakespeare's 'seven ages of man' is a theme with a good many variations, but it is still a very important theme in personal growth and in aging. We may see something like this in the development of organisations also, or even of the whole human race. An interesting question, for instance, is whether the last few centuries of extraordinarily rapid change and growth represent something like adolescence and whether the human race is now approaching something that might be called maturity. However we should be a little wary of parallels. The similarities that we perceive may be illusory and history never quite repeats itself. Furthermore there are some patterns or events which seem to be unique. The Great Depression and the Second World War are unlikely to be repeated in exactly the same form, although it is a very fundamental principle that anything that has existed must have been possible and, unless the system changes, remains possible. But organisms, organisations and even systemic patterns of behaviour such as depressions, recoveries and wars may all have the potential to become extinct. Dinosaurs, duelling and slavery obviously were possible at certain times and in certain places, but they have only a very small probability of being recreated. Extinction is known in social as well as in biological systems. The possibility of events and structures arising which have no parallel must also be taken into consideration. Mutations may have had no parallel in the past. These may be biological mutations or social mutations, such as inventions, or prophetic figures, like Jesus, Buddha or Mohammed, who create whole new social systems. New possibilities of social mutations therefore, even in a system which seems as unchangeable as the United States economy, cannot be wholly ruled out.

Fourth, *probabilities* are important in that they may allow us to guard against possible future disasters. The concept of the 100-year flood is a good example. This is a flood with a one per cent per annum probability of happening, the probability being estimated from past records. It frequently pays to anticipate such events even though the time at which they will happen is not predictable. A 100-year flood is not something that happens once every 100 years. The probability of one happening just a year after one has occurred may still be one per cent. Earthquakes are rather similar, although it is a little more difficult to predict their probabilities, which change as time goes on. Even these uncertain images of the future however can profoundly affect human behaviour. It is unwise to build on a 100-year flood plain. If we build near a fault in the earth's crust, we had better be careful that what we build is earthquake-proof. How far we should protect ourselves against rare events involves our perspective of time and the cost of 'doing something about it', as well as our perception of the rarity of the event. We may decide against building on the 100-year flood plain but may very well build on the flood plain of a 1000-year flood. Some risks have to be taken because it is too costly to avoid them. There is an interesting balance between insurance and prevention. Insurance rates should be less on a building that has fire sprinklers, although the cost–benefit analysis here can often be rather difficult and subtle.

How far these principles apply to economic institutions is an interesting yet difficult question. The Great Depression, which was perhaps something like a 100-year flood, or perhaps even a 1000-year flood, as an improbable event that actually took place, certainly had something to do with the subsequent formation of the Council of Economic Advisors and a good deal of economic model building and statistics. The fact that the stock market collapse of 1987 had practically no impact at all on the general economy, whereas that of 1929 is usually blamed for causing the Great Depression, may be some indication that we are learning to build our economy a little off the flood plain. On the other hand the rise in the interest burden and the creeping rise in poverty suggests that we might be moving towards another kind of flood, for which we are not well prepared.

Wars likewise, especially those which are the result of the breakdown of deterrence, are something like floods, that is events with some probability of happening but the dates of which are not determinable. Wars are not caused so much by conflicts as by the existence of armed forces. Hitler was perhaps a political 500-year flood, a quite improbable event that happened, as did Ghengis Khan and Attila. Political institutions have a lot to do with the technology of the means of destruction. The development of an effective cannon had much to do with the collapse of the feudal system and the creation of the national state. Similarly it could well be that the nuclear weapon and the long-range missile have made national defence obsolete and that we will end up with a situation in which international war becomes extinct, although the institutions through which it will become extinct are still not wholly clear.

Fifth, another possible metaphor here is that of the *precipice*, which is a possible catastrophe that we might avoid through making wise decisions. Not falling over a precipice is a little different from not building on a flood plain. We cannot know when there is going to be a flood but we may perceive that we are moving towards a precipice and draw back from it. Hardly anybody buys insurance in the form of a parachute – it is wiser to turn back from the precipice before you come to it, although of course there are people who like hang gliding. Fire insurance really does not deal very well with arson. In fact it may encourage it. Taboos, moral commandments, 'thou shalt nots' and laws can be thought of as fences in front of possible precipices. Still, even Pandora's box may have some goodies in it. Challenges, as Toynbee remarks,[2] can sometimes produce creative responses. Military defeat often results in economic and cultural expansion on the part of the defeated party, as we saw in Paris after 1871, or in Japan and Germany after the Second World War. The theory of punctuated equilibrium[3] suggests that catastrophes play an important role in the evolutionary process when they open up niches for more complex beings. We may not have been here today if it were not for the catastrophe – whatever it was – that led to the extinction of the dinosaur.

A very important question is whether we are now approaching the edge of a cliff. If so there is still time to turn around. The extraordinary impact of Mr. Gorbachev certainly suggests that somebody decided it was time to turn around. In Iraq, however, we found ourselves approaching the edge of a perhaps smaller cliff but one which we went over as nobody turned around. An uncomfortable question is whether the United States economy is sliding towards something that could well turn out to be a cliff, what with the rise in interest rates, the recession of 1991, the dangerous situation not only in the savings and loans institutions but also in commercial banks, the intractable budget deficit and so on. Whether the United States is indeed sliding towards a major collapse of the fiscal and monetary system I do not know, but the feeling of sliding is very strong, and the need for some kind of turnaround is becoming increasingly pressing.

Sixth, another pattern over time that we have to watch out for, especially in the economy, is the *positive feedback* discussed earlier. The Great Depression was an example of such a process. The stock market crash of 1929 evidently created a good deal of pessimism about the future of profits, which led to a decline in investment, which in turn led to a decline in profits, which led to a further decline in investment, a further decline in profits and so on until, as we have noticed, in 1932 and 1933 gross private domestic investment was almost zero, profits were negative and the system was on the point of collapse.

Cycles in general price levels, especially in organised commodity and securities markets, have a rather similar pattern, as we have already noted. When prices are low but people think they will rise, more people start to buy and so they do rise. This confirms the belief and therefore they rise still further, which makes them rise still further and so on until they are perceived as 'high'. At this point people believe that prices are going to fall, there is an excess of selling and they do fall, which confirms the opinion and they go on falling until they become 'low', at which point the cycle starts all over again.

Arms races are rather similar. One country feels insecure and builds up its armaments, which makes the potential enemy feel insecure and so build up its armaments, which leads to further increases in the armaments of the first country, and then of the second country and so on until not infrequently the situation explodes into war, although sometimes the situation reverses itself, as we have seen with the 'Cold War'. Sometimes it does not, as in the Gulf War. The breakdown of a marriage is often another case of positive feedback. Suspicion and anger on the part of one spouse creates anger and aloofness in the other, which increases the suspicion and anger in the first and so on, very much like an arms race. Again there may be a breakdown ending in divorce. Whether the United States economy is in a situation like this, for instance in the relationship between the government and the people, is an alarming thought. How these positive-feedback processes can be identified and avoided is a critical question for the human race, and one to which we have by no means found any easy answer.

Seventh, a final principle that emerges in our quest to study the future is that *preparations* for the future will change it, for better or worse depending on the accuracy of the images of the future upon which these preparations are founded. Every decision is a choice, a selection, one among a variety of possible images of the future. The power of a decision maker might be measured roughly by the number of people that the decision maker's decisions will affect, and by how much. On the other hand decisions are often offset by other decisions, particularly when there are equilibrium or quasi-equilibrium systems, and power is often something of an illusion.

A difficult question is: what is the optimum degree of decisiveness? Decisiveness is certainly an element in the rise to power. It can also lead to catastrophic decisions. Sometimes, especially where the future is very uncertain, there is a strong case for patience, postponement, even for fiddling around. If we do not know enough to cure a disease, there is a lot to be said for promoting palliatives and painkillers, and this may be as true of politics and society as it sometimes is true of the human body. It is a great mistake to gallop decisively towards a precipice. And frequently what saves us is habit, doing today what we did yesterday, which is probably what saved the United States from total catastrophe, as we have seen, during the Great Depression. The wars that did not happen may be more important historically than the wars that did, but they are very difficult to study.

Sometimes we are pulled into the future by distant dreams and visions of a better world. The Marxists, the Zionists, and the Seventh-Day Adventists share something of this. Certainly without some kind of positive vision of the future we may be driven into despair and destruction.[4] If these visions are illusory, however, they may pull us towards a precipice, as it now appears happened with Marxism.

At the other extreme, we are sometimes pushed by rage, by lust, by fear or the 'don't just stand there, do something' syndrome, which can also be disastrous. When somebody says, 'I had no alternative', one suspects that impatient 'pushing' towards a solution prevented any realistic appraisal of the alternatives, and this so often leads to disaster. Perhaps the surprising thing is that we get along as well as we do, an indication perhaps that something like Adam Smith's 'invisible hand' operates not only in the market but in a great variety of human relationships, as the belief in some sort of social equilibrium would certainly suggest. We still need however to search for principles, both moral and intellectual, and for a learning process that turns our images of the past into wisdom about the future, so that the capacity to make decisions does not lead to too much disappointment. It is strange and perhaps ominous that in the English language we seem to have no word for the opposite of disappointment, that is, for having things turn out better than we expected when we made a decision. Within the learning process there is a power of truth, in the sense that if we believe something that is not so, especially about the future, we are more likely to change this than if we believe something that is so. This could go for our images of value as well as our images of fact.

How then does all this apply to the economy? How can the image of the 60 years from 1929–89, as it has been presented in these chapters, affect our image of the next 60 years? As we have seen, we have to be very careful about projections. In social systems especially we are likely to have 'regions of time',[5] at whose boundaries the parameters of the system change and projections fail. In virtually all time charts these regions are obvious. First there were the prosperous 1920s. Then came the Great Depression from 1929–33 followed by what might be called the 'spontaneous recovery', which was interrupted by a small depression in 1938 but which continued to 1941. Then the United States joined in the Second World War from 1941–5 and there was explosive expansion of the war industry, followed by the 'great disarmament' (1945–7). Then came what might almost be called the 'golden age', from the end of the 1940s to the mid-1970s, when incomes rose steadily and poverty was reduced sharply. This period was interrupted for a time, but not dramatically so, by the Korean and Vietnam Wars. This was followed by what might almost be called the 'silver age', starting in the mid-1970s, in which productivity grew less quickly, the increase in incomes became more hesitant, and poverty began to creep up again.

Perhaps the most striking changes and stabilities in the structure of the United States economy since 1969 were as follows: (1) The dramatic rise in the proportion of national income going to interest. (2) The stabilisation of the proportion of national income going to labour as a result of two offsetting factors – a certain decline in real wages offset by a large increase in the proportion of the population in the labour force, almost wholly due to the increase in the number of women in the labour force. (3) The decline in the proportion of the labour force in agriculture, which was very striking in the earlier period, now seems to have come to an end. No great release of labour from agriculture can be expected in the future. (4) Whether there will be a release of labour from manufacturing as a result of computers, robotisation and so on is an open question. The proportion in manufacturing has declined a little since 1979. (5) The stability of the proportional distribution of income in the earlier years of this study is very striking. Since 1969 or so there has been some redistribution from the poor to the rich, which is disconcerting. Some of this may be due to the rise in interest rates.

Perhaps the all-important question is whether the economic growth and the remarkable rise in per capita income that Americans have enjoyed over this period can continue in spite of, or perhaps partly because of, a doubling of the human population. In the United States birth rates in the case of the native born are now below what is necessary for population expansion. Immigration is a very important factor in the United States but it is very difficult to predict what will happen in the future. The fact that immigrants tend to be of child-bearing age of course means that they have a disproportionate impact on the overall growth of the population.

Whether GCP will continue to grow at the rate it has done since 1929 is a matter of considerable doubt and depends on something that is inherently unpredictable, that is the change in human knowledge and know-how. Obviously we cannot predict what knowledge we will have 60 years from now or we would already know it now. There has of course been a remarkable increase in productivity in some fields as a result of the increase in human know-how, especially in agriculture, to a lesser extent in manufacturing, and to a very small extent in education. The cost of the health services has increased spectacularly, largely because of an increase in know-how that has enabled people to be kept alive longer and at greater expense. Unfortunately accounting for this element in the economy is almost impossible because of the extreme difficulty of computing the value of human capital in terms of earning or productive capacity. Insofar as medical skills are employed to keep alive those who are helpless, unconscious, dependent on very expensive equipment and so on, the economic benefits would almost certainly seem to be negative.

With the growing obsolescence of national defence the war industry may eventually go back to where it was under Herbert Hoover, when it was only 0.5 per cent of the economy. This would release something like 6 per cent of the economy for civilian production, and would certainly offer a better chance to eliminate poverty. A really critical question that might come up in the future is: how will the economy adjust to something more like a stationary state if the population stabilises and no one is growing very much richer? The capital stock may stabilise, which means that net investment would shrink eventually to zero. Of course gross investment still has to sustain depreciation and capital consumption. The disappearance of net investment might create a severe unemployment problem, particularly if it leads to diminishing profits and if we allow interest rates to go on increasing. An examination of the proportions of GCP in Figure 3.3 suggests that these problems are by no means insoluble, but that they will have to be consciously considered, particularly in regard to the role of government. If net investment is zero, then there should be no net saving. And if profits are to be sustained, most of the income from profit must be spent on household purchases. Otherwise it is not inconceivable that another great depression could take place following positive feedback processes. The only offsetting element here would seem to be government. Negative taxes might have to be imposed in order to offset inadequate household expenditure. These may seem very odd considerations today, but in 60 years this scenario may not look wholly unrealistic.

Whether inflation will continue is an interesting and perhaps unanswerable question. Certainly the more the burden of old debt is increased, the more likely it is that inflation will be seen as a solution to this problem. If interest rates could be reduced to their Second World War level, the use of public finance as an instrument for maintaining full employment would become much easier. But to do this would certainly require changes in the philosophy of government.

The future role of the United States in the world economy is also a question involving great uncertainties and a wide range of possible futures. Two major problems may emerge. One is that the abatement of the conflict within the temperate zone between the United States and the Soviet Union and the 'First' and 'Second' Worlds may accentuate the conflict between the temperate zone and the tropics, that is between the rich and the poor countries (there were aspects of such a conflict in the war in Iraq). But it is very difficult to spell out how this might happen. It is not inconceivable that the greatest danger will arise from the development of nuclear weapons in poor countries, for such weapons are, after all, rather cheap and may even be available for purchase. On the other hand threat is a very ineffective form of power. The poor countries certainly will not be able to get rich by taking things away from the rich countries. In fact I think it is almost true to say that the poor very rarely have become rich by redistribution, but nearly always by a learning process which has increased their productivity. There may be some exceptions to this principle, but it is not easy to recall any such cases. The only world which we can look forward to with any satisfaction is certainly a world in which severe poverty, the sort of poverty that creates premature death and a failure to realise the capacity of human beings for the 'good life', is constantly diminished. This does not exclude the possibility that there may be many kinds of 'good life', as Gandhi demonstrated, which do not involve riches in the economic sense.

The second major problem is that of the exhaustion of exhaustible resources, which also involve long-term environmental problems. Oil is unlikely to last more than 100 years unless new sources are discovered. Coal will last a little longer, but at the cost of increased pollution and acceleration of the 'greenhouse effect'. The 'greenhouse effect' is rather uncertain, but it does have the potential to create very large disasters, such as melting of the polar ice caps, which could raise the sea level twenty feet, necessitating the massive relocation of people and causing impoverisation. It is not only fossil fuels that are exhaustible. We seem to be exhausting wood as a resource with great rapidity, with a potentially catastrophic effect on the climate, especially with the destruction of tropical rain forests. In the case of energy however, the world is an open system with respect to the sun, and it is certainly conceivable that solar energy might provide all our future energy needs, although the technology of how to do this is difficult, and the fact that solar energy is very diffuse makes its collection and concentration very space-consuming.

The striking economies in energy use following the dramatic rise in the price of oil after 1973 suggest that there are substantial possibilities for economising almost anything if the relative price is high enough. Nobody will economise on anything that is too cheap. Perhaps one reason why economics seems to have become a much more cheerful science over the last generation, in spite of anxiety about the effect of an ever-increasing population on the earth's diminishing resources, is the belief that changes in the relative price structure do profoundly affect human behaviour, and often positively. As things become scarce their relative price rises, and this offers substantial inducement not only to economise on them but also to find substitutes. Whether substitutes can always be found is of course another matter, and economists are perhaps too optimistic about this and insufficiently sensitive to the limitations on what the earth can offer, and even on human knowledge, even if this is the 'ultimate resource', as Julian Simon calls it.[6] It is a fundamental principle that we cannot discover what is not there. But it will be very difficult to ascertain exactly what is not there until we have made very thorough searches. The future of human knowledge, as we have seen, is therefore profoundly uncertain.

On the other hand there is something to be said for insurance against future shortages and catastrophes, even though this may not be easy. One possible method of such insurance would be to antici- pate future scarcities through the manipulation of the relative price system, which could be done fairly easily through taxation. There is a lot to be said for making expensive something which is plentiful now but which is going to be scarce later on. Then people will economise on it and find substitutes. There is a great deal to be said for high taxes on oil and on water in many parts of the world. Whether this is politically feasible is another matter and depends to a considerable degree on whether the problem is widely understood. Here econom- ists have some responsibility.

Another role of the economy which may turn out to be much more important in the future than it has been in the past is to provide encouragement to maintain existing capital structures and to make them more durable. Economists are perhaps partly responsible for the lack of this because of their obsession with income, production and consumption, and their failure to recognise that riches consist in having the use of things rather than in their consumption. My satis- faction rests on living in my house, wearing my clothes, driving my car, using my furniture, appliances and so on, not on using them up or wearing them out. This is not to deny that there may be some economic benefit from consumption. We like eating as well as being well fed, which is reasonable. We may even like a certain amount of variety and change, and there may be some optimum mix of main- tenance and consumption. Existing institutions do not seem to be able to provide this. One of the great problems in the Third World is the absence of a culture of maintenance of resources, and as these become scarcer and populations increase the case for emphasis on durability and maintenance becomes much stronger. One of the problems here is the failure of accounting to measure adequately the costs of depreciation. This seems especially true in non-profit organisations such as schools, colleges and hospitals. This may indeed be one reason for the breakdown of centrally planned economies. It is important that decision makers recognise that accountants cannot account for everything, and that what they present in the way of numbers is evidence, not truth, albeit very valuable evidence.

In the case of materials however, the earth is virtually a closed system and we may run into the very real problem of what we might call 'materials entropy', that is the exhaustion of mines and the dispersal of materials – metals, phosphorus and so on – in dumps all over the world or in the oceans. Theoretically energy can be used to offset this as we now obtain magnesium from the sea, but it might take more energy than is available. The awful truth is that we do not really know what the carrying capacity of the earth is for the human population at a reasonably high standard of living. If this is one billion, then we are in real trouble, for we will almost certainly go to 10 billion before the present population explosion ceases. We may well see famines such as those in Africa taking place in many other parts of the world , with very large-scale migrations as a result. It is not inconceivable that the greatest problem for the United States economy in the future will be the population explosion in Mexico, which may be very difficult to control.

One question that may have to be faced is whether the dynamics of capitalist societies might contain an element which could lead to some sort of breakdown like the Great Depression. This could be as large as the breakdown which now seems to be taking place in centrally planned economies. This is an aspect of the problem of sustainability which is becoming increasingly ominous. Some aspects of the present system we know cannot be sustained; for instance its dependence on fossil fuels, which could well become very scarce and expensive even by 2050 and will certainly become so by the end of the next century. Nuclear weapons too are a time bomb. No matter how small the probability of their being used, this probability is positive, unless national security can be obtained by the abandonment of national defence organisations.

The history of this century however suggests that there may be more subtle unsustainabilities which could produce something like a collapse of the system of free-market economies in the absence of some change in institutions and public policy. Certainly the experience of the Great Depression, which demonstrated that the prosperity of the 1920s was unsustainable, could foretell a cloud on the horizon of the future. The fact that it did happen shows that it must have been possible. And are we quite sure that we have now made it impossible for something like that to happen again? The rise in the proportion of national income going to interest since 1950 is an indication that something in the system is not sustainable. This cannot go on for another decade or more without inflicting disastrous consequences on free-market economies. Whether it can really be controlled is a still somewhat unanswered question which certainly needs much more attention from the economics profession than it is getting now.

We live in a world that has moved closer and closer to becoming a single system, especially with regard to finance and world trade, and this is a system with nobody in particular in charge. Whether somebody should be in charge is a critical question. There was nobody in charge of evolution until genetic engineering arrived. Having somebody in charge of all evolution could easily lead to disaster. An ecosystem like the wild woods is free private enterprise beyond the dreams of Milton Friedman. It has nothing even remotely resembling a government. Such systems may also be subject to catastrophe, but evolution has never come to an end. There is now an uneasy feeling that as far as the human race is concerned it might do just that unless the extraordinary potential of its 'ultimate resource', the human mind, can be realised and put to good and positive use. Learning about the structure of the economy is part of this process. And economists have a great responsibility to move their own image of the economy towards the truth and to propagate this image widely among the human race.

Notes and References

2 Human Capital

1. The figures are taken back to 1910 to show the impact of the First World War.
2. I call these 'layer cake' diagrammes as the proportionate distribution of aggregates are layered like a cake, the 100 per cent line being the top of the cake!

3 Sizes and Proportional Structures of Total Output and Income

1. For an excellent discussion of the inadequacies of national income statistics, see Herman E. Daly and John B. Cobb, Jr, *For the Common Good* (Boston: Beacon Press, 1989), especially Chapter 3 and the Appendix, 'The Index of Sustainable Economic Welfare'. This index (ISEW), which again must be taken as evidence in an extremely complex situation, starts in 1950 at 2448.0, peaks in 1976 at 3789.5, and is only 3402.8 in 1986. GNP is 3512.2 in 1950 and is 7226.4 in 1986. The ISEW, which is 70.8 per cent of per capita GNP in 1950 but only 47 per cent of per capita GNP by 1986, certainly suggests things that GNP does not take into account or succeeds in exaggerating, which rise especially in the last two or three decades.
   The World Resources Institute has published modifications of national income accounts for various countries to take account of the using up of natural resources as a capital loss. See Robert Repetto et al., *Wasting Assets: Natural Resources in the National Income Accounts* (Washington, DC: World Resources Institute, 1989).
2. The 'statistical discrepancy' arises because GNP is calculated by adding up the value of output; and national income by adding up the income of the factors of production.
3. This is equal to national income, less corporate profits, with inventory valuation and capital consumption adjustments, net interest, contributions for social insurance, and wage accruals less disbursements (a negligible item), plus government transfer payments to persons, personal interest income, personal dividend income and business transfer payments. These have changed somewhat over the years, as we see in Figure 3.1. It is a little difficult to see the value of this particular aggregate.
4. Some of farm and non-farm proprietors' income should be included in labour income, although how much is not easy to say. The larger this proportion, the less will be the rise in the percentage of labour income.

5 Capital Structures

1. The higher the discount rate, the less the present value of a given income in the future. Thus at a rate of 2 per cent, the value of $100 ten years hence will be $82; at 10 per cent, $39.

2. A 'time scatter' is a scatter diagram of a pair of variables, each point representing the magnitude of the two variables at a given time, with arrows leading from each point to the next in time.
3. J. M. Keynes, *The General Theory of Employment, Interest and Money* (London: Macmillan, 1936).

6 The Role of Government

1. *Statistical Abstract of the United States*, 1990.
2. *World Almanac and Book of Facts* (New York: World Almanac, 1990) p. 108.
3. Milton Friedman, 'The Role of Monetary Policy', *American Economic Review*, vol. 58, no. 1 (1968) pp. 1–17.

8 Towards Understanding and Control

1. John Kenneth Galbraith, *Reaganomics: Meaning, Means, and Ends* (New York: Free Press, 1983).
2. There is a small organisation called the Committee on Monetary and Economic Reform (COMER), centred mainly in Canada, which is concerned about this problem, but this concern does not seem to have spread very much to the United States.
3. J. M. Keynes, 'The Economic Consequences of Mr. Churchill'. Reprinted in: *The Collected Writings of John Maynard Keynes*, vol. IX (London: Macmillan, for the Royal Economic Society, 1972) pp. 207–30. (First published 1925.)
4. This figure actually seems high in the light of the figure for gross private domestic investment, which was close to zero. This may mainly represent the repair of old structures.
5. K. E. Boulding, 'Puzzles Over Distribution', *Challenge*, vol. 28, no. 5 (Nov./Dec. 1985) pp. 4–10.
6. J. M. Keynes, *A Treatise on Money*, vol. 1 (New York: Harcourt, Brace and Company, 1930) p. 139.
7. Nicholas Kaldor, 'Alternative Theories of Distribution', in *Essays on Value and Distribution* (London: G. Duckworth, 1960).
8. K. E. Boulding, *A Reconstruction of Economics* (New York: John Wiley & Sons, 1950).
9. K. E. Boulding, 'Economic Theory: The Reconstruction Reconstructed', in *Segments of the Economy – 1956, A Symposium* (Cleveland: Howard Allen, 1957) pp. 7–55. Also in K. E. Boulding, *Collected Papers*, vol. II, Fred R. Glahe (ed.). (Boulder: Colorado Associated University Press, 1971) pp. 35–85.

9 What of the Future?

1. Robert Burns, 'To a Mouse' (1785).
2. Arnold Toynbee, *Change and Habit: The Challenge of Our Time* (New York: Oxford University Press. 1966).
3. See the *Journal of Social and Biological Structures* (special issue on The

Punctuated Equilibrium Debate: Scientific Issues and Implications), vol. 12, no. 2/3 (April/July 1989).

4. Fred Polak, *The Image of the Future*, translated from the Dutch and abridged by Elise Boulding (San Francisco and Amsterdam: Jossey-Bass/ Elsevier, 1973).

5. K. E. Boulding, 'Regions of Time', *Papers of the Regional Science Association* (31st North American Meetings, Denver, November 1984), vol. 57 (1985) pp. 19–32.

6. Julian Simon, *The Ultimate Resource* (Princeton, New Jersey: Princeton University Press, 1981).

Appendix: Data Tables

The curious reader may wonder why I have included in this volume the numbers on which the graphs are based. Partly my motivation is to contrast the mental images of the last 60 years as displayed in the graphs and as represented in the numerical tables, in the light of my view that tables of numbers do not give us a new image of the world unless they are translated into visual patterns in the mind, for which the graphs are essential. It will also be a valuable exercise for the reader to create graphs personally from the numerical data provided. Though the numbers are easily available in libraries, they will present a certain challenge to the curious reader to continue the process of graph-building for other combinations of variables beyond what the limited space available in this book permits. I hope therefore when this work is used as a textbook that teachers will encourage students to draw their own graphs of variables and combinations of variables that interest them, especially if this leads them to seek out other time series that are of interest for graphing.

The statistician may complain – with some legitimacy – that I do not use the reduction of the time series to single numbers, like a coefficient of correlation or parameters of an equation. The loss of information in terms of time patterns which such statistical indexes and numbers necessitate is, however, a serious loss. This loss is least where all the equations are linear, so that graphs can be reduced to one or two coefficients, but linearity is very rare, in social systems especially, and reduction to algebraic coefficients can easily lead to the throwing away of important data. Compare, for instance, the information lost when complex multidimensional functions are reduced to algebraic equations which grossly underestimate the complexity of the data. A linear, or even a multilinear, equation is no real substitute for the image created by the careful contemplation of a scatter diagramme or time chart.

You, the reader, are therefore invited to make personal graphs from the numerical data tables, even if it takes a little time. The very act of constructing a graph, in bringing out the subtle details of complex relationships, involves you in the act of creating knowledge in a fresh way.

The reader will note that the data tables in the Appendix appear in the same order as the graphs in the book. Appendix table names correspond to figure names, designated by 'a', 'b', etc. when more than one figure is included in a table. Figure numbers (2.2 for instance) are included at the top of each data column relating to that figure (2.2A, 2.2B, 2.2C), thus allowing for quick reference. Data common to more than one figure have not always been repeated.

In some cases, the same data category is used in more than one figure, but the data themselves are slightly different. This reflects the fact that minor numerical revisions were made in *The Economic Report of the President* from time to time.

Table A1 (a) Total population of the US, 1929–89 (thousands); (b) live births and deaths in the US, 1910–88 (thousands); (c) total annual increase in population of the US, 1929–89 (thousands)

	(a)	(b)			(c)	
	2.1A	2.2A	2.2B	2.2C	2.3A	2.3B
Year	Population	Births	Deaths	Natural increase	Net immigration	Total annual increase
1910	–	2781	1358	1423	–	–
1911	–	2807	1277	1530	–	–
1912	–	2841	1297	1544	–	–
1913	–	2868	1342	1526	–	–
1914	–	2963	1318	1645	–	–
1915	–	2966	1327	1639	–	–
1916	–	2967	1407	1560	–	–
1917	–	2943	1445	1498	–	–
1918	–	2910	1868	1042	–	–
1919	–	2728	1348	1380	–	–
1920	–	2949	1384	1565	–	–
1921	–	3050	1248	1802	–	–
1922	–	2883	1288	1595	–	–
1923	–	2911	1355	1556	–	–
1924	–	2978	1324	1654	–	–
1925	–	2907	1355	1552	–	–
1926	–	2841	1421	1420	–	–
1927	–	2797	1345	1452	–	–
1928	–	2675	1449	1226	–	–
1929	121 767	2581	1449	1132	126	1258
1930	123 077	2622	1391	1231	79	1310
1931	124 040	2506	1377	1129	–166	963
1932	124 840	2434	1361	1073	–273	800
1933	125 579	2307	1342	965	–226	739
1934	126 734	2396	1397	999	–204	795
1935	127 250	2377	1393	984	–108	876
1936	128 053	2355	1479	876	–73	803
1937	128 825	2413	1450	963	–191	772
1938	129 825	2496	1381	1115	–115	1000
1939	130 880	2466	1388	1078	–23	1055
1940	132 122	2559	1417	1142	100	1242
1941	133 402	2703	1398	1305	–25	1280
1942	134 860	2989	1385	1604	–146	1458
1943	136 739	3104	1460	1644	235	1879
1944	138 397	2939	1411	1528	130	1658
1945	139 928	2858	1402	1456	75	1531
1946	141 389	3411	1396	2015	–554	1461

130

1947	144 126	3817	1445	2372	365	2737
1948	146 631	3637	1444	2193	312	2505
1949	149 188	3649	1444	2205	352	2557
1950	151 684	3632	1452	2180	903	2496
1951	154 287	3823	1482	2341	266	2603
1952	156 954	3913	1497	2416	259	2667
1953	159 565	3965	1518	2447	184	2611
1954	162 391	4078	1481	2597	245	2826
1955	165 275	4105	1529	2576	329	2884
1956	168 221	4218	1564	2654	318	2946
1957	171 274	4308	1633	2675	406	3053
1958	174 141	4255	1648	2607	291	2867
1959	177 830	4245	1657	2588	360	2932
1960	180 671	4258	1712	2546	295	2841
1961	183 691	4268	1702	2566	454	3020
1962	186 538	4167	1757	2410	437	2847
1963	189 242	4098	1814	2284	420	2704
1964	191 889	4027	1798	2229	418	2647
1965	194 303	3760	1828	1932	482	2414
1966	196 560	3606	1863	1743	514	2257
1967	198 712	3521	1851	1670	482	2152
1968	200 706	3502	1930	1572	422	1994
1969	203 212	3600	1922	1678	293	1971
1970	205 052	3731	1921	1810	565	2375
1971	207 661	3556	1928	1628	981	2609
1972	209 896	3258	1964	1294	941	2235
1973	211 909	3137	1973	1164	849	2013
1974	213 854	3160	1934	1226	719	1945
1975	215 973	3144	1893	1251	868	2119
1976	218 035	3168	1909	1259	803	2062
1977	220 239	3327	1900	1427	777	2204
1978	222 585	3333	1928	1405	941	2346
1979	225 055	3494	1906	1588	882	2470
1980	227 757	3612	1986	1626	1076	2702
1981	230 138	3646	1987	1659	722	2381
1982	232 520	3614	1976	1638	744	2382
1983	234 799	3614	2010	1604	675	2279
1984	237 001	3663	2033	1630	572	2202
1985	239 279	3761	2086	1675	603	2278
1986	241 625	3731	2099	1632	714	2346
1987	243 934	3829	2127	1702	607	2309
1988	246 329	3913	2171	1742	653	2395
1989	248 777	–	–	–	–	–

Table A2 Population by age group, 1929–87

Year	2.4A Under 5	2.4B 5–15	2.4C 16–19	2.4D 20–24	2.4E 25–44	2.4F 45–64	2.4G 65 & over	2.4I Under 5	2.4J 5–15	2.4K 16–19	2.4L 20–24	2.4M 25–44	2.4N 45–64	2.4O 65 & over
	(thousands)							(per cent)						
1929	11 734	26 800	9 127	10 694	35 862	21 076	6 474	9.64	22.01	7.50	8.78	29.45	17.31	5.32
1930	11 372	26 983	9 220	10 915	36 309	21 573	6 705	9.24	21.92	7.49	8.87	29.50	17.53	5.45
1931	11 179	26 984	9 259	11 003	36 654	22 031	6 928	9.01	21.75	7.46	8.87	29.55	17.76	5.59
1932	10 903	26 969	9 284	11 077	36 988	22 475	7 147	8.73	21.60	7.44	8.87	29.63	18.00	5.72
1933	10 612	26 897	9 302	11 152	37 319	22 933	7 363	8.45	21.42	7.41	8.88	29.72	18.26	5.86
1934	10 331	26 796	9 331	11 238	37 662	23 435	7 582	8.17	21.20	7.38	8.89	29.80	18.54	6.00
1935	10 170	26 645	9 381	11 317	37 987	23 947	7 804	7.99	20.94	7.37	8.89	29.85	18.82	6.13
1936	10 044	26 415	9 461	11 375	38 288	24 444	8 027	7.84	20.63	7.39	8.88	29.90	19.09	6.27
1937	10 009	26 062	9 578	11 411	38 589	24 917	8 258	7.77	20.23	7.43	8.86	29.95	19.34	6.41
1938	10 176	25 631	9 717	11 453	38 954	25 387	8 508	7.84	19.74	7.48	8.82	30.00	19.55	6.55
1939	10 418	25 179	9 822	11 519	39 354	25 823	8 764	7.96	19.24	7.50	8.80	30.07	19.73	6.70
1940	10 579	24 811	9 895	11 690	39 868	26 249	9 031	8.01	18.78	7.49	8.85	30.17	19.87	6.84
1941	10 850	24 516	9 840	11 807	40 383	26 718	9 288	8.13	18.38	7.38	8.85	30.27	20.03	6.96
1942	11 301	24 231	9 730	11 955	40 861	27 196	9 584	8.38	17.97	7.21	8.86	30.30	20.17	7.11
1943	12 016	24 093	9 607	12 064	41 420	27 671	9 867	8.79	17.62	7.03	8.82	30.29	20.24	7.22
1944	12 524	23 949	9 561	12 062	42 016	28 138	10 147	9.05	17.30	6.91	8.72	30.36	20.33	7.33
1945	12 979	23 907	9 361	12 036	42 521	28 630	10 494	9.28	17.09	6.69	8.60	30.39	20.46	7.50
1946	13 244	24 103	9 119	12 004	43 027	29 064	10 828	9.37	17.05	6.45	8.49	30.43	20.56	7.66
1947	14 406	24 468	9 097	11 814	43 657	29 498	11 185	10.00	16.98	6.31	8.20	30.29	20.47	7.76
1948	14 919	25 209	8 952	11 794	44 288	29 931	11 538	10.17	17.19	6.11	8.04	30.20	20.41	7.87
1949	15 607	25 852	8 788	11 700	44 916	30 405	11 921	10.46	17.33	5.89	7.84	30.11	20.38	7.99
1950	16 410	26 721	8 542	11 680	45 672	30 849	12 397	10.78	17.55	5.61	7.67	29.99	20.26	8.14
1951	17 333	27 279	8 446	11 552	46 103	31 362	12 803	11.19	17.61	5.45	7.46	29.77	20.25	8.27
1952	17 312	28 894	8 414	11 350	46 495	31 884	13 203	10.99	18.34	5.34	7.20	29.51	20.24	8.38
1953	17 638	30 227	8 460	11 062	46 786	32 394	13 617	11.01	18.87	5.28	6.91	29.21	20.22	8.50
1954	18 057	31 480	8 637	10 832	47 001	32 942	14 076	11.08	19.31	5.30	6.64	28.83	20.21	8.63

1955	18 566	32 682	8 744	10 714	47 194	33 506	14 525	11.19	19.70	5.27	6.46	28.44	20.19	8.75
1956	19 003	33 994	8 916	10 616	47 379	34 057	14 938	11.25	20.13	5.28	6.29	28.05	20.16	8.84
1957	19 494	35 272	9 195	10 603	47 440	34 591	15 388	11.33	20.51	5.35	6.17	27.58	20.11	8.95
1958	19 887	36 445	9 543	10 756	47 337	35 109	15 806	11.37	20.84	5.46	6.15	27.07	20.08	9.04
1959	20 175	37 368	10 215	10 969	47 192	35 663	16 248	11.35	21.01	5.74	6.17	26.54	20.05	9.14
1960	20 341	38 494	10 683	11 134	47 140	36 203	16 675	11.26	21.31	5.91	6.16	26.09	20.04	9.23
1961	20 522	39 765	11 025	11 483	47 084	36 722	17 089	11.17	21.65	6.00	6.25	25.63	19.99	9.30
1962	20 469	41 205	11 180	11 959	47 013	37 255	17 457	10.97	22.09	5.99	6.41	25.20	19.97	9.36
1963	20 342	41 626	12 007	12 714	46 994	37 782	17 778	10.75	22.00	6.34	6.72	24.83	19.96	9.39
1964	20 165	42 297	12 736	13 269	46 958	38 338	18 127	10.51	22.04	6.64	6.91	24.47	19.98	9.45
1965	19 824	42 938	13 516	13 746	46 912	38 916	18 451	10.20	22.10	6.96	7.07	24.14	20.03	9.50
1966	19 208	43 702	14 311	14 050	47 001	39 534	18 755	9.77	22.23	7.28	7.15	23.91	20.11	9.54
1967	18 563	44 244	14 200	15 248	47 194	40 193	19 071	9.34	22.27	7.15	7.67	23.75	20.23	9.60
1968	17 913	44 622	14 452	15 786	47 721	40 846	19 365	8.93	22.23	7.20	7.87	23.78	20.35	9.65
1969	17 376	44 840	14 800	16 480	48 064	41 437	19 680	8.57	22.12	7.30	8.13	23.71	20.44	9.71
1970	17 166	44 816	15 289	17 202	48 473	41 999	20 107	8.37	21.86	7.46	8.39	23.64	20.48	9.81
1971	17 244	44 591	15 688	18 159	48 936	42 482	20 561	8.30	21.47	7.55	8.74	23.57	20.46	9.90
1972	17 101	44 203	16 039	18 153	50 482	42 898	21 020	8.15	21.06	7.64	8.65	24.05	20.44	10.01
1973	16 851	43 582	16 446	18 521	51 749	43 235	21 525	7.95	20.57	7.76	8.74	24.42	20.40	10.16
1974	16 487	42 989	16 769	18 975	53 051	43 522	22 061	7.71	20.10	7.84	8.87	24.81	20.35	10.32
1975	16 121	42 508	17 017	19 527	54 302	43 801	22 696	7.46	19.68	7.88	9.04	25.14	20.28	10.51
1976	15 617	42 099	17 194	19 986	55 852	44 008	23 278	7.16	19.31	7.89	9.17	25.62	20.18	10.68
1977	15 564	41 298	17 276	20 499	57 561	44 150	23 892	7.07	18.75	7.84	9.31	26.14	20.05	10.85
1978	15 735	40 428	17 288	20 946	59 400	44 286	24 502	7.07	18.16	7.77	9.41	26.69	19.90	11.01
1979	16 063	39 552	17 242	21 297	61 379	44 390	25 134	7.14	17.57	7.66	9.46	27.27	19.72	11.17
1980	16 458	38 844	17 160	21 584	63 494	44 515	25 704	7.23	17.05	7.53	9.48	27.88	19.54	11.29
1981	16 931	38 190	16 770	21 821	65 619	44 569	26 236	7.36	16.59	7.29	9.48	28.51	19.37	11.40
1982	17 298	37 876	16 255	21 807	67 856	44 601	26 827	7.44	16.29	6.99	9.38	29.18	19.18	11.54
1983	17 650	37 668	15 704	21 700	69 970	44 678	27 428	7.52	16.04	6.69	9.24	29.80	19.03	11.68
1984	17 830	37 657	15 141	21 536	72 048	44 817	27 927	7.52	15.89	6.39	9.09	30.41	18.91	11.79
1985	18 004	37 691	14 819	21 214	74 077	44 934	28 540	7.52	15.75	6.19	8.87	30.96	18.78	11.93
1986	18 152	37 706	14 802	20 608	76 124	45 055	29 167	7.51	15.61	6.13	8.53	31.51	18.65	12.07
1987	18 252	37 685	14 958	19 984	77 897	45 303	29 835	7.48	15.45	6.13	8.19	31.94	18.57	12.23

Appendix: Data Tables

Table A3 Labour force and population of labour force age, 1929–87

Year	2.5A Total population	2.5B Civilian labour force	2.5C Armed forces	2.5D 20–64	2.5E 16–64	2.5F Civilian labour force	2.5G Armed forces	2.5H 20–64	2.5I 16–64
			(thousands)				(per cent)		
1929	121 767	49 180	260	67 632	76 759	40.39	0.5	55.54	63.04
1930	123 077	49 820	260	68 797	78 017	40.48	0.5	55.90	63.39
1931	124 038	50 420	260	69 688	78 947	40.65	0.5	56.18	63.65
1932	124 843	51 000	250	70 540	79 824	40.85	0.5	56.50	63.94
1933	125 578	51 590	250	71 404	80 706	41.08	0.5	56.86	64.27
1934	126 375	52 230	260	72 335	81 666	41.33	0.5	57.24	64.62
1935	127 251	52 870	270	73 251	82 632	41.55	0.5	57.56	64.94
1936	128 054	53 440	300	74 107	83 568	41.73	0.6	57.87	65.26
1937	128 824	54 000	320	74 917	84 495	41.92	0.6	58.15	65.59
1938	129 826	54 610	340	75 794	85 511	42.06	0.6	58.38	65.87
1939	130 879	55 230	370	76 696	86 518	42.20	0.7	58.60	66.11
1940	132 123	55 640	540	77 807	87 702	42.11	1.0	58.89	66.38
1941	133 402	55 910	1 620	78 908	88 748	41.91	2.8	59.15	66.53
1942	134 858	56 410	3 970	80 012	89 742	41.83	6.6	59.33	66.55
1943	136 738	55 540	9 020	81 155	90 762	40.62	14.0	59.35	66.38
1944	138 397	54 630	11 410	82 216	91 777	39.47	17.3	59.41	66.31
1945	139 928	53 860	11 440	83 187	92 548	38.49	17.5	59.45	66.14
1946	141 389	57 520	3 450	84 095	93 214	40.68	5.7	59.48	65.93
1947	144 125	60 168	1 591	84 969	94 066	41.75	2.6	58.96	65.27
1948	146 631	60 621	1 456	86 013	94 965	41.34	2.3	58.66	64.76
1949	149 189	61 286	1 617	87 021	95 809	41.08	2.6	58.33	64.22
1950	152 271	62 208	1 169	88 201	96 743	40.85	1.8	57.92	63.53
1951	154 878	62 017	2 143	89 017	97 463	40.04	3.3	57.48	62.93
1952	157 552	62 138	2 386	89 729	98 143	39.44	3.7	56.95	62.29
1953	160 184	63 015	2 231	90 242	98 702	39.34	3.4	56.34	61.62
1954	163 025	63 643	2 142	90 775	99 412	39.04	3.3	55.68	60.98
1955	165 931	65 023	2 064	91 414	100 158	39.19	3.1	55.09	60.36
1956	168 903	66 552	1 965	92 052	100 968	39.40	2.9	54.50	59.78
1957	171 983	66 929	1 948	92 634	101 829	38.92	2.8	53.86	59.21
1958	174 883	67 639	1 847	93 202	102 745	38.68	2.7	53.29	58.75
1959	177 830	68 369	1 788	93 824	104 039	38.45	2.5	52.76	58.50
1960	180 670	69 628	1 861	94 477	105 160	38.54	2.6	52.29	58.21
1961	183 690	70 459	1 900	95 289	106 314	38.36	2.6	51.87	57.88
1962	186 538	70 614	2 061	96 227	107 407	37.86	2.8	51.59	57.58
1963	189 243	71 833	2 006	97 490	109 497	37.96	2.7	51.52	57.86
1964	191 890	73 091	2 018	98 565	111 301	38.09	2.7	51.37	58.00
1965	194 303	74 455	1 946	99 574	113 090	38.32	2.5	51.25	58.20
1966	196 561	75 770	2 122	100 585	114 896	38.55	2.7	51.17	58.45
1967	198 713	77 347	2 218	102 635	116 835	38.92	2.8	51.65	58.80
1968	200 705	78 737	2 253	104 353	118 805	39.23	2.8	51.99	59.19
1969	202 677	80 734	2 238	105 981	120 781	39.83	2.7	52.29	59.59
1970	205 052	82 771	2 118	107 674	122 963	40.37	2.5	52.51	59.97
1971	207 661	84 382	1 973	109 577	125 265	40.63	2.3	52.77	60.32
1972	209 896	87 034	1 813	111 533	127 572	41.47	2.0	53.14	60.78
1973	211 909	89 429	1 774	113 505	129 951	42.20	1.9	53.56	61.32

1974	213 854	91 949	1 721	115 548	132 317	43.00	1.8	54.03 61.87
1975	215 972	93 775	1 678	117 630	134 647	43.42	1.8	54.47 62.34
1976	218 034	96 158	1 668	119 846	137 040	44.10	1.7	54.97 62.85
1977	220 240	99 009	1 656	122 210	139 486	44.96	1.6	55.49 63.33
1978	222 585	102 251	1 631	124 632	141 920	45.94	1.6	55.99 63.76
1979	225 057	104 962	1 597	127 066	144 308	46.64	1.5	56.46 64.12
1980	227 759	106 940	1 604	129 593	146 753	46.95	1.5	56.90 64.43
1981	230 136	108 670	1 645	132 009	148 779	47.22	1.5	57.36 64.65
1982	232 520	110 204	1 668	134 264	150 519	47.40	1.5	57.74 64.73
1983	234 798	111 550	1 676	136 348	152 052	47.51	1.5	58.07 64.76
1984	236 956	113 544	1 697	138 401	153 542	47.92	1.5	58.41 64.80
1985	239 279	115 461	1 706	140 225	155 044	48.25	1.5	58.60 64.80
1986	241 614	117 834	1 706	141 787	156 589	48.77	1.4	58.68 64.81
1987	243 914	119 865	1 737	143 184	158 142	49.14	1.4	58.70 64.84

Table A4 Population in non-labour force, labour force and employment, 1929–89

Year	2.6A Male employmt l. force	2.6B Male unemploymt	2.6C Male l. force	2.6D Female employmt	2.6E Female unemploymt	2.6F Female l. force	2.6G Total l. force	2.6H Male employmt	2.6I Male unemploymt	2.6J Female employmt	2.6K Female unemploymt	2.6L Total
	(thousands)									*(per cent)*		
1929	–	–	–	–	–	–	49 180	–	–	–	–	40.39
1930	–	–	–	–	–	–	49 820	–	–	–	–	40.48
1931	–	–	–	–	–	–	50 420	–	–	–	–	40.65
1932	–	–	–	–	–	–	51 000	–	–	–	–	40.85
1933	–	–	–	–	–	–	51 590	–	–	–	–	41.08
1934	–	–	–	–	–	–	52 230	–	–	–	–	41.33
1935	–	–	–	–	–	–	52 870	–	–	–	–	41.55
1936	–	–	–	–	–	–	53 440	–	–	–	–	41.73
1937	–	–	–	–	–	–	54 000	–	–	–	–	41.92
1938	–	–	–	–	–	–	54 610	–	–	–	–	42.06
1939	–	–	–	–	–	–	55 230	–	–	–	–	42.20
1940	–	–	–	–	–	–	55 640	–	–	–	–	42.11
1941	–	–	–	–	–	–	55 910	–	–	–	–	41.91
1942	–	–	–	–	–	–	56 410	–	–	–	–	41.83
1943	–	–	–	–	–	–	55 540	–	–	–	–	40.62
1944	–	–	–	–	–	–	54 630	–	–	–	–	39.47
1945	–	–	–	–	–	–	53 860	–	–	–	–	38.49
1946	–	–	–	–	–	–	57 520	–	–	–	–	40.68
1947	40 995	1692	42 687	16 045	619	16 664	59 351	28.44	1.17	11.13	0.43	41.18
1948	41 725	1559	43 284	16 617	717	17 334	60 618	28.46	1.06	11.33	0.49	41.34
1949	40 925	2572	43 497	16 723	1065	17 788	61 285	27.43	1.72	11.21	0.71	41.08
1950	41 578	2239	43 817	17 340	1049	18 389	62 206	27.41	1.48	11.43	0.69	41.01
1951	41 780	1221	43 001	18 181	834	19 015	62 016	27.08	0.79	11.78	0.54	40.20
1952	41 682	1185	42 867	18 568	698	19 266	62 133	26.56	0.75	11.83	0.44	39.59
1953	42 430	1202	43 632	18 749	632	19 381	63 013	26.59	0.75	11.75	0.40	39.49
1954	41 619	2344	43 963	18 490	1188	19 678	63 641	25.63	1.44	11.39	0.73	39.19
1955	42 621	1854	44 475	19 551	998	20 549	65 024	25.79	1.12	11.83	0.60	39.34

Year												
1956	43 379	1711	45 090	20 419	1039	21 548	66 548	25.79	1.02	12.14	0.62	39.56
1957	43 357	1841	45 198	20 714	1018	21 732	66 930	25.31	1.07	12.09	0.59	39.08
1958	42 423	3098	45 521	20 613	1504	22 117	67 638	24.36	1.78	11.84	0.86	38.84
1959	43 466	2420	45 886	21 164	1320	22 484	68 370	24.44	1.36	11.90	0.74	38.45
1960	43 904	2486	46 390	21 874	1366	23 240	69 630	24.30	1.38	12.11	0.76	38.54
1961	43 656	2997	46 653	22 090	1717	23 807	70 460	23.77	1.63	12.03	0.93	38.36
1962	44 177	2423	46 600	22 525	1488	24 013	70 613	23.68	1.30	12.08	0.80	37.85
1963	44 657	2472	47 129	23 105	1598	24 703	71 832	23.60	1.31	12.21	0.84	37.96
1964	45 474	2205	47 679	23 831	1581	25 412	73 091	23.70	1.15	12.42	0.82	38.09
1965	46 340	1914	48 254	24 748	1452	26 200	74 454	23.85	0.99	12.74	0.75	38.32
1966	46 919	1551	48 470	25 976	1324	27 300	75 770	23.87	0.79	13.22	0.67	38.55
1967	47 479	1508	48 987	26 893	1468	28 361	77 348	23.89	0.76	13.53	0.74	38.92
1968	48 114	1419	49 533	27 807	1397	29 204	78 737	23.97	0.71	13.85	0.70	39.23
1969	48 818	1403	50 221	29 084	1429	30 513	80 734	24.02	0.69	14.31	0.70	39.73
1970	48 990	2238	51 228	29 688	1855	31 543	82 771	23.89	1.09	14.48	0.90	40.37
1971	49 390	2789	52 179	29 976	2227	32 203	84 382	23.86	1.35	14.48	1.08	40.76
1972	50 896	2659	53 555	31 257	2222	33 479	87 034	24.37	1.27	14.97	1.06	41.68
1973	52 349	2275	54 624	32 715	2089	34 804	89 428	24.93	1.08	15.58	0.99	42.58
1974	53 024	2714	55 738	33 769	2441	36 210	91 948	25.02	1.28	15.94	1.15	43.39
1975	51 857	4442	56 299	33 989	3486	37 475	93 774	24.01	2.06	15.74	1.61	43.42
1976	53 138	4036	57 174	35 615	3369	38 984	96 158	24.70	1.88	16.55	1.57	44.70
1977	54 728	3667	58 395	37 289	3324	40 613	99 008	25.24	1.69	17.20	1.53	45.66
1978	56 479	3142	59 621	39 569	3061	42 630	102 251	25.82	1.44	18.09	1.40	46.75
1979	57 607	3120	60 727	41 217	3018	44 235	104 962	25.60	1.39	18.31	1.34	46.64
1980	57 186	4267	61 453	42 117	3370	45 487	106 940	25.11	1.87	18.49	1.48	46.95
1981	57 397	4577	61 974	43 000	3696	46 696	108 670	24.94	1.99	18.68	1.61	47.22
1982	56 271	6179	62 450	43 256	4499	47 755	110 205	24.20	2.66	18.60	1.93	47.40
1983	56 787	6260	63 047	44 047	4457	48 504	111 551	24.19	2.67	18.76	1.90	47.51
1984	59 091	4744	63 835	45 915	3794	49 709	113 544	24.93	2.00	19.37	1.60	47.91
1985	59 891	4521	64 412	47 259	3791	51 050	115 462	25.03	1.89	19.75	1.58	48.25
1986	60 892	4530	65 422	48 706	3707	52 413	117 835	25.20	1.87	20.16	1.53	48.77
1987	62 107	4101	66 208	50 334	3324	53 658	119 866	25.46	1.68	20.63	1.36	49.14
1988	63 273	3655	66 928	51 696	3046	54 742	121 670	25.69	1.48	20.99	1.24	49.39
1989	64 315	3525	67 840	53 027	3003	56 030	123 870	25.85	1.42	21.32	1.21	49.79

Table A5 Employment by sector, 1929–89 (per cent)

Year	2.7A Agri- culture	2.7B Manufac- turing	2.7C Services	2.7D Finance, insurance & real estate	2.7E Whole- sale & retail trade	2.7F Trans- portation & public utilities	2.7G Construc- tion	2.7H Mining	2.7I State govt	2.7J Federal govt	2.7K Armed forces	2.7L Misc.	2.7M Unemploy- ment
1929	21.1	21.6	6.9	3.0	12.4	7.9	3.1	2.2	5.1	1.1	0.5	11.8	3.1
1930	20.6	19.1	6.7	2.9	11.6	7.4	2.8	2.0	5.2	1.1	0.5	11.4	8.7
1931	20.3	16.1	6.3	2.7	10.4	6.4	2.4	1.7	5.3	1.1	0.5	10.8	15.8
1932	19.8	13.5	5.7	2.6	9.1	5.5	1.9	1.4	5.2	1.1	0.5	10.1	23.5
1933	19.5	14.3	5.5	2.5	9.2	5.2	1.6	1.4	5.0	1.1	0.5	9.6	24.7
1934	18.9	16.2	5.8	2.5	10.1	5.2	1.7	1.7	5.0	1.2	0.5	9.6	21.6
1935	19.0	17.1	5.9	2.5	10.2	5.2	1.7	1.7	5.1	1.4	0.5	9.6	20.0
1936	18.6	18.3	6.2	2.6	10.8	5.5	2.2	1.8	5.3	1.5	0.6	9.9	16.8
1937	18.1	19.9	6.4	2.6	11.5	5.8	2.1	1.9	5.4	1.5	0.6	10.1	14.2
1938	17.6	17.2	6.3	2.6	11.2	5.2	1.9	1.6	5.6	1.5	0.6	9.7	18.9
1939	17.3	18.5	6.3	2.6	11.6	5.3	2.1	1.5	5.6	1.6	0.7	10.0	17.1
1940	17.0	19.6	6.5	2.6	12.0	5.4	2.3	1.6	5.7	1.8	1.0	10.0	14.5
1941	15.8	22.9	6.8	2.7	12.5	5.7	3.2	1.7	5.8	2.3	2.8	8.2	9.7
1942	15.3	25.3	6.7	2.5	11.8	5.7	3.6	1.6	5.4	3.7	6.6	7.3	4.4
1943	14.1	27.3	6.4	2.3	10.8	5.6	2.5	1.4	4.9	4.5	14.0	4.6	1.7
1944	13.6	26.2	6.3	2.2	10.7	5.8	1.7	1.4	4.7	4.4	17.3	4.8	1.0
1945	13.1	23.8	6.5	2.3	11.2	6.0	1.8	1.3	4.8	4.3	17.5	5.9	1.6
1946	13.6	24.1	7.7	2.7	13.7	6.7	2.8	1.4	5.5	3.7	5.7	8.7	3.7
1947	12.9	25.5	8.2	2.8	14.7	6.8	3.3	1.6	5.9	3.1	2.6	8.7	3.8
1948	12.3	25.1	8.3	2.9	14.9	6.7	3.5	1.6	6.1	3.0	2.3	9.4	3.7
1949	12.2	23.0	8.3	2.9	14.7	6.4	3.5	1.5	6.3	3.0	2.6	9.9	5.8
1950	11.3	24.0	8.5	3.0	14.8	6.4	3.7	1.4	6.5	3.0	1.8	10.4	5.2
1951	10.5	25.6	8.6	3.0	15.2	6.6	4.1	1.4	6.4	3.6	3.3	8.4	3.2
1952	10.1	25.8	8.8	3.2	15.5	6.6	4.1	1.4	6.5	3.8	3.7	7.7	2.9
1953	9.6	26.9	8.9	3.2	15.7	6.6	4.1	1.3	6.7	3.5	3.4	7.2	2.8
1954	9.4	24.8	9.1	3.3	15.6	6.2	4.0	1.2	6.9	3.3	3.3	7.5	5.4
1955	9.6	25.2	9.3	3.4	15.7	6.2	4.2	1.2	7.0	3.3	3.1	7.6	4.3

1956	4.0	7.5	2.9	3.2	7.4	1.2	4.4	6.2	15.8	3.5	9.5	25.2	9.2
1957	4.2	7.7	2.8	3.2	7.8	1.2	4.3	6.2	15.8	3.5	9.7	24.9	8.6
1958	6.6	8.8	2.7	3.2	8.1	1.1	4.1	5.7	15.5	3.6	9.7	22.9	8.0
1959	5.3	8.3	2.5	3.2	8.3	1.0	4.3	5.7	15.9	3.6	10.1	23.8	7.9
1960	5.4	8.6	2.6	3.2	8.5	1.0	4.1	5.6	15.9	3.7	10.3	23.5	7.6
1961	6.5	9.0	2.6	3.1	8.7	0.9	4.0	5.4	15.7	3.7	10.5	22.6	7.2
1962	5.4	8.5	2.8	3.2	9.0	0.9	4.1	5.4	15.9	3.8	11.0	23.2	6.8
1963	5.5	8.7	2.7	3.2	9.3	0.9	4.1	5.3	16.0	3.8	11.2	23.0	6.3
1964	5.0	8.7	2.7	3.1	9.6	0.8	4.1	5.3	16.2	3.9	11.5	23.0	6.0
1965	4.4	7.8	2.5	3.1	10.1	0.8	4.2	5.3	16.6	3.9	11.8	23.6	5.7
1966	3.7	6.4	2.7	3.3	10.6	0.8	4.3	5.3	17.0	3.9	12.2	24.7	5.1
1967	3.7	5.9	2.8	3.4	10.9	0.8	4.1	5.4	17.1	4.0	12.6	24.4	4.8
1968	3.5	5.2	2.8	3.4	11.2	0.7	4.1	5.3	17.4	4.1	13.0	24.4	4.7
1969	3.4	4.7	2.7	3.3	11.4	0.7	4.3	5.4	17.7	4.2	13.5	24.3	4.3
1970	4.8	5.1	2.5	3.2	11.6	0.7	4.2	5.3	17.7	4.3	13.6	22.8	4.1
1971	5.8	5.5	2.3	3.1	11.8	0.7	4.3	5.2	17.8	4.4	13.7	21.6	3.9
1972	5.5	5.6	2.0	3.0	12.0	0.7	4.4	5.1	18.0	4.4	13.8	21.6	3.9
1973	4.8	5.3	1.9	2.9	12.1	0.7	4.5	5.1	18.2	4.4	14.1	22.1	3.8
1974	5.5	5.4	1.8	2.9	12.2	0.7	4.3	5.0	18.1	4.4	14.3	21.4	3.8
1975	8.3	5.8	1.8	2.9	12.5	0.8	3.7	4.8	17.9	4.4	14.6	19.2	3.6
1976	7.6	6.2	1.7	2.8	12.4	0.8	3.7	4.7	18.1	4.4	14.9	19.4	3.4
1977	6.9	6.2	1.6	2.7	12.3	0.8	3.8	4.7	18.4	4.4	15.2	19.6	3.3
1978	6.0	5.7	1.6	2.7	12.4	0.8	4.1	4.7	18.8	4.5	15.6	19.7	3.3
1979	5.8	5.3	1.5	2.6	12.4	0.9	4.2	4.8	18.9	4.7	16.1	19.7	3.1
1980	7.0	5.1	1.5	2.6	12.3	0.9	4.0	4.7	18.7	4.8	16.5	18.7	3.1
1981	7.5	5.3	1.5	2.5	12.0	1.0	3.8	4.7	18.6	4.8	16.9	18.3	3.1
1982	9.5	5.9	1.5	2.4	11.7	1.0	3.5	4.5	18.3	4.8	17.0	16.8	3.0
1983	9.5	6.4	1.5	2.4	11.6	0.8	3.5	4.4	18.4	4.8	17.4	16.3	3.0
1984	7.4	6.2	1.5	2.4	11.5	0.8	3.8	4.5	19.2	4.9	18.0	16.8	2.9
1985	7.1	5.5	1.5	2.5	11.5	0.8	4.0	4.5	19.7	5.1	18.8	16.4	2.7
1986	6.9	5.8	1.4	2.4	11.5	0.6	4.0	4.4	19.8	5.3	19.3	15.9	2.6
1987	6.1	5.8	1.4	2.4	11.6	0.6	4.1	4.4	20.0	5.4	20.0	15.7	2.5
1988	5.4	5.0	1.4	2.4	11.7	0.6	4.2	4.5	20.4	5.4	20.7	15.7	2.6
1989	5.2	4.4	1.3	2.4	11.7	0.6	4.2	4.5	20.6	5.4	21.4	15.6	2.5

Table A6   Employment by sector, 1929–89 (16 years of age and over,* thousands)

Year	2.8A Agri-culture	2.8B Manufac-turing	2.8C Services	2.8D Finance, insurance & real estate	2.8E Whole-sale & retail trade	2.8F Trans-portation & public utilities	2.8G Construc-tion	2.8H Mining	2.8I State govt	2.8J Federal govt	2.8K Armed forces	2.8L Misc.	2.8M Unemploy-ment	2.8N Labour force
1929	10 450	10 702	3 425	1494	6 123	3916	1512	1087	2 532	533	260	5856	1 550	49 440
1930	10 340	9 562	3 361	1460	5 797	3685	1387	1009	2 622	526	260	5731	4 340	50 080
1931	10 290	8 170	3 169	1392	5 284	3254	1229	873	2 704	560	260	5475	8 020	50 680
1932	10 170	6 931	2 918	1326	4 683	2816	985	731	2 666	559	250	5155	12 060	51 250
1933	10 090	7 397	2 861	1280	4 755	2672	824	744	2 601	565	250	4971	12 830	51 840
1934	9 900	8 501	3 045	1304	5 281	2750	877	883	2 647	652	260	5050	11 340	52 490
1935	10 110	9 069	3 128	1320	5 431	2786	927	897	2 728	753	270	5111	10 610	53 140
1936	10 000	9 827	3 312	1373	5 809	2973	1160	946	2 842	826	300	5342	9 030	53 740
1937	9 820	10 794	3 503	1417	6 265	3134	1127	1015	2 923	833	320	5469	7 700	54 320
1938	9 690	9 440	3 458	1410	6 179	2863	1070	891	3 054	829	340	5336	10 390	54 950
1939	9 610	10 278	3 502	1447	6 426	2936	1165	854	3 090	905	370	5537	9 480	55 600
1940	9 540	10 985	3 665	1485	6 750	3038	1311	925	3 206	996	540	5619	8 120	56 180
1941	9 100	13 192	3 905	1525	7 210	3274	1814	957	3 320	1340	1 620	4713	5 560	57 530
1942	9 250	15 280	4 066	1509	7 118	3460	2198	992	3 270	2213	3 970	4394	2 660	60 380
1943	9 080	17 602	4 130	1481	6 982	3647	1587	925	3 174	2905	9 020	2957	1 070	64 560
1944	8 950	17 328	4 145	1461	7 058	3829	1108	892	3 116	2928	11 410	3145	670	66 040
1945	8 580	15 524	4 222	1481	7 314	3906	1147	836	3 137	2808	11 440	3865	1 040	65 300
1946	8 320	14 703	4 697	1675	8 376	4061	1683	862	3 341	2254	3 450	5278	2 270	60 970
1947	7 890	15 545	5 025	1728	8 955	4166	2009	955	3 582	1892	1 591	5291	2 311	60 941
1948	7 629	15 582	5 181	1800	9 272	4189	2198	994	3 787	1863	1 456	5848	2 276	62 080
1949	7 658	14 441	5 240	1828	9 264	4001	2194	930	3 948	1908	1 617	6239	3 637	62 903
1950	7 160	15 241	5 357	1888	9 386	4034	2364	901	4 098	1928	1 169	6561	3 288	63 377
1951	6 726	16 393	5 547	1956	9 742	4226	2637	929	4 087	2302	2 143	5416	2 055	64 160
1952	6 500	16 632	5 699	2035	10 004	4248	2668	898	4 188	2420	2 386	4957	1 883	64 524
1953	6 260	17 549	5 835	2111	10 247	4290	2659	866	4 340	2305	2 231	4717	1 834	65 246
1954	6 205	16 314	5 969	2200	10 235	4084	2646	791	4 563	2188	2 142	4914	3 532	65 785
1955	6 450	16 882	6 240	2298	10 535	4141	2839	792	4 727	2187	2 064	5081	2 852	67 087
1956	6 283	17 243	6 497	2389	10 858	4244	3039	822	5 069	2209	1 965	5144	2 750	68 517

1957	5 947	17 174	6 708	2438	10 886	4241	2962	828	5 399	2217	1 948	5270	2 859	68 877
1958	5 586	15 945	6 765	2481	10 750	3976	2817	751	5 648	2191	1 847	6126	4 602	69 486
1959	5 565	16 675	7 087	2549	11 127	4011	3004	732	5 850	2233	1 788	5797	3 740	70 157
1960	5 458	16 796	7 378	2629	11 391	4004	2926	712	6 083	2270	1 861	6129	3 852	71 489
1961	5 200	16 326	7 620	2688	11 337	3903	2859	672	6 315	2279	1 900	6547	4 714	72 359
1962	4 944	16 853	7 982	2754	11 566	3906	2948	650	6 550	2340	2 061	6210	3 911	72 675
1963	4 687	16 995	8 277	2830	11 778	3903	3010	635	6 868	2358	2 006	6422	4 070	73 839
1964	4 523	17 274	8 660	2911	12 160	3951	3097	634	7 248	2348	2 018	6499	3 786	75 109
1965	4 361	18 062	9 036	2977	12 716	4036	3232	632	7 696	2378	1 946	5961	3 366	76 401
1966	3 979	19 214	9 498	3058	13 245	4158	3317	627	8 220	2564	2 122	5014	2 875	77 892
1967	3 844	19 447	10 045	3185	13 606	4268	3248	613	8 672	2719	2 218	4724	2 975	79 565
1968	3 817	19 781	10 567	3337	14 099	4318	3350	606	9 102	2737	2 253	4206	2 817	80 990
1969	3 606	20 167	11 169	3512	14 705	4442	3575	619	9 437	2758	2 238	3912	2 832	82 972
1970	3 463	19 367	11 548	3645	15 040	4515	3588	623	9 823	2731	2 118	4335	4 093	84 889
1971	3 394	18 623	11 797	3772	15 352	4476	3704	609	10 185	2696	1 973	4758	5 016	86 355
1972	3 484	19 151	12 276	3908	15 949	4541	3889	628	10 649	2684	1 813	4994	4 882	88 847
1973	3 470	20 154	12 857	4046	16 607	4656	4097	642	11 068	2663	1 774	4804	4 365	91 203
1974	3 515	20 077	13 441	4148	16 987	4725	4020	697	11 446	2724	1 721	5014	5 156	93 670
1975	3 408	18 323	13 892	4165	17 060	4542	3525	752	11 937	2748	1 678	5494	7 929	95 453
1976	3 331	18 997	14 551	4271	17 755	4582	3576	779	12 138	2733	1 668	6039	7 406	97 826
1977	3 283	19 682	15 303	4467	18 516	4713	3851	813	12 399	2727	1 656	6263	6 991	100 665
1978	3 387	20 505	16 252	4724	19 542	4923	4229	851	12 919	2753	1 631	5963	6 202	103 882
1979	3 347	21 040	17 112	4975	20 192	5136	4463	958	13 174	2773	1 597	5654	6 137	106 559
1980	3 364	20 285	17 890	5160	20 310	5146	4346	1027	13 375	2866	1 604	5533	7 637	108 544
1981	3 368	20 170	18 619	5298	20 547	5165	4188	1139	13 259	2772	1 645	5873	8 273	110 315
1982	3 401	18 781	19 036	5341	20 457	5082	3905	1128	13 098	2739	1 668	6558	10 678	111 872
1983	3 383	18 434	19 694	5468	20 881	4954	3948	952	13 096	2774	1 676	7249	10 717	113 226
1984	3 321	19 378	20 797	5689	22 100	5159	4383	966	13 216	2807	1 697	7190	8 539	115 241
1985	3 179	19 260	22 000	5955	23 073	5238	4673	927	13 519	2875	1 706	6451	8 312	117 167
1986	3 163	18 965	23 053	6283	23 683	5255	4816	777	13 794	2899	1 706	6909	8 237	119 540
1987	3 028	19 024	24 236	6547	24 327	5372	4967	717	14 067	2943	1 737	7032	7 425	121 602
1988	3 169	19 403	25 600	6676	25 139	5548	5125	721	14 402	2971	1 709	6215	6 701	123 378
1989	3 199	19 611	26 889	6814	25 807	5703	5302	722	14 739	2988	1 688	5567	6 528	125 557

* 1929–46 data includes those greater than or equal to 14 years old.

Table A7 (a) Per capita national account index, 1929–89; (b) per capita real net product of the civilian labour force, 1929–89

Year	3.1A Personal income	3.1B NCP	3.1C Natl income	3.1D NNP	3.1E GNP	3.1F GCP	3.2A NCP	3.2B Labour force	3.2C NCP/ L. force
			(1982 dollars/capita)				(1982 dollars)	(thousands)	(billions 1982 $)
1929	4 898	5 438	5 012	5 469	5 931	6 123	662	49 180	13 465
1930	4 288	4 573	4 221	4 606	5 080	5 562	563	49 820	11 297
1931	4 036	4 144	3 667	4 183	4 693	5 576	514	50 420	10 196
1932	3 398	3 416	2 883	3 453	3 968	5 189	426	51 000	8 363
1933	3 233	3 302	2 754	3 343	3 836	5 098	415	51 590	8 038
1934	3 439	3 650	3 143	3 714	4 208	5 368	461	52 230	8 831
1935	3 795	4 059	3 600	4 116	4 589	5 734	517	52 870	9 769
1936	4 264	4 594	4 040	4 681	5 173	6 218	588	53 440	11 008
1937	4 406	4 873	4 389	4 949	5 444	6 343	628	54 000	11 625
1938	4 126	4 566	4 065	4 655	5 136	6 333	593	54 610	10 855
1939	4 403	4 951	4 397	5 031	5 514	6 648	648	11 733	11 733
1940	4 582	5 249	4 751	5 385	5 845	6 833	693	55 640	12 463
1941	5 231	5 595	5 687	6 345	6 817	7 546	746	55 910	13 351
1942	6 230	5 025	6 946	7 516	8 020	8 390	678	56 410	12 014
1943	7 333	4 933	8 248	8 795	9 333	9 490	675	55 540	12 146
1944	7 825	5 283	8 623	9 417	9 984	10 086	731	54 630	13 385
1945	7 793	5 793	8 248	9 149	9 714	9 871	811	53 860	15 051
1946	6 537	6 695	6 595	7 291	7 743	8 043	947	57 520	16 457
1947	6 015	6 319	6 223	6 634	7 384	7 675	911	60 168	15 136
1948	6 080	6 721	6 459	7 051	7 560	7 847	986	60 621	16 257
1949	5 941	6 474	6 210	6 868	7 427	7 883	966	61 286	15 759
1950	6 303	6 929	6 673	7 324	7 953	8 388	1051	62 208	16 895
1951	6 629	7 055	7 212	7 927	8 609	8 894	1088	62 017	17 551
1952	6 824	6 920	7 301	8 070	8 785	9 049	1086	62 138	17 479
1953	6 976	7 015	7 395	8 200	8 992	9 252	1119	63 015	17 763
1954	6 785	6 849	7 066	7 827	8 722	9 217	1112	63 643	17 476

Year									
1955	6 900	7 261	7 481	8 130	9 029	9 430	1200	65 023	18 457
1956	7 043	7 281	7 538	8 140	9 059	9 437	1225	66 552	18 404
1957	7 050	7 234	7 480	8 132	9 049	9 441	1239	66 929	18 511
1958	6 966	6 957	7 251	7 848	8 832	9 459	1212	67 639	17 912
1959	7 101	7 316	7 569	8 171	9 171	9 688	1301	68 369	19 030
1960	7 333	7 588	7 611	8 399	9 230	9 756	1371	69 628	19 690
1961	7 433	7 643	7 660	8 482	9 314	9 963	1404	70 459	19 926
1962	7 616	7 947	7 954	8 826	9 656	10 205	1482	70 614	20 994
1963	7 768	8 220	8 160	9 060	9 898	10 476	1556	71 833	21 656
1964	8 082	8 636	8 516	9 439	10 293	10 839	1657	73 091	22 672
1965	8 405	9 087	8 911	9 862	10 736	11 231	1766	74 455	23 713
1966	8 733	9 421	9 332	10 319	11 222	11 652	1852	75 770	24 439
1967	9 035	9 476	9 500	10 499	11 444	11 889	1883	77 347	24 346
1968	9 346	9 780	9 768	10 820	11 798	12 223	1963	78 737	24 929
1969	9 556	9 936	9 868	10 911	11 918	12 339	2019	80 734	25 009
1970	9 658	9 866	9 668	10 759	11 791	12 389	2023	82 771	24 443
1971	9 727	10 133	9 772	10 936	11 998	12 738	2097	84 382	24 857
1972	10 108	10 583	10 237	11 377	12 489	13 215	2210	87 034	25 394
1973	10 598	11 198	10 800	11 940	13 076	13 734	2352	89 429	26 295
1974	10 575	10 947	10 517	11 670	12 871	13 611	2320	91 949	25 230
1975	10 255	10 521	10 065	11 217	12 480	13 620	2272	93 775	24 232
1976	10 691	11 130	10 618	11 812	13 133	14 208	2394	96 158	24 901
1977	11 016	11 570	11 087	12 260	13 641	14 659	2509	99 009	25 337
1978	11 477	12 108	11 641	12 791	14 246	15 151	2648	102 251	25 899
1979	11 498	11 984	11 574	12 677	14 179	15 046	2697	104 962	25 696
1980	11 571	11 709	11 289	12 440	13 997	15 056	2667	106 940	24 937
1981	11 653	11 729	11 295	12 503	14 111	15 255	2699	108 670	24 839
1982	11 486	11 135	10 831	11 968	13 616	15 053	2589	110 204	23 493
1983	11 636	11 456	11 147	12 335	13 960	15 420	2690	111 550	24 113
1984	12 179	12 233	11 865	13 151	14 778	15 961	2899	113 544	25 534
1985	12 531	12 506	12 187	13 482	15 130	16 285	2992	115 461	25 916
1986	12 824	12 706	12 411	13 716	15 389	16 528	3070	117 834	26 054
1987	13 191	13 069	12 799	14 099	15 798	16 826	3188	119 865	26 597
1988	13 603	13 618	13 295	14 616	16 334	17 267	3355	121 669	27 571
1989	14 095	13 931	13 574	14 895	16 655	17 569	3466	123 869	27 979

Note: Net civilian product (NCP) = gross capacity product (GCP) – national defence – capital consumption.

Table A8 Major components of the gross capacity product, 1929–89

Year	3.3A PCE	3.3B State & local govt pur.	3.3C Fed. grants	3.3D Fed. nondef. pur.	3.3E Natl def. pur.	3.3F GPDI	3.3G Net exprs	3.3H Unrealised product (unemploy)	3.3I GNP	3.3J GCP	3.4A PCE	3.4B State & loc g pur.	3.4C Fed. grts	3.4D Fed. nondef. pur.	3.4E Natl def. pur.	3.4F GPDI	3.4G Net exports	3.4H Unreal. product (unemploy)
	(constant 1982 dollars, billions)										*(per cent)*							
1929	471.4	74.9	1.0	10.6	5.3	139.2	4.7	25.9	709.6	733.1	72.0	6.8	0.1	0.9	0.5	15.6	1.0	3.1
1930	439.7	81.7	1.0	10.9	6.5	97.5	2.3	64.5	642.8	704.1	70.1	7.8	0.1	1.0	0.6	10.6	1.0	8.8
1931	422.1	82.3	3.3	12.4	6.7	60.2	-1.0	113.3	588.1	699.3	66.6	8.3	0.3	1.2	0.7	6.5	0.6	15.9
1932	384.9	79.1	1.2	13.4	6.1	22.6	-0.5	159.7	509.2	666.5	63.5	8.6	0.1	1.4	0.7	1.3	0.5	23.9
1933	378.7	65.7	5.8	19.0	7.1	22.7	-1.4	166.1	498.5	663.8	61.4	7.5	0.7	2.1	0.8	2.1	0.5	24.8
1934	390.5	58.5	17.6	24.2	11.0	35.3	0.1	148.3	536.7	685.4	61.4	6.3	1.9	2.6	1.2	4.2	0.7	21.7
1935	412.1	60.3	18.7	24.2	9.9	60.9	-5.9	146.0	580.2	726.2	61.2	6.0	1.9	2.4	1.0	7.2	0.1	20.1
1936	451.6	71.1	7.8	40.2	15.2	82.1	-4.2	133.0	662.2	796.9	62.0	6.4	0.7	3.7	1.4	8.7	0.1	17.0
1937	467.9	70.3	0.7	36.8	13.7	99.9	-0.3	114.3	695.3	811.3	62.6	6.1	0.8	3.3	1.2	11.4	0.4	14.3
1938	457.1	74.3	8.6	41.7	15.6	63.1	6.0	153.6	664.2	820.0	60.8	6.5	0.8	3.8	1.4	6.4	1.2	19.1
1939	480.5	79.4	10.9	41.5	13.8	86.0	6.1	147.2	716.6	865.5	60.8	6.6	0.9	3.5	1.4	8.6	1.1	17.3
1940	502.6	76.9	9.7	41.1	24.2	111.8	8.2	130.6	772.9	905.0	60.4	6.1	0.8	3.3	2.0	11.4	1.5	14.5
1941	531.1	74.4	8.2	30.2	130.2	138.8	3.9	92.5	909.4	1009.3	58.0	5.2	0.6	2.3	9.9	13.1	1.1	9.8
1942	527.6	67.9	8.8	21.0	398.4	76.7	-7.7	40.9	1080.3	1133.6	53.1	4.1	0.5	1.6	29.6	6.2	0.1	4.8
1943	539.9	62.3	8.5	12.8	638.4	50.4	-23.0	11.6	1276.2	1300.0	50.7	3.4	0.5	0.8	40.6	3.2	-1.0	1.9
1944	557.1	60.3	8.0	16.3	711.4	56.4	-23.8	11.3	1380.2	1397.0	50.6	3.1	0.4	0.9	40.9	3.6	-0.8	1.2
1945	592.7	62.7	7.8	9.3	624.6	76.5	-18.9	26.3	1354.8	1381.0	55.0	3.4	0.4	0.5	33.9	5.2	-0.2	1.9
1946	655.0	69.0	8.6	22.8	133.3	178.1	27.0	47.6	1096.9	1141.4	65.1	4.0	0.5	1.3	7.4	14.3	3.5	3.9
1947	666.6	76.2	11.7	24.5	68.0	177.9	42.4	42.7	1066.7	1110.0	66.2	4.5	0.7	1.5	4.1	14.3	4.9	3.9
1948	681.8	81.1	12.3	36.8	69.3	208.2	19.2	43.8	1108.7	1152.5	64.3	4.9	0.7	2.2	4.2	17.3	2.6	3.8
1949	695.4	93.5	13.0	41.6	80.3	168.8	18.8	67.1	1109.0	1178.5	64.4	5.7	0.8	2.6	5.0	13.2	2.3	5.9
1950	733.2	100.9	13.3	28.0	85.1	234.9	4.7	71.0	1203.7	1271.1	63.1	5.7	0.8	1.5	4.7	18.1	0.7	5.3
1951	748.7	102.2	13.2	26.2	184.7	235.2	14.6	48.7	1328.2	1373.5	60.4	5.6	0.7	1.4	9.8	17.5	1.3	3.3
1952	771.4	104.1	13.2	33.5	238.1	211.8	6.9	43.6	1380.0	1422.7	60.4	5.7	0.7	1.8	12.7	14.8	0.9	3.0
1953	802.5	109.2	13.9	44.9	247.5	216.6	-2.7	46.2	1435.3	1478.2	60.8	5.7	0.7	2.3	12.8	14.3	0.3	2.9
1954	822.7	119.4	14.0	33.8	207.0	212.6	2.5	86.6	1416.2	1498.6	60.8	6.3	0.7	1.7	10.6	13.7	0.7	5.5
1955	873.8	128.8	14.6	28.8	187.5	259.8	0.0	70.4	1494.9	1563.7	60.7	6.4	0.7	1.4	9.2	16.4	0.7	4.4

Year																		
1956	899.8	133.6	14.7	26.0	185.8	257.8	4.3	68.8	1525.6	1590.8	60.6	6.7	0.7	1.3	9.1	16.3	1.2	4.1
1957	919.7	139.1	17.9	25.8	194.8	243.4	7.0	73.2	1551.1	1620.8	60.5	6.9	0.9	1.3	9.5	15.1	1.5	4.3
1958	932.9	147.1	23.3	34.4	192.1	221.4	-10.3	110.5	1539.2	1651.5	60.1	7.2	1.1	1.7	9.4	13.0	0.7	6.8
1959	979.4	148.6	27.6	33.3	188.6	270.3	-18.2	94.3	1629.1	1723.9	60.3	7.0	1.3	1.6	8.8	14.3	0.3	5.5
1960	1005.1	157.3	25.8	36.9	181.9	260.5	-4.0	98.6	1665.3	1762.2	60.6	7.3	1.2	1.7	8.3	14.3	1.1	5.5
1961	1025.2	166.4	27.8	40.2	188.6	259.1	-2.7	126.9	1708.7	1831.4	59.6	7.5	1.3	1.8	8.4	13.5	1.3	6.7
1962	1069.0	170.1	30.0	47.9	198.1	288.6	-7.5	107.9	1799.4	1904.1	59.5	7.5	1.3	2.1	8.6	14.4	1.1	5.5
1963	1108.4	178.8	33.2	52.8	191.4	307.1	-1.9	116.7	1873.3	1986.5	59.3	7.6	1.4	2.2	8.0	14.5	1.3	5.7
1964	1170.6	189.5	37.1	58.0	182.6	325.9	5.9	112.0	1973.3	2081.5	59.7	7.7	1.5	2.3	7.4	14.5	1.6	5.2
1965	1236.4	204.0	38.5	62.1	178.9	367.0	-2.7	101.7	2087.6	2186.0	59.7	8.0	1.5	2.4	6.9	15.7	1.3	4.5
1966	1298.9	211.1	47.7	61.4	208.1	390.5	-13.7	91.6	2208.3	2295.5	59.5	8.0	1.8	2.3	7.7	16.0	0.9	3.8
1967	1337.7	222.1	49.7	61.9	235.3	374.4	-16.9	97.0	2271.4	2361.1	59.3	8.4	1.9	2.3	8.6	14.8	0.9	3.8
1968	1405.9	233.1	54.9	63.4	239.0	391.8	-29.7	95.5	2365.6	2453.4	59.7	8.5	2.0	2.3	8.5	14.8	0.6	3.6
1969	1456.7	239.7	55.9	60.1	224.8	410.3	-34.9	98.6	2423.3	2511.2	59.9	8.7	2.0	2.1	7.9	15.3	0.6	3.5
1970	1492.0	242.1	62.2	57.7	201.6	381.5	-30.0	133.6	2416.2	2540.7	59.9	8.9	2.3	2.1	7.2	13.9	0.8	4.9
1971	1538.8	246.7	69.2	62.9	180.7	419.3	-39.8	162.7	2484.8	2640.6	59.0	8.8	2.5	2.2	6.3	14.7	0.5	5.9
1972	1621.9	240.2	84.5	64.8	176.7	465.4	-49.4	159.1	2608.5	2763.3	59.0	8.3	2.9	2.2	6.0	15.7	0.2	5.6
1973	1689.6	250.4	84.9	61.4	164.5	520.8	-31.5	145.4	2744.1	2885.5	58.6	8.4	2.8	2.0	5.4	16.7	1.2	4.9
1974	1674.0	263.7	83.1	64.4	158.2	481.3	0.8	165.7	2729.3	2891.2	58.7	8.9	2.8	2.2	5.3	15.4	1.0	5.6
1975	1711.9	260.6	94.0	68.6	155.3	383.3	18.9	252.7	2695.0	2945.4	58.0	8.7	3.1	2.3	5.1	12.6	1.8	8.5
1976	1803.9	257.5	98.5	69.8	151.9	453.5	-11.0	238.5	2826.7	3062.5	58.5	8.3	3.2	2.2	4.8	14.7	1.0	7.7
1977	1883.8	255.1	102.1	76.4	153.3	521.3	-35.5	228.1	2958.6	3184.7	58.7	7.9	3.2	2.3	4.7	16.1	0.1	7.1
1978	1961.0	261.7	108.7	75.1	154.7	576.9	-26.8	206.2	3115.2	3317.6	58.6	7.8	3.2	2.2	4.5	17.4	0.2	6.1
1979	2004.4	269.4	103.6	73.0	158.7	575.2	3.6	201.0	3192.4	3389.0	58.8	7.9	3.0	2.1	4.6	17.1	0.7	5.8
1980	2000.4	270.7	102.9	76.5	166.9	509.3	57.0	247.0	3187.1	3430.7	58.9	7.9	3.0	2.2	4.9	14.9	1.1	7.1
1981	2024.2	276.0	94.1	80.1	179.3	545.5	49.4	267.4	3248.8	3516.1	58.0	7.8	2.7	2.3	5.1	15.6	1.0	7.6
1982	2050.7	285.1	83.9	78.9	193.8	447.3	26.3	340.1	3166.0	3506.1	58.5	8.1	2.4	2.3	5.5	12.8	0.8	9.7
1983	2146.0	291.6	82.3	66.4	206.2	504.0	-19.9	350.7	3279.1	3627.3	59.3	8.1	2.3	1.8	5.7	13.3	-0.2	9.6
1984	2249.3	301.8	85.2	70.2	215.7	658.4	-84.0	288.7	3501.4	3785.3	59.6	8.1	2.3	1.9	5.7	16.3	-1.4	7.5
1985	2354.8	318.4	86.8	85.5	230.7	637.0	-104.3	290.6	3678.7	3899.5	60.8	8.5	2.3	2.2	6.0	14.9	-1.8	7.2
1986	2446.4	337.2	90.3	77.5	242.6	639.6	-129.7	293.9	3717.9	3997.7	61.5	8.8	2.3	1.9	6.1	14.5	-2.1	7.0
1987	2513.7	358.8	83.3	73.2	248.8	674.0	-115.7	272.3	3853.7	4108.4	62.4	9.2	2.1	1.8	6.1	14.5	-2.3	6.2
1988	2598.4	369.7	86.5	67.5	241.5	716.8	-74.9	253.1	4024.4	4258.6	62.6	9.2	2.2	1.6	5.8	14.5	-1.4	5.5
1989	2668.5	380.0	88.6	78.7	235.5	724.5	-56.3	255.2	4142.6	4374.4	62.8	9.3	2.2	1.8	5.5	14.1	-0.9	5.3

Table A9 National income by type of income, 1929–89

Year	3.5A Compensation to employees income	3.5B Farm proptrs income	3.5C Non-farm proptrs income	3.5D Rent income	3.5E Net interest	3.5F Corporate rate profits	3.5G Total natl income	3.5H Compensation to employees income	3.5I Farm proptrs income	3.5J Non-farm proptrs income	3.5K Rent	3.5L Net interest	3.5M Corporate rate profits
	(billions of dollars)							(per cent)					
1929	51.1	6.1	8.3	4.9	4.7	9.6	84.7	60.33	7.20	9.80	5.79	5.55	11.33
1930	46.9	4.3	6.9	4.2	4.9	6.3	73.5	63.81	5.85	9.39	5.71	6.67	8.57
1931	39.8	3.4	5.2	3.4	4.9	1.6	58.3	68.27	5.83	8.92	5.83	8.40	2.74
1932	31.1	2.1	3.1	2.7	4.6	-1.6	42.0	74.05	5.00	7.38	6.43	10.95	-3.81
1933	29.6	2.5	2.9	2.0	4.1	-1.5	39.4	75.13	6.35	7.36	5.08	10.41	-3.81
1934	34.3	2.9	4.3	1.6	4.1	1.1	48.3	71.01	6.00	8.90	3.31	8.49	2.28
1935	37.4	5.2	5.1	1.6	4.1	2.7	56.1	66.67	9.27	9.09	2.85	7.31	4.81
1936	43.0	4.3	6.3	1.7	3.8	5.0	64.0	67.19	6.72	9.84	2.66	5.94	7.81
1937	48.0	6.0	6.8	1.9	3.7	5.8	72.2	66.48	8.31	9.42	2.63	5.12	8.03
1938	45.0	4.4	6.5	2.4	3.6	3.9	65.8	68.39	6.69	9.88	3.65	5.47	5.93
1939	48.2	4.4	7.1	2.6	3.6	5.5	71.2	67.70	6.18	9.97	3.65	5.06	7.72
1940	52.2	4.4	8.2	2.7	3.3	8.8	79.6	65.58	5.53	10.30	3.39	4.15	11.06
1941	64.8	6.4	10.8	3.2	3.3	14.3	102.8	63.04	6.23	10.51	3.11	3.21	13.91
1942	85.3	10.1	13.8	4.1	3.1	19.7	136.2	62.63	7.42	10.13	3.01	2.28	14.46
1943	109.6	12.0	16.8	4.6	2.7	24.0	169.7	64.58	7.07	9.90	2.71	1.59	14.14
1944	121.3	11.9	18.1	4.8	2.3	24.2	182.6	66.43	6.52	9.91	2.63	1.26	13.25
1945	123.3	12.4	19.1	5.0	2.2	19.7	181.6	67.90	6.83	10.52	2.75	1.21	10.85
1946	119.6	14.8	21.5	5.8	1.8	17.2	180.7	66.19	8.19	11.90	3.21	1.00	9.52
1947	130.1	15.1	20.4	5.8	2.3	22.9	196.6	66.17	7.68	10.38	2.95	1.17	11.65
1948	142.1	17.5	22.9	6.4	2.4	30.3	221.5	64.15	7.90	10.34	2.89	1.08	13.68
1949	142.0	12.8	23.1	6.7	2.6	28.0	215.2	65.99	5.95	10.73	3.11	1.21	13.01

1950	155.4	13.6	25.2	7.7	3.0	34.9	239.8	64.80	5.67	10.51	3.21	1.25	14.55
1951	181.6	16.0	28.0	8.3	3.5	39.9	277.3	65.49	5.77	10.10	2.99	1.26	14.39
1952	196.3	15.0	29.4	9.4	3.9	37.5	291.6	67.32	5.14	10.08	3.22	1.34	12.86
1953	210.4	13.0	30.4	10.7	4.4	37.7	306.3	68.69	4.24	9.92	3.49	1.44	12.31
1954	209.4	12.4	31.1	11.6	5.2	36.6	306.3	68.36	4.05	10.15	3.79	1.70	11.95
1955	225.9	11.3	34.0	12.0	5.8	47.1	336.3	67.17	3.36	10.11	3.57	1.72	14.01
1956	244.7	11.1	35.8	12.4	6.5	45.7	356.3	68.68	3.12	10.05	3.48	1.82	12.83
1957	257.8	11.0	37.8	13.1	7.8	45.3	372.8	69.15	2.95	10.14	3.51	2.09	12.15
1958	259.8	13.1	38.5	13.9	9.5	40.3	375.0	69.28	3.49	10.27	3.71	2.53	10.75
1959	281.2	10.8	40.9	14.6	10.2	51.4	409.2	68.72	2.64	10.00	3.57	2.49	12.56
1960	296.7	11.6	40.5	15.3	11.3	49.5	424.9	69.83	2.73	9.53	3.60	2.66	11.65
1961	305.6	12.0	42.3	15.8	12.9	50.3	439.0	69.61	2.73	9.64	3.60	2.94	11.46
1962	327.4	12.1	44.4	16.5	14.6	58.3	473.3	69.17	2.56	9.38	3.49	3.08	12.32
1963	345.5	11.9	45.7	17.1	16.3	63.6	500.3	69.06	2.38	9.13	3.42	3.26	12.71
1964	371.0	10.7	49.8	17.3	18.2	70.7	537.6	69.01	1.99	9.26	3.22	3.39	13.15
1965	399.8	13.0	52.1	18.1	20.9	81.3	585.2	68.32	2.22	8.90	3.09	3.57	13.89
1966	443.0	14.0	55.5	18.6	24.3	86.6	642.0	69.00	2.18	8.64	2.90	3.79	13.49
1967	475.5	12.7	58.4	19.6	27.4	84.1	677.7	70.16	1.87	8.62	2.89	4.04	12.41
1968	524.7	12.8	62.6	18.4	29.8	90.7	739.1	70.99	1.73	8.47	2.49	4.03	12.27
1969	578.4	14.6	64.7	18.4	34.6	87.4	798.1	72.47	1.83	8.11	2.31	4.34	10.95
1970	618.3	14.7	65.4	18.2	41.2	74.7	832.6	74.26	1.77	7.85	2.19	4.95	8.97
1971	659.4	15.5	71.4	18.6	46.3	87.1	898.1	73.42	1.73	7.95	2.07	5.16	9.70
1972	726.2	19.4	79.0	17.9	51.0	100.7	994.1	73.05	1.95	7.95	1.80	5.13	10.13
1973	812.8	33.7	85.3	18.0	59.6	113.3	1122.7	72.40	3.00	7.60	1.60	5.31	10.09
1974	891.3	27.5	91.3	16.1	75.5	101.7	1203.5	74.06	2.29	7.59	1.34	6.27	8.45
1975	948.7	25.4	100.0	13.5	83.8	117.6	1289.1	73.59	1.97	7.76	1.05	6.50	9.12
1976	1057.9	20.6	117.1	11.9	88.8	145.2	1441.4	73.39	1.43	8.12	0.83	6.16	10.07

continued on p. 148

Table A9   continued

Year	3.5A Compensation to employees	3.5B Farm proprtrs income	3.5C Non-farm proprtrs income	3.5D Rent	3.5E Net interest	3.5F Corporate profits	3.5G Total natl income	3.5H Compensation to employees income	3.5I Farm proprtrs income	3.5J Non-farm proprtrs income	3.5K Rent	3.5L Net interest	3.5M Corporate profits
			(billions of dollars)							(per cent)			
1977	1176.6	20.5	132.4	8.2	105.3	174.8	1617.8	72.73	1.27	8.18	0.51	6.51	10.80
1978	1329.2	27.0	149.2	9.3	126.3	197.2	1838.2	72.31	1.47	8.12	0.51	6.87	10.73
1979	1491.4	31.7	160.1	5.6	158.3	200.1	2047.3	72.85	1.55	7.82	0.27	7.73	9.77
1980	1638.2	20.5	160.1	6.6	200.9	177.2	2203.5	74.35	0.93	7.27	0.30	9.12	8.04
1981	1807.4	30.7	156.1	13.3	248.1	188.0	2443.5	73.97	1.26	6.39	0.54	10.15	7.69
1982	1907.0	24.6	150.9	13.6	272.3	150.0	2518.4	75.72	0.98	5.99	0.54	10.81	5.96
1983	2020.7	12.4	178.4	13.2	281.0	213.7	2719.5	74.30	0.46	6.56	0.49	10.33	7.86
1984	2213.9	30.5	204.0	8.5	304.8	266.9	3028.6	73.10	1.01	6.74	0.28	10.06	8.81
1985	2367.5	30.2	225.6	9.2	319.0	282.3	3234.0	73.21	0.93	6.98	0.28	9.86	8.73
1986	2511.4	34.7	247.2	11.6	325.5	282.1	3412.6	73.59	1.02	7.24	0.34	9.54	8.27
1987	2690.0	41.6	270.0	13.4	351.7	298.7	3665.4	73.39	1.13	7.37	0.37	9.60	8.15
1988	2907.6	39.8	288.0	15.7	392.9	328.6	3972.6	73.19	1.00	7.25	0.40	9.89	8.27
1989	3145.4	46.3	305.9	8.0	461.1	298.2	4265.0	73.75	1.09	7.17	0.19	10.81	6.99

Table A10 (a) Average gross weekly earnings and real compensation per hour, 1947–89; (b) percentage share of aggregate income received by each fifth of families, 1947–87

	(a) (1977 dollars)		(b) (per cent)					
	3.6A Average gross weekly	3.6B Real compen- sation/	3.7A	3.7B	3.7C	3.7D	3.7E	3.7F
Year	earnings	hour	Lowest fifth	2nd fifth	3rd fifth	4th fifth	Highest fifth	Top 5%
1947	123.52	45.20	5.0	11.9	17.0	23.1	43.0	17.5
1948	123.43	45.50	4.9	12.1	17.3	23.2	42.5	17.1
1949	127.84	46.70	4.5	11.9	17.3	23.5	42.8	16.9
1950	133.83	49.60	4.5	12.0	17.4	23.4	42.7	17.3
1951	134.87	50.50	5.0	12.4	17.6	23.4	41.6	16.8
1952	138.47	52.50	4.9	12.3	17.4	23.4	42.0	17.4
1953	144.58	55.60	4.7	12.5	18.0	23.9	40.9	15.7
1954	145.32	57.20	4.5	12.1	17.7	23.9	41.8	16.3
1955	153.21	58.80	4.8	12.3	17.8	23.7	41.4	16.4
1956	157.90	61.80	5.0	12.5	17.9	23.7	40.9	16.1
1957	158.04	63.60	5.1	12.7	18.1	23.8	40.3	15.6
1958	157.40	64.80	5.2	12.5	17.9	23.7	40.7	15.6
1959	163.78	67.10	4.9	12.3	17.9	23.8	41.1	15.9
1960	164.97	68.90	4.8	12.2	17.8	24.0	41.2	15.9
1961	167.21	70.80	4.7	11.9	17.5	23.8	42.1	16.6
1962	172.16	73.20	5.0	12.1	17.6	24.0	41.3	15.7
1963	175.17	75.10	5.0	12.1	17.7	24.0	41.2	15.8
1964	178.38	78.00	5.1	12.0	17.7	24.0	41.2	15.9
1965	183.21	79.60	5.2	12.2	17.8	23.9	40.9	15.5
1966	184.37	82.70	5.6	12.4	17.8	23.8	40.4	15.6
1967	184.83	84.80	5.5	12.4	17.9	23.9	40.3	15.2
1968	187.83	87.80	5.6	12.4	17.9	23.7	40.6	15.6
1969	189.44	89.10	5.6	12.4	17.7	23.7	40.6	15.6
1970	186.94	90.20	5.4	12.2	17.6	23.8	41.0	15.6
1971	190.58	92.10	5.5	12.0	17.6	23.8	41.1	15.7
1972	198.41	94.90	5.4	11.9	17.5	23.9	41.3	15.9
1973	198.35	96.70	5.5	11.9	17.5	24.0	41.1	15.5
1974	190.12	95.40	5.5	12.0	17.5	24.0	41.0	15.5
1975	184.16	95.90	5.4	11.8	17.6	24.1	41.1	15.5
1976	186.85	98.70	5.4	11.8	17.6	24.1	41.1	15.6
1977	189.00	100.00	5.2	11.6	17.5	24.2	41.5	15.7
1978	189.31	100.80	5.2	11.6	17.5	24.1	41.6	15.6
1979	183.41	99.40	5.2	11.6	17.5	24.1	41.6	15.8
1980	172.74	96.70	5.1	11.6	17.5	24.3	41.5	15.3
1981	170.13	96.00	5.0	11.3	17.4	24.4	41.9	15.4
1982	168.09	97.10	4.7	11.2	17.1	24.3	42.7	16.0
1983	171.26	97.80	4.7	11.1	17.1	24.3	42.8	15.9

continued on p. 150

Appendix: Data Tables

Table A10   continued

| | (a) (1977 dollars) | | (b) (per cent) | | | | | |
| | 3.6A Average gross weekly earnings | 3.6B Real compensation/ hour | 3.7A Lowest fifth | 3.7B 2nd fifth | 3.7C 3rd fifth | 3.7D 4th fifth | 3.7E Highest fifth | 3.7F Top 5% |
Year								
1984	172.78	97.50	4.7	11.0	17.0	24.4	42.9	16.0
1985	170.42	98.00	4.6	10.9	16.9	24.2	43.4	16.7
1986	171.07	101.10	4.6	10.9	16.9	24.2	43.4	16.8
1987	169.28	101.20	4.6	10.8	16.9	24.1	43.6	16.9
1988	167.81	101.80	–	–	–	–	–	–
1989	166.52	102.20	–	–	–	–	–	–

Table A11 Families, distribution by total income, 1947–88 (per cent)

Year	3.8A Under $2500	3.8B $2500–$4999	3.8C $5000–$7499	3.8D $7500–$9999	3.8E $10 000–$12 499	3.8F $12 500–$14 999	3.8G $15 000–$19 999	3.8H $20 000–$24 999	3.8I $25 000–$34 999	3.8J $35 000–$49 999	3.8K $50 000 & over
1947	4.7	6.8	10.1	7.7	—	—	—	—	—	—	—
1948	5.7	6.9	10.0	7.9	—	—	—	—	—	—	—
1949	6.8	7.1	8.7	9.2	—	—	—	—	—	—	—
1950	6.8	6.5	7.7	8.4	—	—	—	—	—	—	—
1951	5.8	5.9	7.4	8.0	12.8	8.8	—	—	—	—	—
1952	5.5	5.8	7.1	7.2	12.7	8.7	23.1	10.7	—	—	—
1953	5.9	5.3	6.4	6.3	10.3	7.4	23.8	11.5	—	—	—
1954	6.0	6.0	7.0	6.4	10.6	7.5	22.6	11.1	—	—	—
1955	4.8	5.6	6.4	6.2	9.6	7.0	22.8	11.6	—	—	—
1956	4.4	4.8	5.9	5.9	8.5	6.3	22.7	11.9	—	—	—
1957	4.4	4.8	6.0	6.1	8.2	6.1	23.5	12.2	—	—	—
1958	3.9	4.6	6.5	6.4	8.3	6.1	23.0	12.0	—	—	—
1959	3.6	4.5	5.8	6.2	7.8	5.8	21.3	11.7	—	—	—
1960	3.7	4.3	5.8	6.0	7.6	5.6	20.2	11.4	—	—	—
1961	3.7	4.3	5.7	6.0	7.5	5.6	19.1	11.0	—	—	—
1962	3.1	4.0	5.5	5.8	7.4	5.5	19.2	11.1	—	—	—
1963	3.6	2.9	5.3	5.7	6.4	6.2	18.1	10.7	—	—	—
1964	3.1	2.8	5.0	5.8	6.3	6.1	17.1	10.4	—	—	—
1965	2.8	2.7	4.9	5.2	5.8	5.7	16.6	10.2	—	—	—
1966	2.0	2.2	4.8	4.7	5.4	5.2	16.1	10.1	–	—	—
1967	1.5	2.8	4.5	4.9	4.5	5.2	12.6	12.7	23.5	17.6	10.4
1968	1.4	2.4	3.8	4.5	4.9	4.7	11.4	13.4	23.3	19.2	11.1

continued on p. 152

Note: All income figures in column headings are in constant 1985 dollars.

Table A11   continued

Year	3.8A Under $2500	3.8B $2500–$4999	3.8C $5000–$7499	3.8D $7500–$9999	3.8E $10 000–$12 499	3.8F $12 500–$14 999	3.8G $15 000–$19 999	3.8H $20 000–$24 999	3.8I $25 000–$34 999	3.8J $35 000–$49 999	3.8K $50 000– & over
1969	1.3	2.3	3.8	4.1	4.7	4.8	10.4	12.6	22.6	20.5	12.9
1970	1.5	2.3	3.8	4.4	4.7	5.2	10.8	12.2	22.9	19.3	13.0
1971	1.4	2.2	3.9	4.5	4.8	5.5	10.9	11.6	22.7	19.4	13.1
1972	1.2	2.0	3.6	4.4	4.7	5.0	10.2	11.1	21.7	20.5	15.6
1973	1.2	1.9	3.5	4.3	4.7	4.9	10.1	10.8	21.0	21.0	16.5
1974	1.3	1.8	3.5	4.5	4.9	5.0	10.6	11.3	21.5	20.4	15.2
1975	1.3	2.0	3.9	5.0	5.2	5.2	11.1	11.2	21.1	20.0	13.9
1976	1.3	1.9	3.7	4.7	5.3	4.9	10.8	10.8	21.0	20.6	14.9
1977	1.3	2.0	3.7	4.8	5.2	5.1	10.3	10.5	20.1	21.1	15.9
1978	1.4	2.1	3.6	4.5	4.8	5.0	10.4	10.1	20.3	20.9	17.1
1979	1.4	2.1	3.8	4.2	4.8	5.1	10.6	10.0	20.3	21.0	16.8
1980	1.5	2.4	4.2	4.7	5.0	5.4	11.1	10.6	20.5	19.5	15.1
1981	1.8	2.5	4.3	4.8	5.6	5.7	11.0	11.1	19.6	18.9	14.6
1982	2.1	3.0	4.4	4.9	5.7	5.4	10.9	11.4	19.5	17.9	14.8
1983	2.1	3.1	4.3	4.9	5.5	5.3	11.0	10.7	19.2	18.3	15.6
1984	1.9	2.9	4.2	4.7	5.5	5.0	10.6	10.4	18.7	19.0	17.0
1985	1.9	2.9	4.2	4.3	5.2	5.0	10.5	10.3	18.6	18.8	18.3
1986	– 4.8 –		– 7.8 –		– 9.9 –		– 20.0 –		18.3	19.0	19.7
1987	– 4.7 –		– 7.6 –		– 9.7 –		– 19.6 –		17.9	19.1	20.5
1988	– 4.6 –		– 7.5 –		– 10.0 –		– 19.4 –		17.8	19.0	20.9

Note: All income figures in column headings are in constant 1985 dollars.

Table A12 (a) Implicit price deflators, 1929–89; (b) federal government deficit or surplus vs consumer price index, 1929–89; (c) purchasing power* of the various forms of liquid assets, 1959–89

	(a)							(b)		(c)				
	4.1A	4.2A	4.2B	4.3A	4.3B	4.3C Govt purch. of goods & servs		4.4A Federal deficit(-) or surplus(+) (blns $)	4.4B Consumer price index (1967=100)	4.5A	4.5B	4.5C	4.5D	4.5E
Year	GNP	PCE	GPDI	Exports	Imports		(1982 = 100)			Currency	M1	M2 (billions of dollars)	M3	L
1929	15.1	17.9	10.7	17.0	13.8	9.2		1.2	51.3	–	–	–	–	–
1930	14.6	17.2	10.2	14.8	11.8	9.0		0.3	50.0	–	–	–	–	–
1931	13.1	15.3	9.3	11.6	9.6	8.6		-2.1	45.6	–	–	–	–	–
1932	11.8	13.5	8.0	9.7	7.8	7.9		-1.5	40.0	–	–	–	–	–
1933	11.6	13.0	8.0	9.5	7.1	8.1		-1.3	38.8	–	–	–	–	–
1934	12.3	13.9	8.5	11.6	8.1	8.6		-2.9	40.1	–	–	–	–	–
1935	12.5	14.1	8.7	12.0	8.7	8.7		-2.6	41.1	–	–	–	–	–
1936	12.5	14.3	8.9	12.4	8.9	8.8		-3.6	41.5	–	–	–	–	–
1937	13.0	14.8	10.0	13.2	9.9	9.1		-0.4	43.0	–	–	–	–	–
1938	12.8	14.5	10.0	12.5	9.2	8.9		-2.1	42.2	–	–	–	–	–
1939	12.7	13.9	11.1	12.7	11.3	9.4		-2.2	41.6	–	–	–	–	–
1940	13.0	14.1	11.5	13.6	11.6	9.5		-1.3	42.0	–	–	–	–	–
1941	13.8	15.2	12.4	14.6	12.3	10.6		-5.1	44.1	–	–	–	–	–
1942	14.7	16.8	13.2	17.2	13.1	12.4		-33.1	48.8	–	–	–	–	–
1943	15.1	18.4	13.8	18.5	13.6	12.5		-46.6	51.8	–	–	–	–	–
1944	15.3	19.4	14.2	20.2	14.1	12.3		-54.5	52.7	–	–	–	–	–
1945	15.7	20.2	14.5	21.1	14.6	11.8		-42.1	53.9	–	–	–	–	–
1946	19.4	22.0	16.7	22.0	17.4	12.3		3.5	58.5	–	–	–	–	–

continued on p. 154

* Liquid assets/GNP deflator.

Table A12 continued

	(a)						(b)		(c)				
	4.1A	4.2A	4.2B	4.3A	4.3B	4.3C	4.4A	4.4B	4.5A	4.5B	4.5C	4.5D	4.5E
Year	GNP	PCE	GPDI	Exports	Imports	Govt purch. of goods & servs	Federal deficit(-) or surplus(+) (blns $)	Consumer price index (1967=100)	Currency	M1	M2	M3	L
									(billions of dollars)				
1947	22.1	24.3	19.8	24.6	20.9	14.7	13.4	66.9	—	—	—	—	—
1948	23.6	25.7	21.7	26.5	22.4	16.3	8.3	72.1	—	—	—	—	—
1949	23.5	25.6	22.2	25.2	21.2	17.3	-2.6	71.4	—	—	—	—	—
1950	23.9	26.2	22.9	24.4	22.5	16.8	9.2	72.1	—	—	—	—	—
1951	25.1	27.8	24.6	27.4	26.7	18.3	6.5	77.8	—	—	—	—	—
1952	25.5	28.4	25.0	27.4	25.3	19.4	-3.7	79.5	—	—	—	—	—
1953	25.9	29.0	25.5	27.0	24.1	19.8	-7.1	80.1	—	—	—	—	—
1954	26.3	29.1	25.6	26.9	24.1	20.1	-6.0	80.5	—	—	—	—	—
1955	27.2	29.5	26.3	27.5	23.5	20.8	4.4	80.2	—	—	—	—	—
1956	28.1	30.1	27.8	28.6	23.8	21.9	6.1	81.4	—	—	—	—	—
1957	29.1	31.0	29.0	29.7	23.8	22.9	2.3	84.3	—	—	—	—	—
1958	29.7	31.6	28.9	29.6	22.7	24.1	-10.3	86.6	—	—	—	—	—
1959	30.4	32.3	29.3	29.9	23.1	24.6	-1.1	87.3	28.80	461	980	986	1279
1960	30.9	32.9	29.7	30.4	23.4	24.9	3.0	88.7	28.70	455	1011	1020	1306
1961	31.2	33.3	29.7	30.9	23.1	25.4	-3.9	89.6	29.30	465	1075	1093	1381
1962	31.9	33.9	29.9	31.0	22.9	26.3	-4.2	90.6	30.30	464	1137	1164	1461
1963	32.4	34.4	30.1	31.1	23.6	26.9	0.3	91.7	32.30	473	1214	1253	1555
1964	32.9	35.0	30.4	31.4	24.1	27.6	-3.3	92.9	33.90	488	1291	1345	1643
1965	33.8	35.6	31.1	32.5	24.7	28.5	0.5	94.5	36.00	497	1359	1427	1729
1966	35.0	36.7	32.4	33.7	25.7	29.8	-1.8	97.2	38.00	492	1371	1443	1756

Year													
1967	35.9	37.6	33.4	34.5	26.2	31.2	-13.2	100.0	40.00	511	1460	1552	1857
1968	37.7	39.3	34.8	35.2	26.6	33.1	-6.0	104.2	43.00	524	1502	1608	1933
1969	39.8	41.0	37.2	36.6	27.4	35.1	8.4	109.8	45.70	513	1481	1545	1918
1970	42.0	42.9	39.0	38.7	29.0	38.1	-12.4	116.3	48.60	511	1496	1613	1943
1971	44.4	44.9	41.2	40.4	30.2	41.0	-22.0	121.3	52.00	514	1605	1748	2034
1972	46.5	46.7	43.2	41.7	32.0	43.8	-16.8	125.3	56.30	536	1731	1905	2200
1973	49.5	49.6	45.6	47.1	35.5	47.1	-5.6	133.1	60.80	531	1739	1990	2308
1974	54.0	54.8	50.3	56.3	50.4	52.2	-11.6	147.7	67.00	508	1682	1982	2316
1975	59.3	59.2	56.9	62.1	54.1	57.7	-69.4	161.2	72.80	485	1725	1977	2305
1976	63.1	62.6	60.7	64.8	55.7	61.5	-53.5	170.5	79.50	486	1844	2079	2404
1977	67.3	66.7	65.6	68.0	59.8	65.8	-46.0	181.5	87.40	493	1912	2189	2534
1978	72.2	71.6	71.9	72.8	65.8	70.4	-29.3	195.4	96.10	497	1924	2281	2647
1979	78.6	78.2	78.9	81.6	77.1	76.8	-16.1	217.4	104.90	491	1909	2299	2697
1980	85.7	86.6	86.3	90.2	96.0	85.5	-61.3	246.8	115.20	481	1906	2323	2716
1981	94.0	94.6	94.2	97.5	101.6	93.4	-63.8	272.4	122.50	467	1911	2380	2765
1982	100.0	100.0	100.0	100.0	100.0	100.0	-145.9	289.1	132.60	476	1955	2444	2854
1983	103.9	104.1	99.8	101.3	97.4	104.0	-176.0	298.4	146.30	503	2104	2593	3037
1984	107.7	108.1	100.2	103.2	97.1	108.6	-170.0	311.1	156.10	512	2198	2769	3271
1985	110.9	111.6	100.6	101.0	95.2	112.3	-197.0	322.2	167.80	560	2315	2887	3454
1986	113.8	114.3	102.9	99.8	93.7	114.5	-207.0	328.2	180.50	638	2470	3071	3635
1987	117.4	119.8	103.1	99.5	99.0	118.5	-161.0	340.2	196.40	641	2479	3133	3694
1988	121.3	124.5	104.6	103.3	102.7	123.4	-146.0	354.2	211.80	652	2531	3228	3852
1989	126.3	130.0	106.8	106.3	104.9	128.7	-150.0	371.3	222.10	632	2547	3198	3831

* Liquid assets/GNP deflator.

Table A13 (a) Average currency held per capita, 1929–89; (b) per capita currency plus demand deposits and GNP deflators, 1929–89; (c) components of M1, 1929–89

	(a)					(b)						(c)		
	4.6A Currency	4.6B Popu-lation	4.6C Currency/ capita	4.6D GNP deflator	4.6E Real currency	4.7A Currency	4.7B Demand deposits	4.7C Other M1	4.7D Total M1	4.7E M1/ Capita	4.7F GNP deflator	4.8A Currency	4.8B Demand deposits	4.8C Other M1
Year	(bln $)	(thousands)	($)	(1929=100)	(1982 $)	(billions of dollars)				($)	(1982=100)	(per cent of total M1)		
1929	3.56	121 767	29	100.0	203	3.56	22.81	0	26.4	217	14.4	13.5	86.5	0
1930	3.61	123 077	29	101.4	201	3.61	20.97	0	24.6	200	14.6	14.7	85.3	0
1931	4.47	124 040	36	91.0	275	4.47	17.41	0	21.9	176	13.1	20.4	79.6	0
1932	4.67	124 840	37	82.0	317	4.67	15.73	0	20.4	163	11.8	22.9	77.1	0
1933	4.78	125 579	38	81.0	327	4.78	15.04	0	19.8	158	11.6	24.1	75.9	0
1934	4.65	126 374	37	85.4	298	4.65	18.46	0	23.1	183	12.3	20.1	79.9	0
1935	4.92	127 250	39	86.8	310	4.92	22.11	0	27.0	212	12.5	18.2	81.8	0
1936	5.52	128 053	43	86.8	344	5.52	25.48	0	31.0	242	12.5	17.8	82.2	0
1937	5.64	128 825	44	90.3	336	5.64	23.96	0	29.6	230	13.0	19.1	80.9	0
1938	5.77	129 825	44	88.9	347	5.77	25.99	0	31.8	245	12.8	18.2	81.8	0
1939	6.40	130 880	49	88.2	387	6.40	29.79	0	36.2	277	12.7	17.7	82.3	0
1940	7.32	132 122	55	90.3	426	7.32	34.94	0	42.3	320	13.0	17.3	82.7	0
1941	9.61	133 402	72	95.8	522	9.61	38.99	0	48.6	364	13.8	19.8	80.2	0
1942	13.95	134 860	103	102.1	704	13.95	48.92	0	62.9	466	14.7	22.2	77.8	0
1943	18.84	136 739	138	104.9	912	18.84	60.80	0	79.6	582	15.1	23.7	76.3	0
1944	23.50	138 397	170	106.3	1110	23.50	66.93	0	90.4	653	15.3	26.0	74.0	0
1945	26.49	139 928	189	109.0	1206	26.49	75.85	0	102.3	731	15.7	25.9	74.1	0
1946	26.73	141 389	189	134.7	974	26.73	83.31	0	110.0	778	19.4	24.3	75.7	0
1947	26.48	144 126	184	153.5	831	26.48	87.12	0	113.6	788	22.1	23.3	76.7	0
1948	26.08	146 631	178	163.9	754	26.08	85.52	0	111.6	761	23.6	23.4	76.6	0
1949	25.41	149 188	170	163.2	725	25.41	85.75	0	111.2	745	23.5	22.9	77.1	0
1950	25.40	151 684	167	166.0	701	25.40	92.27	0	117.7	776	23.9	21.6	78.4	0

1951	26.31	154 287	171	174.3	679	26.31	98.23	0	124.5	807	25.1	21.1	78.9	0
1952	27.50	156 954	175	177.1	687	27.50	101.50	0	129.0	822	25.5	21.3	78.7	0
1953	28.10	159 565	176	179.9	680	28.10	102.45	0	130.6	818	25.9	21.5	78.5	0
1954	27.85	162 391	171	182.6	652	27.85	106.55	0	134.4	828	26.3	20.7	79.3	0
1955	28.29	165 275	171	188.9	629	28.09	109.92	0	138.0	835	27.2	20.4	79.6	0
1956	28.80	168 221	171	195.1	609	28.80	111.50	0	140.3	834	28.1	20.5	79.5	0
1957	28.90	171 274	169	202.1	580	28.90	110.40	0	139.3	813	29.1	20.7	79.3	0
1958	29.20	174 141	168	206.3	565	29.20	115.50	0	144.7	831	29.7	20.2	79.8	0
1959	28.80	177 830	162	211.1	533	28.80	110.80	0.4	140.0	787	30.4	20.6	79.1	0.3
1960	28.70	180 671	159	214.6	514	28.70	111.60	0.4	140.7	779	30.9	20.4	79.3	0.3
1961	29.30	183 691	160	216.7	511	29.30	115.50	0.4	145.2	790	31.2	20.2	79.5	0.3
1962	30.30	186 538	162	221.5	509	30.30	117.10	0.5	147.9	793	31.9	20.5	79.2	0.3
1963	32.30	189 242	171	225.0	527	32.20	120.60	0.6	153.4	811	32.4	21.0	78.6	0.4
1964	33.90	191 889	177	228.5	537	33.90	125.80	0.7	160.4	836	32.9	21.1	78.4	0.4
1965	36.00	194 303	185	234.7	548	36.00	131.30	0.6	167.9	864	33.8	21.4	78.2	0.4
1966	38.00	196 560	193	243.1	552	38.00	133.40	0.7	172.1	876	35.0	22.1	77.5	0.4
1967	40.00	198 712	201	249.3	561	40.00	142.50	0.8	183.3	922	35.9	21.8	77.7	0.4
1968	43.00	200 706	214	261.8	568	43.00	153.60	0.9	197.5	984	37.7	21.8	77.8	0.5
1969	45.70	203 216	225	276.4	565	45.70	157.30	1.0	204.0	1004	39.8	22.4	77.1	0.5
1970	48.60	205 052	237	291.7	564	48.60	164.70	1.2	214.5	1046	42.0	22.7	76.8	0.6
1971	52.00	207 000	251	308.3	566	52.00	175.10	1.3	228.4	1103	44.4	22.8	76.7	0.6
1972	56.30	208 837	270	322.9	580	56.30	191.60	1.5	249.4	1194	46.5	22.6	76.8	0.6
1973	60.80	210 000	290	343.8	585	60.80	200.30	1.9	263.0	1252	49.5	23.1	76.2	0.7
1974	67.00	211 909	316	375.0	586	67.00	205.10	2.3	274.4	1295	54.0	24.4	74.7	0.8
1975	72.80	215 973	337	411.8	568	72.80	211.60	3.2	287.6	1332	59.3	25.3	73.6	1.1
1976	79.50	215 142	370	438.2	586	79.50	221.60	5.4	306.5	1425	63.1	25.9	72.3	1.8
1977	87.40	216 817	403	467.4	599	87.40	236.80	7.3	331.5	1529	67.3	26.4	71.4	2.2
1978	96.10	218 717	439	501.4	609	96.10	250.60	12.1	358.8	1640	72.2	26.8	69.8	3.4
1979	104.90	225 055	466	545.8	593	104.90	257.70	23.5	386.1	1716	78.6	27.2	66.7	6.1
1980	115.20	227 757	506	595.1	590	115.20	261.50	35.5	412.2	1810	85.7	27.9	63.4	8.6
1981	122.50	230 138	532	652.8	566	122.50	231.50	85.1	439.1	1908	94.0	27.9	52.7	19.4

continued on p. 158

Table A13 continued

| | (a) | | | | | (b) | | | | | | (c) | | |
Year	4.6A Currency (bln $)	4.6B Population (thousands)	4.6C Currency/capita ($)	4.6D GNP deflator (1929=100)	4.6E Real currency (1982 $)	4.7A Currency	4.7B Demand deposits	4.7C Other M1	4.7D Total M1	4.7E M1/Capita ($)	4.7F GNP deflator (1982=100)	4.8A Currency deposits	4.8B Demand deposits	4.8C Other M1
						(billions of dollars)				($)		(per cent of total M1)		
1982	132.60	232 520	570	694.4	570	132.60	234.20	109.6	476.4	2049	100.0	27.8	49.2	23.0
1983	146.30	234 799	623	721.5	600	146.30	238.70	137.1	522.1	2224	103.9	28.0	45.7	26.3
1984	156.10	237 001	659	747.9	612	156.10	244.20	151.6	551.9	2329	107.7	28.3	44.2	27.5
1985	167.80	239 279	701	770.1	632	167.80	267.30	185.4	620.5	2593	110.9	27.0	43.1	29.9
1986	180.50	241 625	747	790.3	656	180.50	303.20	242.2	725.9	3004	113.8	24.9	41.8	33.4
1987	196.40	243 934	805	815.3	686	196.40	288.30	267.6	752.3	3084	117.4	26.1	38.3	35.6
1988	211.80	246 329	860	842.4	709	211.80	288.60	289.9	790.3	3208	121.3	26.8	36.5	36.7
1989	222.10	248 777	893	877.1	707	222.10	281.20	294.3	797.6	3206	126.3	27.8	35.3	36.9

Table A14   (a) Consumer price indexes, 1913–89; (b) consumer price indexes, 1935–88; (c) consumer price indexes, 1935–89; (d) common stock price indexes, 1929–86

	(a)				(b)			(c)		(d)		
	4.9A	4.9B	4.10A	4.10B	4.11A	4.11B	4.11C	4.12A	4.12B	4.13A	4.13B	4.13C
Year	All items	Rent & residential	Food (1967=100)	Clothing & upkeep	Commodities	Durables (1967=100)	Non-durables	Transportation (1967=100)	Medical care	Implicit GNP deflator	Standard & Poor's index (1929=100)	Dow J. Industl average
1913	29.7	49.6	29.2	29.2	—	—	—	—	—	—	—	—
1914	30.1	49.6	29.8	29.4	—	—	—	—	—	—	—	—
1915	30.4	49.9	29.4	30.1	—	—	—	—	—	—	—	—
1916	32.7	50.5	33.1	33.0	—	—	—	—	—	—	—	—
1917	38.4	50.1	42.6	39.6	—	—	—	—	—	—	—	—
1918	45.1	51.0	49.0	53.6	—	—	—	—	—	—	—	—
1919	51.8	55.2	54.6	71.1	—	—	—	—	—	—	—	—
1920	60.0	64.9	61.5	84.6	—	—	—	—	—	—	—	—
1921	53.6	74.5	46.7	65.2	—	—	—	—	—	—	—	—
1922	50.2	76.7	43.7	53.0	—	—	—	—	—	—	—	—
1923	51.1	78.6	45.1	53.1	—	—	—	—	—	—	—	—
1924	51.2	81.5	44.7	52.6	—	—	—	—	—	—	—	—
1925	52.5	81.8	48.4	51.6	—	—	—	—	—	—	—	—
1926	53.0	81.0	50.0	50.8	—	—	—	—	—	—	—	—
1927	52.0	79.7	48.2	49.7	—	—	—	—	—	—	—	—
1928	51.3	77.8	47.7	49.0	—	—	—	—	—	—	—	—
1929	51.3	76.0	48.3	48.5	—	—	—	—	—	100.0	100.00	100.00
1930	50.0	73.9	45.9	47.5	—	—	—	—	—	100.3	80.82	77.88
1931	45.6	70.0	37.8	43.2	—	—	—	—	—	91.2	52.50	46.24
1932	40.9	62.8	31.5	38.2	—	—	—	—	—	81.8	26.63	22.42
1933	38.8	54.1	30.6	36.9	—	—	—	—	—	79.9	34.44	27.39
1934	40.1	50.7	34.1	40.4	–	–	–	–	–	85.8	37.82	33.84
1935	41.1	50.6	36.5	40.8	40.5	45.2	39.0	36.3	31.8	86.6	40.74	42.28
1936	41.5	51.9	36.9	41.1	41.0	45.8	39.6	36.0	31.9	86.8	59.45	56.57

continued on p. 160

Note: For columns 4.9A and 4.9B, data cycle 1984 may not be in exactly the same classifications as before.

Table A14   continued

	(a)				(b)			(c)		(d)		
Year	4.9A All items	4.9B Rent & residential (1967=100)	4.10A Food (1967=100)	4.10B Clothing & upkeep	4.11A Commodities	4.11B Durables (1967=100)	4.11C Non-durables	4.12A Transportation (1967=100)	4.12B Medical care (1967=100)	4.13A Implicit GNP deflator	4.13B Standard & Poor's index (1929=100)	4.13C Dow J. Industl average
1937	43.0	54.2	38.4	43.2	42.6	48.7	41.1	35.7	32.3	90.5	59.22	53.12
1938	42.2	56.0	35.6	43.0	41.0	49.6	39.2	36.0	32.4	88.7	44.16	44.38
1939	41.6	56.0	34.6	42.4	40.2	48.5	38.4	36.1	32.5	87.0	46.35	47.83
1940	42.0	56.2	35.2	42.8	40.6	48.1	38.9	36.1	32.5	89.0	42.35	45.64
1941	44.1	57.2	38.4	44.8	43.3	51.4	41.6	36.3	32.7	94.5	37.74	41.38
1942	48.8	58.5	45.1	52.3	49.6	58.4	47.6	38.2	33.7	100.7	33.32	36.67
1943	51.8	58.5	50.3	54.6	54.0	60.3	51.8	38.2	35.4	103.4	44.20	45.71
1944	52.7	58.6	49.6	58.5	54.7	65.9	52.2	38.2	36.9	106.3	47.92	49.45
1945	53.9	58.8	50.7	61.5	56.3	70.9	53.7	38.2	37.9	107.5	58.26	58.15
1946	58.5	59.2	58.1	67.5	62.4	74.1	59.6	39.0	40.1	132.9	65.64	64.78
1947	66.9	61.1	70.6	78.2	75.0	80.3	71.9	40.3	43.5	151.4	58.30	60.37
1948	72.1	65.1	76.6	83.3	80.4	86.2	77.2	44.9	46.4	161.6	59.68	61.83
1949	71.4	68.0	73.5	80.1	78.3	87.4	74.9	50.0	48.1	161.0	58.53	62.45
1950	72.1	70.4	74.5	79.0	78.8	88.4	75.4	53.3	49.2	163.7	70.71	74.55
1951	77.8	73.2	82.8	86.1	85.9	95.1	82.5	58.3	51.7	171.9	85.86	88.88
1952	79.5	76.2	84.3	85.3	87.0	96.4	83.4	62.4	55.0	174.7	94.16	94.57
1953	80.1	80.3	83.0	84.6	86.7	95.7	83.2	66.4	57.0	177.4	95.04	94.73
1954	80.5	83.2	82.8	84.5	85.9	93.3	83.2	69.2	58.7	180.1	114.10	118.00
1955	80.2	84.3	81.6	84.1	85.1	91.5	82.5	69.4	60.4	186.3	155.61	151.17
1956	81.4	85.9	82.2	85.8	85.9	91.5	83.7	70.5	62.8	192.5	179.17	169.59
1957	84.3	87.5	84.9	87.3	88.6	94.4	86.3	73.8	65.5	199.3	170.56	162.20
1958	86.6	89.1	88.5	87.5	90.6	95.9	88.6	78.5	68.7	203.4	177.71	176.00
1959	87.3	90.4	87.1	88.2	90.7	97.3	88.2	81.2	72.0	208.2	220.52	216.23
1960	88.7	91.7	88.0	89.6	91.5	96.7	89.4	83.3	74.9	211.6	214.64	215.83

1961	89.6	92.9	89.1	90.4	92.0	96.6	90.2	85.3	77.7	213.7	254.69	231.98
1962	90.6	94.0	89.9	90.9	92.8	97.6	90.9	86.6	80.2	218.5	239.74	217.60
1963	91.7	95.0	91.2	91.9	93.6	97.9	92.0	87.5	82.6	221.9	268.52	243.83
1964	92.9	95.9	92.4	92.7	94.6	98.4	93.0	89.6	84.6	225.3	312.72	285.89
1965	94.5	96.9	94.4	93.7	95.7	98.5	94.6	92.9	87.3	231.5	338.85	312.12
1966	97.2	98.2	99.1	96.1	98.2	100.0	98.1	96.8	92.0	239.7	327.67	299.98
1967	100.0	100.0	100.0	100.0	100.0	103.1	100.0	100.0	100.0	245.9	353.31	296.71
1968	104.2	102.4	103.6	105.5	103.7	107.0	103.9	104.0	107.3	258.2	379.32	312.20
1969	109.8	105.7	108.9	111.5	108.4	111.8	108.9	111.3	116.0	272.6	376.02	299.86
1970	116.3	110.1	114.9	116.1	113.5	116.5	114.0	123.1	124.2	287.7	319.83	254.05
1971	121.3	115.2	118.4	119.8	117.4	118.9	117.7	133.0	133.3	304.1	377.75	301.59
1972	125.3	119.2	123.5	122.3	120.9	121.9	121.7	136.0	138.2	318.5	419.68	332.05
1973	133.1	124.3	141.4	126.8	129.9	130.6	132.8	136.9	144.3	339.0	412.87	317.32
1974	147.7	130.6	161.7	136.2	145.5	145.5	151.0	141.9	159.1	369.9	318.41	253.38
1975	161.2	137.3	175.4	142.3	158.4	154.3	163.2	152.7	179.1	406.2	331.13	261.07
1976	170.5	144.7	180.8	147.6	165.2	163.2	169.2	174.3	197.1	432.2	392.04	323.10
1977	181.5	153.5	192.2	154.2	174.7	173.9	178.9	188.4	216.7	461.0	315.91	310.52
1978	195.4	164.0	211.4	159.6	187.1	191.1	192.0	197.4	235.4	494.5	369.02	284.53
1979	217.4	176.0	234.5	166.6	208.4	210.4	215.9	212.8	258.3	538.4	395.89	292.19
1980	246.8	191.6	254.6	178.4	233.9	227.1	245.0	242.6	287.4	587.0	456.50	303.40
1981	272.4	208.2	274.6	186.9	253.6	241.1	266.3	271.6	318.2	643.8	492.12	318.71
1982	289.1	224.0	285.7	191.8	263.8	253.0	273.6	294.4	356.0	684.9	460.07	318.61
1983	298.4	236.9	291.7	196.5	271.5	266.8	279.0	303.6	387.0	711.6	616.49	399.10
1984	310.6	336.9	294.6	198.1	280.4	271.1	287.1	310.9	378.5	739.0	616.68	409.27
1985	322.4	351.3	302.8	203.6	286.4	270.6	293.6	318.9	404.2	763.7	718.06	472.19
1986	326.0	357.4	314.2	205.5	283.7	274.6	289.9	300.0	435.3	784.2	910.22	596.33
1987	340.4	370.5	325.2	215.5	292.7	280.2	301.1	318.3	460.6	-	-	-
1988	355.5	385.3	341.6	225.6	303.0	-	313.2	327.8	492.4	-	-	-
1989	372.0	400.3	360.3	227.9	-	-	-	340.0	534.2	-	-	-

Note: For columns 4.9A and 4.9B data after 1984 may not be in exactly the same classifications as before.

Table A15   Balance sheets for the US economy, 1945–88 (per cent)

Year	5.1A Net Worth	5.1B Foreign direct invest. in US	5.1C Prof. tax. payable & trade debt	5.1D Loans	5.1E Mortg.	5.1F Corporate & tax exempt bonds	5.1G Resid. & non-res. struct. & equip.	5.1H Inventories	5.1I Land	5.1J Liquid assets	5.1K Consumer & trade credit	5.1L Foreign direct invest.	5.1M Misc. assets
1945	64.32	1.25	12.54	5.78	4.32	11.77	36.02	14.30	15.15	19.34	11.32	3.62	0.26
1946	65.80	1.06	12.19	6.28	4.33	10.34	44.99	17.11	9.35	14.22	10.97	3.06	0.30
1947	66.18	0.94	12.45	6.42	4.21	9.80	45.99	17.46	9.11	12.67	11.41	3.01	0.35
1948	66.41	0.91	12.11	6.01	4.28	10.28	46.59	17.61	9.08	11.86	11.29	3.15	0.42
1949	67.69	0.93	10.88	5.25	4.40	10.85	47.76	15.67	9.42	12.45	10.82	3.39	0.48
1950	65.45	0.94	13.87	5.66	4.19	9.89	45.98	16.66	9.02	12.13	12.50	3.26	0.45
1951	65.22	0.91	13.95	6.13	4.05	9.74	45.93	17.43	9.00	11.61	12.30	3.25	0.47
1952	65.61	0.94	12.85	6.16	4.09	10.35	46.42	16.81	9.26	10.98	12.56	3.49	0.49
1953	66.09	0.96	12.34	5.87	4.10	10.64	46.82	16.47	9.74	10.88	11.85	3.68	0.56
1954	68.01	1.03	9.67	5.71	4.38	11.20	46.96	15.48	10.49	10.51	12.18	3.83	0.56
1955	65.51	1.00	13.03	5.76	4.24	10.46	46.22	15.49	10.39	10.49	13.02	3.81	0.57
1956	65.10	0.98	12.32	6.22	4.17	10.21	47.17	15.60	10.82	8.77	13.00	4.04	0.60
1957	66.44	0.97	11.52	6.18	4.20	10.69	47.83	15.01	11.48	8.19	12.53	4.29	0.66
1958	66.19	0.99	11.22	5.93	4.49	11.17	47.31	14.07	12.10	8.27	13.08	4.44	0.72
1959	65.37	1.01	11.73	6.24	4.70	10.96	46.33	14.14	12.26	8.57	13.35	4.55	0.79
1960	64.60	1.02	11.52	6.74	4.95	11.16	46.24	14.16	12.67	7.62	13.62	4.72	0.96
1961	63.70	1.05	11.78	6.78	5.32	11.37	45.48	13.90	12.96	7.80	13.91	4.94	1.02
1962	62.91	1.04	11.87	6.96	5.71	11.52	45.40	14.09	12.75	7.39	14.14	5.11	1.13
1963	61.73	1.03	12.52	7.16	6.07	11.49	44.65	14.12	12.35	7.97	14.35	5.29	1.27

Year													
1964	61.22	1.03	12.79	7.52	6.08	11.37	44.54	14.24	12.07	7.59	14.75	5.47	1.35
1965	60.20	1.00	13.51	8.23	5.89	11.16	44.60	14.29	11.57	7.21	15.31	5.63	1.39
1966	59.94	0.64	13.64	8.61	5.75	11.41	45.39	14.89	11.05	6.46	15.44	5.37	1.40
1967	59.50	0.98	12.99	8.89	5.57	12.08	46.20	15.01	10.37	6.22	15.30	5.45	1.46
1968	58.60	0.98	13.70	9.21	5.30	12.22	46.85	14.88	9.49	6.18	15.68	5.28	1.64
1969	58.36	0.97	13.92	9.85	4.77	12.13	47.22	14.98	8.95	5.67	16.19	5.23	1.76
1970	58.49	1.02	13.28	9.88	4.51	12.82	48.54	14.57	8.55	5.33	15.79	5.39	1.83
1971	58.90	0.98	13.24	9.37	4.34	13.16	49.00	14.19	8.10	5.57	15.63	5.40	2.10
1972	58.77	0.96	13.56	9.68	4.15	12.88	48.49	14.07	7.96	5.70	16.07	5.28	2.44
1973	58.32	1.17	14.27	10.55	3.75	11.94	47.59	14.78	7.70	5.74	16.41	5.22	2.55
1974	63.52	1.23	9.37	11.26	3.28	11.35	50.62	16.26	7.77	5.17	13.04	4.93	2.21
1975	65.11	1.25	8.82	10.03	2.98	11.81	52.06	15.26	7.44	5.67	12.33	5.17	2.08
1976	65.47	1.27	8.79	9.79	2.83	11.84	51.79	15.52	7.38	5.78	12.12	5.24	2.18
1977	65.24	1.29	8.71	10.21	2.68	11.86	51.81	15.58	7.51	5.36	12.34	5.06	2.34
1978	65.14	1.38	9.38	10.37	2.47	11.26	51.84	15.67	7.64	5.18	12.62	4.93	2.13
1979	64.77	1.55	9.83	10.99	2.21	10.65	51.11	15.95	7.61	5.17	13.09	5.08	1.99
1980	65.34	2.09	9.62	10.62	2.01	10.32	51.47	15.59	7.98	4.93	12.74	5.23	2.06
1981	68.09	2.43	8.82	8.69	1.98	10.00	51.78	15.05	8.25	4.92	11.89	5.02	3.09
1982	68.25	2.68	8.30	9.23	1.18	10.35	52.65	14.18	8.62	5.74	11.13	4.59	3.10
1983	67.30	2.82	8.84	9.41	1.20	10.43	52.23	13.31	8.74	6.31	11.48	4.44	3.48
1984	65.07	3.15	8.87	10.69	1.24	10.98	50.63	14.18	8.88	6.67	11.64	4.25	3.75
1985	63.22	3.37	9.05	11.14	0.98	12.24	50.26	13.76	9.04	7.19	11.63	4.35	3.77
1986	60.85	3.84	8.69	11.68	1.35	13.60	49.66	13.17	9.17	8.38	11.13	4.55	3.94
1987	59.06	4.32	8.64	11.52	1.94	14.52	49.15	13.66	9.10	8.16	11.41	5.09	3.44
1988	57.74	4.71	8.14	12.18	1.98	15.25	49.62	14.12	9.00	7.75	11.09	5.09	3.34

Table A16 Balance sheets of the household sector, 1945–88 (per cent)

Year	5.2A Net worth	5.2B Loans and other	5.2C Consumer credit	5.2D Mortg.	5.2E Resid. & non-res. struct. & equip.	5.2F Consumer durables	5.2G Land	5.2H Currency & depos.	5.2I Credit market instruments	5.2J Corporate equit.	5.2K Equity in non-corp. business	5.2L Misc. assets
1945	95.03	1.19	1.09	2.69	11.05	6.95	2.09	15.16	13.71	15.96	26.81	8.27
1946	94.87	0.76	1.42	2.94	12.28	7.27	2.10	15.35	12.56	13.68	28.31	8.46
1947	94.31	0.66	1.75	3.28	13.97	7.95	2.25	14.28	11.74	12.25	29.11	8.44
1948	93.68	0.63	2.02	3.67	15.19	8.75	2.29	13.41	11.40	11.48	28.83	8.65
1949	92.95	0.68	2.31	4.07	15.17	9.56	2.30	13.08	11.22	12.11	27.54	9.01
1950	92.39	0.73	2.55	4.33	15.95	10.19	2.46	12.11	9.97	13.16	27.38	8.78
1951	92.27	0.69	2.45	4.59	16.40	10.73	2.45	11.85	9.15	14.04	26.79	8.60
1952	91.63	0.70	2.76	4.91	16.74	10.97	2.58	12.08	8.61	14.52	25.64	8.86
1953	90.82	0.75	3.02	5.41	17.10	11.33	2.73	12.41	8.94	13.34	24.91	9.24
1954	90.75	0.80	2.85	5.61	16.73	10.65	2.81	12.08	8.21	17.54	22.96	9.03
1955	90.14	0.79	3.09	5.98	16.79	10.34	3.07	11.67	8.02	19.48	21.64	8.99
1956	89.77	0.78	3.12	6.33	16.89	10.51	3.36	11.57	7.89	19.38	21.40	9.00
1957	89.16	0.78	3.25	6.82	17.39	10.88	3.89	12.04	8.09	16.65	21.65	9.41
1958	89.53	0.83	2.95	6.69	16.36	10.14	3.86	11.70	7.32	20.87	20.54	9.21
1959	88.94	0.86	3.20	7.01	16.29	9.88	4.18	11.76	7.51	21.15	19.86	9.37
1960	88.33	0.89	3.33	7.46	16.58	9.84	4.05	12.13	7.67	20.22	19.76	9.74
1961	88.45	0.93	3.17	7.45	15.85	9.14	4.03	11.92	7.24	23.48	18.62	9.72
1962	87.51	0.96	3.44	8.09	16.46	9.32	4.38	13.01	7.34	20.34	19.05	10.10
1963	87.14	1.03	3.58	8.26	15.74	9.09	4.30	13.41	6.97	22.19	18.13	10.17

1964	86.83	1.02	3.72	8.43	15.70	8.90	4.37	13.75	6.76	22.71	17.47	10.34
1965	86.65	1.04	3.84	8.48	15.35	8.68	4.43	14.04	6.46	23.65	16.97	10.43
1966	86.16	1.09	3.96	8.78	16.15	9.22	4.64	14.40	6.83	20.79	17.28	10.68
1967	86.69	1.20	3.76	8.35	15.42	9.11	4.49	14.44	6.35	23.46	16.09	10.64
1968	87.00	1.29	3.71	8.01	15.45	9.07	4.52	14.17	6.15	25.05	15.18	10.42
1969	86.44	1.16	3.95	8.44	16.64	9.75	4.74	14.10	7.15	21.38	15.56	10.68
1970	86.27	1.35	3.92	8.47	17.09	10.08	4.81	14.90	6.91	19.93	15.32	10.96
1971	86.22	1.40	3.95	8.43	17.23	9.76	4.55	15.62	6.21	20.84	14.62	11.17
1972	85.99	1.44	4.01	8.56	17.47	9.50	4.74	16.04	5.91	20.60	14.40	11.33
1973	85.07	1.42	4.36	9.15	19.29	9.97	5.29	16.88	6.42	15.26	16.16	10.73
1974	84.68	1.45	4.36	9.51	20.94	10.92	5.84	17.42	7.05	10.32	17.29	10.23
1975	85.32	1.36	4.07	9.25	20.10	10.66	5.56	17.23	6.95	12.04	16.95	10.52
1976	85.38	1.36	4.03	9.23	20.06	10.31	5.68	17.31	6.63	12.51	16.90	10.61
1977	84.61	1.36	4.27	9.76	21.19	10.36	5.83	17.64	6.54	10.81	17.16	10.47
1978	84.31	1.33	4.36	10.00	22.15	10.22	6.20	17.12	6.50	9.69	17.84	10.29
1979	84.09	1.30	4.37	10.24	21.86	10.06	6.11	16.63	6.85	10.43	17.98	10.10
1980	84.78	1.38	3.87	9.96	21.06	9.78	6.27	16.18	6.58	12.19	17.62	10.34
1981	84.51	1.47	3.86	10.16	21.46	9.89	6.18	17.06	6.88	10.89	17.16	10.49
1982	84.51	1.54	3.83	10.12	20.65	9.76	5.72	17.64	7.11	11.76	15.97	11.39
1983	85.63	1.46	3.63	9.28	18.85	9.20	7.11	16.76	5.33	11.12	18.90	12.73
1984	84.92	1.37	4.08	9.64	18.63	9.23	7.04	17.81	5.88	10.65	17.92	12.84
1985	84.25	1.40	4.45	9.90	17.69	9.18	6.68	17.61	6.69	12.12	16.29	13.74
1986	83.46	1.03	4.02	10.50	17.92	9.39	7.11	16.76	6.16	13.51	13.67	15.48
1987	83.06	2.80	4.02	11.12	18.35	9.72	7.29	16.54	6.64	12.16	13.40	15.91
1988	82.89	1.72	4.00	11.38	18.02	9.91	7.16	16.32	6.92	11.97	12.94	16.77

Table A17 Consumer credit outstanding as percentage of GCP, 1929–89

Year	5.3A GCP	5.3B Non-install. credit	5.3C Auto-mobile loans	5.3D Other install. credit	5.3E Non-install. credit	5.3F Auto-mobile loans	5.3G Other install credit
		(billions of dollars)				*(per cent)*	
1929	107.3	3 592	1 384	2 140	3.35	1.29	1.99
1930	99.8	3 329	986	2 036	3.34	0.99	2.04
1931	90.8	2 852	684	1 779	3.14	0.75	1.96
1932	76.6	2 354	356	1 316	3.07	0.46	1.72
1933	74.6	2 162	493	1 230	2.90	0.66	1.65
1934	83.8	2 219	614	1 385	2.65	0.73	1.65
1935	91.1	2 373	992	1 825	2.60	1.09	2.00
1936	100.0	2 628	1 372	2 375	2.63	1.37	2.38
1937	106.5	2 830	1 494	2 624	2.66	1.40	2.46
1938	105.4	2 684	1 099	2 587	2.55	1.04	2.45
1939	110.3	2 719	1 497	3 006	2.47	1.36	2.73
1940	117.6	2 824	2 071	3 443	2.40	1.76	2.93
1941	139.3	3 087	2 458	3 627	2.22	1.76	2.60
1942	166.8	2 817	742	2 424	1.69	0.44	1.45
1943	196.4	2 765	355	1 781	1.41	0.18	0.91
1944	214.0	2 935	397	1 779	1.37	0.19	0.83
1945	217.5	3 203	455	2 007	1.47	0.21	0.92
1946	221.0	4 212	981	3 191	1.91	0.44	1.44
1947	244.7	4 903	1 924	4 771	2.00	0.79	1.95
1948	271.9	5 415	3 018	5 978	1.99	1.11	2.20
1949	276.7	5 774	4 555	7 035	2.09	1.65	2.54

1950	304.4	8 129	6 035	9 131	2.67	1.98	3.00
1951	344.8	8 765	5 981	9 878	2.54	1.73	2.86
1952	362.5	9 645	7 651	12 470	2.66	2.11	3.44
1953	382.7	9 899	9 702	14 168	2.59	2.54	3.70
1954	394.2	10 557	9 755	14 715	2.68	2.47	3.73
1955	424.6	12 076	13 485	16 324	2.84	3.18	3.84
1956	446.5	12 843	14 499	18 161	2.88	3.25	4.07
1957	471.3	13 218	15 493	19 421	2.80	3.29	4.12
1958	490.1	13 620	14 267	20 469	2.78	2.91	4.18
1959	524.7	15 457	16 641	23 780	2.95	3.17	4.53
1960	545.3	15 700	18 108	26 227	2.88	3.32	4.81
1961	572.1	16 902	17 656	27 782	2.95	3.09	4.86
1962	608.0	17 856	20 001	30 374	2.94	3.29	5.00
1963	643.6	19 550	22 891	34 165	3.04	3.56	5.31
1964	685.4	21 315	25 865	38 809	3.11	3.77	5.66
1965	738.3	23 134	29 378	43 436	3.13	3.98	5.88
1966	802.5	23 677	31 024	47 138	2.95	3.87	5.87
1967	848.6	24 933	31 136	50 647	2.94	3.67	5.97
1968	926.0	27 119	34 352	55 760	2.93	3.71	6.02
1969	998.9	27 547	36 946	62 435	2.76	3.70	6.25
1970	1 067.8	27 695	36 348	67 557	2.59	3.40	6.33
1971	1 171.8	30 624	40 522	75 912	2.61	3.46	6.48
1972	1 284.7	34 751	47 835	83 423	2.70	3.72	6.49
1973	1 429.3	37 691	53 740	99 170	2.64	3.76	6.94
1974	1 560.2	37 162	54 241	107 962	2.38	3.48	6.92
1975	1 746.9	37 920	56 989	110 054	2.17	3.26	6.30
1976	1 931.5	40 380	66 821	120 961	2.09	3.46	6.26
1977	2 142.6	42 333	80 948	140 527	1.98	3.78	6.56

continued on p. 168

Table A17   continued

Year	5.3A GCP	5.3B Non-install. credit	5.3C Auto-mobile loans	5.3D Other install. credit	5.3E Non-intall. credit	5.3F Auto-mobile loans	5.3G Other install credit
		(billions of dollars)				(per cent)	
1978	2 395.8	46 296	98 739	163 237	1.93	4.12	6.81
1979	2 662.6	51 024	112 475	184 008	1.92	4.22	6.91
1980	2 940.8	51 820	111 936	185 630	1.76	3.81	6.31
1981	3 303.7	55 915	118 956	191 726	1.69	3.60	5.80
1982	3 506.1	57 579	124 218	199 318	1.64	3.54	5.68
1983	3 761.8	62 514	143 799	224 069	1.66	3.82	5.95
1984	4 074.1	69 230	173 704	268 834	1.70	4.26	6.60
1985	4 321.5	74 654	209 636	308 119	1.73	4.85	7.13
1986	4 544.8	74 138	247 313	324 734	1.65	5.44	7.15
1987	4 818.5	71 439	265 976	341 745	1.48	5.52	7.09
1988	5 159.2	69 407	281 174	378 333	1.35	5.48	7.33
1989	5 520.3	64 673	289 266	422 533	1.17	5.24	3.65

Table A18 Mortgage debt outstanding 1939–89

	Percentage of GCP			Type of property							
	5.4A	5.4B Total mortgage debt	5.4C Total mortgage debt	5.5A Farm	5.5B 1–4 family	5.5C Multi-family	5.5D Commer-cial	5.5E Farm	5.5F 1–4 family	5.5G Multi-family	5.5H Commer-cial
Year	GCP										
	(billions of dollars)		(per cent)	(billions of dollars)				(per cent)			
1939	110.1	35.5	32.25	6.6	16.3	5.6	7.0	18.59	45.92	15.77	19.72
1940	117.4	36.5	31.10	6.5	17.4	5.7	6.9	17.81	47.67	15.62	18.90
1941	138.9	37.7	27.14	6.4	18.4	5.9	7.0	16.98	48.81	15.65	18.57
1942	166.3	36.7	22.06	6.0	18.2	5.8	6.7	16.35	49.59	15.80	18.26
1943	195.9	35.3	18.02	5.4	17.8	5.8	6.3	15.30	50.42	16.43	17.85
1944	213.6	34.6	16.20	4.9	17.9	5.6	6.2	14.16	51.73	16.18	17.92
1945	216.9	35.5	16.37	4.8	18.6	5.7	6.4	13.52	52.39	16.06	18.03
1946	220.6	41.7	18.90	4.9	23.0	6.1	7.7	11.75	55.16	14.63	18.47
1947	244.5	49.0	20.04	5.1	28.2	6.6	9.1	10.41	57.55	13.47	18.57
1948	271.6	56.3	20.73	5.3	33.3	7.5	10.2	9.41	59.15	13.32	18.12
1949	276.4	62.6	22.65	5.6	37.6	8.6	10.8	8.95	60.06	13.74	17.25
1950	304.1	72.9	23.97	6.1	45.2	10.1	11.5	8.37	62.00	13.85	15.78
1951	344.4	82.4	23.92	6.7	51.7	11.5	12.5	8.13	62.74	13.96	15.17
1952	362.2	91.4	25.24	7.2	58.5	12.3	13.4	7.88	64.00	13.46	14.66
1953	382.3	101.2	26.47	7.7	66.1	12.9	14.5	7.61	65.32	12.75	14.33
1954	393.6	113.7	28.88	8.2	75.7	13.5	16.3	7.21	66.58	11.87	14.34
1955	423.9	129.8	30.62	9.0	88.2	14.3	18.3	6.93	67.95	11.02	14.10
1956	446.1	144.4	32.37	9.8	99.0	14.9	20.7	6.79	68.56	10.32	14.34
1957	470.5	156.5	33.26	10.4	107.6	15.3	23.2	6.65	68.75	9.78	14.82

continued on p. 170

Table A18   continued

Year	Percentage of GCP			Type of property							
	5.4A GCP	5.4B Total mortgage debt	5.4C Total mortgage debt	5.5A Farm	5.5B 1–4 family	5.5C Multi-family	5.5D Commercial	5.5E Farm	5.5F 1–4 family	5.5G Multi-family	5.5H Commercial
	(billions of dollars)	(billions of dollars)	(per cent)	(billions of dollars)				(per cent)			
1958	489.2	171.7	35.10	11.1	117.7	16.8	26.1	6.46	68.55	9.78	15.20
1959	523.7	190.9	36.45	12.1	130.9	18.7	29.2	6.34	68.57	9.80	15.30
1960	544.6	207.4	38.08	12.8	141.9	20.3	32.4	6.17	68.42	9.79	15.62
1961	571.0	228.0	39.93	13.9	154.6	23.0	36.5	6.10	67.81	10.09	16.01
1962	607.3	251.4	41.40	15.2	169.3	25.8	41.1	6.05	67.34	10.26	16.35
1963	642.3	278.4	43.34	16.8	186.4	29.0	46.2	6.03	66.95	10.42	16.59
1964	684.3	305.9	44.70	18.9	203.4	33.6	50.0	6.18	66.49	10.98	16.35
1965	737.6	333.4	45.20	21.2	220.5	37.2	54.5	6.36	66.14	11.16	16.35
1966	801.6	356.4	44.46	23.1	232.9	40.3	60.1	6.48	65.35	11.31	16.86
1967	848.1	381.1	44.94	25.1	247.3	43.9	64.8	6.59	64.89	11.52	17.00
1968	924.9	411.0	44.44	27.5	264.8	47.3	71.4	6.69	64.43	11.51	17.37
1969	998.0	441.7	44.26	29.4	283.2	52.2	76.9	6.66	64.12	11.82	17.41
1970	1066.9	473.6	44.39	30.5	297.4	60.1	85.6	6.44	62.80	12.69	18.07
1971	1170.7	524.3	44.79	32.4	325.9	70.1	95.9	6.18	62.16	13.37	18.29
1972	1283.3	597.4	46.55	35.4	366.5	82.8	112.7	5.93	61.35	13.86	18.87
1973	1427.6	672.5	47.11	39.8	407.9	93.1	131.7	5.92	60.65	13.84	19.58
1974	1558.6	732.5	47.00	44.9	440.7	100.0	146.9	6.13	60.16	13.65	20.05
1975	1743.2	791.9	45.43	49.9	482.1	100.6	159.3	6.30	60.88	12.70	20.12
1976	1928.8	878.6	45.55	55.4	546.3	105.7	171.2	6.31	62.18	12.03	19.49
1977	2139.1	1 010.3	47.23	63.9	642.7	114.0	189.7	6.32	63.61	11.28	18.78
1978	2392.5	1 163.0	48.61	72.8	753.5	124.9	211.8	6.26	64.79	10.74	18.21

Year											
1979	2662.6	1 328.5	49.92	86.8	870.5	134.9	236.3	6.53	65.53	10.15	17.79
1980	2938.8	1 460.4	49.69	97.5	965.1	142.3	255.5	6.68	66.08	9.74	17.50
1981	3300.1	1 566.6	47.47	107.2	1039.8	142.1	277.5	6.84	66.37	9.07	17.71
1982	3500.1	1 637.9	46.80	111.3	1080.0	145.7	300.9	6.80	65.94	8.90	18.37
1983	3761.8	1 832.3	48.71	113.7	1205.5	160.7	352.4	6.21	65.79	8.77	19.23
1984	4074.1	2 061.1	50.59	112.4	1344.0	185.4	419.3	5.45	65.21	9.00	20.34
1985	4321.5	2 303.3	53.30	105.9	1501.4	214.5	481.5	4.60	65.18	9.31	20.90
1986	4544.8	2 618.3	57.61	95.8	1719.7	247.8	555.0	3.66	65.68	9.46	21.20
1987	4818.5	2 977.3	61.79	88.9	1959.6	274.0	654.9	2.99	65.82	9.20	22.00
1988	5159.2	3 265.5	63.29	86.8	2187.0	290.8	701.0	2.66	66.97	8.91	21.47
1989	5520.3	3 453.9	62.57	86.6	2331.2	302.1	734.0	2.51	67.49	8.75	21.25

Table A19 Mortgage debt outstanding by holder, 1939–89

Year	5.6A Total mortgage debt	5.6B Savings institutions	5.6C Commercial banks	5.6D Life insurance co.	5.6E Federal & related agencies	5.6F Individuals & others	5.6G Savings institutions	5.6H Commercial banks	5.6I Life insurance co.	5.6J Federal & related agencies	5.6K Individuals & others
	(billions of dollars)						(per cent)				
1939	35.5	8.6	4.3	5.7	5.0	11.9	24.23	12.11	16.06	14.08	33.52
1940	36.5	9.0	4.6	6.0	4.9	12.0	24.66	12.60	16.44	13.42	32.88
1941	37.6	9.4	4.9	6.4	4.7	12.2	25.00	13.03	17.02	12.50	32.45
1942	36.6	9.2	4.7	6.7	4.3	11.7	25.14	12.84	18.31	11.75	31.97
1943	35.3	9.0	4.5	6.7	3.6	11.5	25.50	12.75	18.98	10.20	32.58
1944	34.7	9.1	4.4	6.7	3.0	11.5	26.22	12.68	19.31	8.65	33.14
1945	35.5	9.6	4.8	6.6	2.4	12.1	27.04	13.52	18.59	6.76	34.08
1946	41.7	11.5	7.2	7.2	2.0	13.8	27.58	17.27	17.27	4.80	33.09
1947	49.0	13.8	9.4	8.7	1.8	15.3	28.16	19.18	17.76	3.67	31.22
1948	56.2	16.1	10.9	10.8	1.8	16.6	28.65	19.40	19.22	3.20	29.54
1949	62.6	18.3	11.6	12.9	2.3	17.5	29.23	18.53	20.61	3.67	27.96
1950	72.9	21.9	13.7	16.1	2.8	18.4	30.04	18.79	22.09	3.84	25.24
1951	82.3	25.5	14.7	19.3	3.5	19.3	30.98	17.86	23.45	4.25	23.45
1952	91.4	29.8	15.9	21.3	4.1	20.4	32.57	17.38	23.28	4.48	22.30
1953	101.4	34.9	16.9	23.3	4.6	21.7	34.42	16.67	22.98	4.54	21.40
1954	113.7	41.1	18.6	26.0	4.8	23.2	36.15	16.36	22.87	4.22	20.40
1955	129.9	48.9	21.0	29.4	5.3	25.3	37.64	16.17	22.63	4.08	19.48
1956	144.5	55.5	22.7	33.0	6.2	27.1	38.41	15.71	22.84	4.29	18.75
1957	156.5	61.2	23.3	35.2	7.7	29.1	39.11	14.89	22.49	4.92	18.59
1958	171.8	68.9	25.5	37.1	8.0	32.3	40.10	14.84	21.59	4.66	18.80
1959	190.7	78.1	28.1	39.2	10.2	35.1	40.95	14.74	20.56	5.35	18.41

1960	18.51	5.54	20.14	13.88	41.93	38.4	11.5	41.8	28.8	87.0	207.5
1961	18.91	5.35	19.39	13.34	43.00	43.1	12.2	44.2	30.4	98.0	227.9
1962	18.42	5.01	18.66	13.72	44.19	46.3	12.6	46.9	34.5	111.1	251.4
1963	17.78	4.24	18.14	14.15	45.69	49.5	11.8	50.5	39.4	127.2	278.4
1964	17.22	3.99	18.04	14.38	46.37	52.7	12.2	55.2	44.0	141.9	306.0
1965	16.56	4.05	18.00	14.91	46.47	55.2	13.5	60.0	49.7	154.9	333.3
1966	16.33	4.91	18.12	15.26	45.39	58.2	17.5	64.6	54.4	161.8	356.5
1967	16.11	5.48	17.71	15.48	45.21	61.4	20.9	67.5	59.0	172.3	381.1
1968	16.07	6.10	17.02	15.98	44.82	66.1	25.1	70.0	65.7	184.3	411.2
1969	16.17	7.04	16.31	16.01	44.46	71.4	31.1	72.0	70.7	196.3	441.5
1970	16.76	8.09	15.71	15.47	43.97	79.4	38.3	74.4	73.3	208.3	473.7
1971	15.95	8.85	14.40	15.74	45.06	83.6	46.4	75.5	82.5	236.2	524.2
1972	15.54	9.14	12.87	16.62	45.82	92.8	54.6	76.9	99.3	273.7	597.3
1973	15.22	9.63	12.10	17.70	45.34	102.4	64.8	81.4	119.1	305.0	672.7
1974	14.71	11.22	11.77	18.04	44.27	107.7	82.2	86.2	132.1	324.2	732.4
1975	13.84	12.77	11.26	17.20	44.93	109.6	101.1	89.2	136.2	355.8	791.9
1976	13.02	13.28	10.46	17.21	46.03	114.4	116.7	91.9	151.3	404.6	878.9
1977	12.33	13.91	9.58	17.72	46.46	124.6	140.5	96.8	179.0	469.4	1010.3
1978	12.41	14.67	9.13	18.40	45.40	144.3	170.6	106.2	214.0	528.0	1163.1
1979	13.12	16.26	8.91	18.46	43.25	174.3	216.0	118.4	245.2	574.6	1328.5
1980	14.16	17.58	8.98	17.99	41.29	206.8	256.8	131.1	262.7	603.1	1460.5
1981	15.12	18.47	8.79	18.14	39.48	236.8	289.4	137.7	284.2	618.5	1566.6
1982	15.95	21.70	8.67	18.39	35.29	261.2	355.4	142.0	301.3	578.1	1638.0
1983	15.87	23.65	8.24	18.04	34.20	290.8	433.4	151.0	330.5	626.7	1832.4
1984	15.73	23.83	7.60	18.41	34.43	324.2	491.1	156.7	379.5	709.7	2061.2
1985	15.62	25.27	7.46	18.63	33.02	359.8	582.0	171.8	429.2	760.5	2303.3
1986	15.61	28.09	7.40	19.19	29.71	408.6	735.4	193.8	502.5	778.0	2618.3
1987	15.16	29.07	6.88	19.92	28.97	450.0	863.1	204.3	591.4	860.0	2968.8
1988	15.13	29.12	6.54	20.60	28.62	491.4	945.9	212.4	669.2	929.6	3248.5
1989	15.01	29.93	6.83	21.37	26.87	518.5	1033.7	235.8	738.0	928.0	3454.0

Table A20 (a) Private domestic investment as percentage of GCP, 1929–89; (b) capital consumption as percentage of GCP, 1929–89; (c) real NPDI, 1929–89; (d) increase in real capital, 1929–89

	(a)					(b)		(c)	(d)		
	5.7A	5.7B	5.7C	5.7D	5.7E	5.8A Capital consumption	5.8B Capital consumption	5.9A	5.10A Cumulation of NPDI	5.10B Real GCP changes	5.10C Cumulation of real GCP
Year	GCP	NPDI	GPDI	NPDI	GPDI	(blns $)	(per cent)	Real NPDI			
	(billions of dollars)			(per cent)				(billions of 1982 dollars)			
1929	107.3	6.7	16.6	6.24	15.47	9.9	9.20	46.6	46.6	–	–
1930	99.8	–	10.3	–	10.32	–	–	24.0	70.6	−51.6	−51.6
1931	90.8	–	5.7	–	6.28	–	–	2.3	72.9	−68.4	−120.1
1932	76.6	–	0.9	–	1.17	–	–	−24.6	48.3	−120.8	−240.8
1933	74.6	−6.1	1.5	−8.18	2.01	7.6	10.19	−52.5	−4.2	−17.9	−258.8
1934	83.8	–	2.9	–	3.46	–	–	−40.5	−44.7	75.1	−183.7
1935	91.1	–	6.3	–	6.92	–	–	−31.3	−76.0	58.4	−125.3
1936	100.0	–	8.5	–	8.50	–	–	−22.3	−98.3	71.1	−54.2
1937	106.5	–	11.7	–	10.99	–	–	−13.1	−111.4	49.9	−4.3
1938	105.4	–	6.4	–	6.07	–	–	−4.7	−116.0	−8.3	−12.6
1939	110.3	0.5	9.5	0.45	8.61	9.0	8.16	4.0	−112.1	37.6	25.0
1940	117.6	4.1	13.5	3.49	11.48	9.4	7.99	31.5	−80.5	56.1	81.1
1941	139.3	8.0	18.3	5.74	13.14	10.3	7.39	58.0	−22.6	156.3	237.4
1942	166.8	−1.0	10.3	−0.60	6.18	11.3	6.77	−6.8	−29.4	186.4	423.8
1943	196.4	−5.3	6.3	−2.70	3.21	11.6	5.91	−35.1	−64.5	196.2	619.9
1944	214.0	−4.2	7.8	−1.96	3.64	12.0	5.61	−27.5	−91.9	115.2	735.1
1945	217.5	−1.1	11.3	−0.51	5.20	12.4	5.70	−7.0	−98.9	20.9	756.0
1946	221.0	17.3	31.5	7.83	14.25	14.2	6.43	89.2	−9.8	19.4	775.4

174

Year											
1947	244.7	17.5	35.1	7.15	14.34	17.6	7.19	79.2	69.4	108.0	883.4
1948	271.9	26.7	47.1	9.82	17.32	20.4	7.50	113.1	182.6	114.8	998.1
1949	276.7	14.5	36.5	5.24	13.19	22.0	7.95	61.7	244.3	20.5	1018.7
1950	304.4	31.5	55.1	10.35	18.10	23.6	7.75	131.8	376.1	115.9	1134.5
1951	344.8	33.3	60.5	9.66	17.55	27.2	7.89	132.7	508.7	160.8	1295.3
1952	362.5	24.4	53.6	6.73	14.79	29.2	8.06	95.7	604.4	69.6	1364.9
1953	382.7	24.0	54.9	6.27	14.35	30.9	8.07	92.7	697.1	77.9	1442.8
1954	394.2	21.6	54.1	5.48	13.72	32.5	8.24	82.1	779.2	42.9	1485.7
1955	424.6	35.3	69.7	8.31	16.42	34.4	8.10	129.8	909.0	111.4	1597.1
1956	446.5	34.6	72.7	7.75	16.28	38.1	8.53	123.1	1032.1	78.9	1676.0
1957	471.3	29.9	71.0	6.34	15.06	41.1	8.72	102.7	1134.9	83.9	1759.9
1958	490.1	20.8	63.6	4.24	12.98	42.8	8.73	70.0	1204.9	62.9	1822.8
1959	524.7	35.5	80.1	6.77	15.27	44.6	8.50	116.8	1321.7	113.6	1936.3
1960	545.3	31.8	78.2	5.83	14.34	46.4	8.51	102.9	1424.6	67.7	2004.1
1961	572.1	29.4	77.2	5.14	13.49	47.8	8.36	94.2	1518.8	84.5	2088.5
1962	608.0	38.2	87.6	6.28	14.41	49.4	8.13	119.7	1638.6	113.7	2202.3
1963	643.6	41.8	93.2	6.49	14.48	51.4	7.99	129.0	1767.6	108.1	2310.4
1964	685.4	45.7	99.6	6.67	14.53	53.9	7.86	138.9	1906.5	127.6	2438.0
1965	738.3	58.8	116.2	7.96	15.74	57.4	7.77	174.0	2080.5	157.7	2595.7
1966	802.5	66.5	128.6	8.29	16.02	62.1	7.74	190.0	2270.5	182.8	2778.5
1967	848.6	58.3	125.7	6.87	14.81	67.4	7.94	162.4	2432.9	129.6	2908.1
1968	926.0	63.1	137.0	6.81	14.79	73.9	7.98	167.4	2600.2	203.6	3111.7
1969	998.9	71.8	153.2	7.19	15.34	81.4	8.15	180.4	2780.6	183.7	3295.4
1970	1067.8	60.0	148.8	5.62	13.94	88.8	8.32	142.9	2923.5	164.2	3459.6
1971	1171.8	74.9	172.4	6.39	14.71	97.5	8.32	168.7	3092.2	233.7	3693.3
1972	1284.7	94.1	202.0	7.32	15.72	107.9	8.40	202.4	3294.5	242.2	3935.5
1973	1427.6	120.7	238.8	8.45	16.73	118.1	8.26	243.8	3538.4	291.5	4227.0
1974	1558.6	103.4	240.9	6.63	15.46	137.5	8.81	191.5	3729.9	242.5	4469.6
1975	1743.2	57.8	219.6	3.32	12.60	161.8	9.26	97.5	3827.3	311.3	4780.9

continued on p. 176

Table A20 continued

		(a)				(b)		(c)			(d)	
	5.7A	5.7B	5.7C	5.7D	5.7E	5.8A Capital consumption	5.8B Capital consumption	5.9A Real NPDI	5.10A Cumulation of NPDI	5.10B Real GCP changes	5.10C Cumulation of real GCP	
Year	GCP	NPDI	GPDI	NPDI	GPDI							
	(billions of dollars)			(per cent)		(blns $)	(per cent)	(billions of constant $, 1982=100)				
1976	1928.8	98.4	277.6	5.10	14.39	179.2	9.28	155.9	3983.3	294.2	5075.0
1977	2139.1	142.5	344.0	6.66	16.08	201.5	9.40	211.7	4195.0	312.4	5387.4
1978	2392.5	186.9	416.8	7.81	17.42	229.9	9.60	258.9	4453.9	351.1	5738.5
1979	2661.5	189.1	454.9	7.11	17.09	265.8	9.98	240.6	4694.5	342.2	6080.7
1980	2938.8	133.1	436.9	4.53	14.87	303.8	10.33	155.3	4849.8	323.6	6404.2
1981	3300.1	167.7	515.5	5.08	15.62	347.8	10.53	178.4	5028.2	384.4	6788.6
1982	3500.1	64.1	447.3	1.83	12.78	383.2	10.93	64.1	5092.3	200.0	6988.6
1983	3761.8	105.7	502.3	2.81	13.35	396.6	10.53	101.7	5194.0	251.9	7240.5
1984	4074.1	249.4	664.9	6.12	16.32	415.5	10.33	231.6	5425.6	290.0	7530.4
1985	4321.5	205.9	643.1	4.76	14.88	437.2	10.12	185.7	5611.2	223.1	7753.5
1986	4544.8	199.3	659.4	4.39	14.51	460.1	10.12	175.1	5786.4	196.2	7949.7
1987	4818.5	213.2	699.9	4.42	14.53	486.7	10.10	181.6	5968.0	233.2	8182.9
1988	5159.2	236.7	750.3	4.59	14.54	513.6	10.10	195.1	6163.1	280.9	8463.8
1989	5520.3	224.9	777.1	4.07	14.08	552.2	10.10	178.1	6341.2	285.9	8749.6

Table A21   (a) Interest rate vs interest as percentage of national income, 1929–89; (b) real rate of return and interest rate, 1929–89

	(a)		*(b)*			
	5.11A *Federal* *discount* *rate*	*5.11B* *Net* *interest*	*5.12A* *Commercl* *paper* *4–6 mo.*	*5.12B* *Rate of* *inflation*	*5.12C* *Real* *interest* *rate*	*5.12D* *Bond* *yields*
Year	*(per cent)*		*(per cent)*	*(1929 = 0)*	*(per cent)*	
1929	5.16	5.55	5.85	0.00	5.85	4.73
1930	3.04	6.67	3.59	−2.59	6.18	4.55
1931	2.11	8.40	2.64	−8.96	11.60	4.58
1932	2.82	10.95	2.73	−10.15	12.88	5.01
1933	2.56	10.41	1.73	−5.31	7.04	4.49
1934	1.54	8.49	1.02	3.44	−2.42	4.00
1935	1.50	7.31	0.76	2.62	−1.86	3.60
1936	1.50	5.94	0.75	1.02	−0.27	3.24
1937	1.33	5.12	0.94	3.54	−2.60	3.26
1938	1.00	5.47	0.81	−1.79	2.60	3.19
1939	1.00	5.06	0.59	−1.49	2.08	3.01
1940	1.00	4.15	0.56	0.84	−0.28	2.84
1941	1.00	3.21	0.53	5.01	−4.48	2.77
1942	1.00	2.28	0.66	10.81	−10.15	2.83
1943	1.00	1.59	0.69	6.17	−5.48	2.73
1944	1.00	1.26	0.73	1.62	−0.89	2.72
1945	1.00	1.21	0.75	2.26	−1.51	2.62
1946	1.00	1.00	0.81	8.45	−7.64	2.53
1947	1.00	1.17	1.03	14.36	−13.33	2.61
1948	1.34	1.08	1.44	8.07	−6.63	2.82
1949	1.50	1.21	1.49	−1.24	2.73	2.66
1950	1.59	1.25	1.45	1.26	0.19	2.62
1951	1.75	1.26	2.16	7.88	−5.72	2.86
1952	1.75	1.34	2.33	1.92	0.41	2.96
1953	1.99	1.44	2.52	0.75	1.77	3.20
1954	1.60	1.70	1.58	0.75	0.83	2.90
1955	1.89	1.72	2.18	−0.37	2.55	3.06
1956	2.77	1.82	3.31	1.49	1.82	3.36
1957	3.12	2.09	3.81	3.31	0.50	3.89
1958	2.15	2.53	2.46	2.85	−0.39	3.79
1959	3.36	2.49	3.97	0.69	3.28	4.38
1960	3.53	2.66	3.85	1.72	2.13	4.41
1961	3.00	2.94	2.97	1.01	1.96	4.35
1962	3.00	3.08	3.26	1.00	2.26	4.33
1963	3.23	3.26	3.55	1.32	2.23	4.26
1964	3.55	3.39	3.97	1.31	2.66	4.40

Note: Bond yields = yields on Moody's AAP industrial bank.

continued on p. 178

Appendix: Data Tables

Table A21   (a) Interest rate vs interest as percentage of national income, 1929–89; (b) real rate of return and interest rate, 1929–89

	(a)		(b)			
Year	*5.11A* Federal discount rate (per cent)	*5.11B* Net interest	*5.12A* Commercl paper 4–6 mo. (per cent)	*5.12B* Rate of inflation (1929=0)	*5.12C* Real interest rate (per cent)	*5.12D* Bond yields
1965	4.04	3.57	4.38	1.61	2.77	4.49
1966	4.50	3.79	5.55	2.86	2.69	5.13
1967	4.19	4.04	5.10	3.09	2.01	5.51
1968	5.16	4.03	5.90	4.19	1.71	6.18
1969	5.87	4.34	7.83	5.46	2.37	7.03
1970	5.95	4.95	7.71	5.72	1.99	8.04
1971	4.88	5.16	5.11	4.38	0.73	7.39
1972	4.50	5.13	4.73	3.21	1.52	7.21
1973	6.44	5.31	8.15	6.22	1.93	7.44
1974	7.83	6.27	9.84	11.04	−1.20	8.57
1975	6.25	6.50	6.32	9.13	−2.81	8.83
1976	5.50	6.16	5.34	5.76	−0.42	8.43
1977	5.46	6.51	5.61	6.50	−0.89	8.02
1978	7.46	6.87	7.99	7.59	0.40	8.73
1979	10.28	7.73	10.91	11.35	−0.44	9.63
1980	11.77	9.12	12.29	13.50	−1.21	11.94
1981	13.42	10.15	14.76	10.32	4.44	14.17
1982	11.02	10.81	11.89	6.16	5.73	13.79
1983	8.50	10.33	8.89	3.21	5.68	12.04
1984	8.80	10.06	10.16	4.32	5.84	12.71
1985	7.69	9.86	8.01	3.56	4.45	11.37
1986	6.33	9.54	6.39	1.86	4.53	9.02
1987	5.66	9.60	6.85	3.65	3.20	9.38
1988	6.20	9.89	7.68	4.14	3.54	9.71
1989	6.93	10.81	8.80	4.82	3.98	9.26

Note: Bond yields = yields on Moody's AAA industrial bonds.

Table A22 Components of manufacturers' inventories, 1953–89 (per cent)

| | By stage of process | | | By durability of goods | | | | | |
| | Durable & non-durable | | | Non-durable goods industries | | | Durable goods industries | | |
Year	5.13A Materials & supplies	5.13B Work in process	5.13C Finished goods	5.14A Materials & supplies	5.14B Work in process	5.14C Finished goods	5.14D Materials & supplies	5.14E Work in process	5.14F Finished goods
1953	39.20	29.92	30.88	18.86	5.61	16.80	20.34	24.31	14.08
1954	38.54	29.18	32.28	19.60	5.85	17.79	18.94	23.32	14.49
1955	39.36	29.56	31.08	18.97	5.70	17.00	20.39	23.85	14.08
1956	38.31	29.71	31.98	17.72	5.38	17.04	20.58	24.34	14.95
1957	37.40	30.29	32.31	16.93	5.53	16.64	20.47	24.77	15.68
1958	37.21	30.29	32.50	17.24	5.63	16.90	19.97	24.66	15.60
1959	37.50	30.23	32.27	17.15	5.56	16.71	20.35	24.67	15.56
1960	36.14	29.23	34.63	16.89	5.48	17.44	19.25	23.75	17.19
1961	36.02	29.72	34.25	17.30	5.67	17.74	18.73	24.06	16.51
1962	35.33	30.05	34.62	16.72	5.67	17.98	18.61	24.38	16.63
1963	35.05	30.44	34.51	16.62	5.67	17.98	18.43	24.77	16.53
1964	34.86	31.07	34.07	15.98	5.54	17.76	18.88	25.53	16.31
1965	34.87	32.09	33.04	15.32	5.58	17.12	19.54	26.51	15.92
1966	34.18	33.54	32.28	14.31	5.39	16.26	19.87	28.14	16.02
1967	33.27	34.76	31.97	13.84	5.22	15.97	19.44	29.53	16.00
1968	32.74	35.52	31.75	13.56	5.35	16.12	19.17	30.17	15.63
1969	31.99	36.18	31.83	12.96	5.22	15.90	19.04	30.96	15.93
1970	31.81	34.55	33.64	12.94	5.19	16.18	18.87	29.36	17.46
1971	32.58	33.43	34.00	13.33	5.52	16.58	19.25	27.91	17.42
1972	32.83	33.97	33.20	13.56	5.53	16.01	19.27	28.44	17.19
1973	35.43	33.90	30.66	14.55	5.38	14.76	20.88	28.52	15.91
1974	37.30	32.18	30.52	15.02	5.18	15.32	22.28	27.00	15.20
1975	35.93	32.64	31.43	14.72	5.53	15.43	21.21	27.12	16.00
1976	36.18	32.12	31.70	14.75	5.67	15.32	21.43	26.45	16.38
1977	35.75	32.57	31.68	14.48	5.82	15.44	21.27	26.75	16.24
1978	35.42	33.51	31.07	13.93	5.66	14.91	21.50	27.85	16.15
1979	35.31	34.42	30.26	13.46	5.70	14.26	21.85	28.72	16.01
1980	34.56	35.09	30.36	13.70	5.95	14.27	20.86	29.13	16.08
1981	33.85	34.38	31.76	13.36	5.69	15.02	20.49	28.70	16.74
1982	32.99	33.93	33.08	14.08	5.96	15.55	18.91	27.97	17.52
1983	33.53	34.06	32.41	14.28	6.03	15.59	19.26	28.03	16.81
1984	32.80	34.87	32.33	13.42	5.67	15.56	19.38	29.20	16.77
1985	32.12	35.47	32.40	13.12	5.78	15.74	19.00	29.70	16.67
1986	32.18	35.37	32.45	13.14	5.49	15.49	19.05	29.88	16.96
1987	31.89	35.85	32.26	13.39	5.66	15.53	18.50	30.18	16.73
1988	31.78	36.05	32.17	13.35	5.45	15.22	18.42	30.61	16.95
1989	30.90	37.02	32.08	12.61	5.67	15.29	18.28	31.35	16.79

Appendix: Data Tables

Table A23 Manufacturing and trade, 1948–89 (per cent)

	Shares of inventories			Shares of sales		
	5.15A	*5.15B*	*5.15C*	*5.16A*	*5.16B*	*5.16D*
Year	*Manufacturing*	*Wholesalers*	*Retail trade*	*Manufacturing*	*Wholesalers*	*Retail trade*
1948	54.30	15.36	30.91	49.11	19.31	31.58
1949	54.59	14.99	30.41	47.73	19.28	33.00
1950	52.54	15.69	32.25	48.28	19.94	31.79
1951	53.64	13.56	31.84	50.08	19.83	30.09
1952	56.60	13.88	29.03	50.24	19.59	30.17
1953	57.67	13.97	28.43	51.77	18.86	29.36
1954	56.89	14.28	28.64	50.29	19.36	30.35
1955	56.45	14.71	28.83	51.22	19.14	29.64
1956	57.27	14.93	27.74	51.31	19.45	29.25
1957	58.22	14.50	27.01	51.43	18.75	29.83
1958	57.81	14.67	27.53	50.27	18.92	30.80
1959	57.47	14.75	28.05	50.71	19.24	30.05
1960	56.95	14.99	27.95	50.77	19.16	30.08
1961	57.13	15.27	27.71	50.56	19.60	29.84
1962	57.57	14.93	27.50	50.80	19.30	29.90
1963	57.63	14.97	27.79	50.81	19.40	29.79
1964	56.52	15.29	28.21	50.67	19.72	29.62
1965	56.35	15.42	28.27	51.06	19.44	29.49
1966	56.72	15.24	28.46	51.46	19.48	29.05
1967	58.26	17.20	24.21	51.22	21.51	27.28
1968	58.03	16.92	25.02	50.94	21.22	27.84
1969	58.27	17.06	25.05	50.67	21.49	27.84
1970	57.49	18.16	24.69	48.85	22.23	28.92
1971	54.72	18.78	26.44	47.88	22.57	29.56
1972	53.76	19.29	27.10	48.14	22.68	29.18
1973	53.36	19.44	27.01	47.43	24.83	27.74
1974	55.05	19.93	24.75	47.65	26.97	25.38
1975	55.58	19.81	24.83	47.47	25.66	26.87
1976	54.85	20.11	24.88	48.34	24.90	26.76
1977	53.77	20.68	25.35	49.27	24.53	26.20
1978	52.84	21.74	25.72	48.70	25.58	25.72
1979	53.71	22.07	24.57	48.28	26.66	25.07
1980	51.95	24.15	23.86	47.09	28.58	24.33
1981	51.76	23.93	24.27	47.13	28.60	24.27
1982	54.22	22.26	23.38	46.84	27.61	25.55
1983	52.96	22.08	24.96	46.43	27.19	26.39
1984	51.96	22.10	25.94	46.06	27.75	26.19
1985	49.99	22.40	27.60	45.44	27.34	27.22
1986	48.36	23.32	28.35	44.46	27.30	28.24
1987	47.25	23.21	29.54	44.31	27.49	28.20
1988	46.99	23.66	29.35	44.80	27.25	27.95
1989	47.08	23.36	29.56	44.20	27.72	28.09

Table A24 (a) Gross private domestic investment as percentage of GCP, 1929–89; (b) government expenditure by components as percentage of GCP, 1929–89

	(a)										(b)			
	5.17A	5.17B	5.17C	5.17D	5.17E	5.17F	5.17G	5.17H	5.17I	5.17J	6.1A	6.1B	6.1C	6.1D
Year	Total GPDI	Prod. durable equip.	Non-residential struct.	Residential invest.	Changes in business inventories	Total GPDI	Prod. durable equip.	Non-residential struct.	Residential invest.	Changes in business inventories	State & local govt purch.	Federal govt purch.	Federal non-defence purch.	Defence purch.
	(billions of dollars)					(per cent)					(per cent)			
1929	16.7	5.5	5.5	4.0	1.7	15.6	5.13	5.13	3.73	1.58	6.8	0.1	0.9	0.5
1930	10.3	4.3	4.0	2.3	-0.3	10.3	4.27	4.02	2.34	-0.30	7.8	0.1	1.0	0.6
1931	5.7	2.7	2.3	1.7	-1.1	6.3	2.99	2.57	1.89	-1.18	8.3	0.3	1.2	0.7
1932	0.9	1.5	1.2	0.7	-2.5	1.2	1.94	1.59	0.96	-3.26	8.6	0.1	1.4	0.7
1933	1.3	1.5	0.9	0.6	-1.7	1.7	1.99	1.24	0.76	-2.27	7.5	0.7	2.1	0.8
1934	2.9	2.2	1.0	0.9	-1.1	3.5	2.60	1.24	1.04	-1.36	6.3	1.9	2.6	1.2
1935	6.3	2.9	1.2	1.2	1.0	7.0	3.19	1.35	1.31	1.12	6.0	1.9	2.4	1.0
1936	8.5	4.0	1.6	1.6	1.3	8.5	3.97	1.63	1.60	1.33	6.4	0.7	3.7	1.4
1937	11.7	4.9	2.4	1.9	2.4	11.0	4.59	2.30	1.81	2.30	6.1	0.8	3.3	1.2
1938	6.4	3.5	1.9	2.0	-1.1	6.0	3.31	1.80	1.92	-1.00	6.5	0.8	3.8	1.4
1939	9.4	4.0	2.0	2.9	0.5	8.5	3.60	1.77	2.66	0.47	6.6	0.9	3.5	1.2
1940	13.5	5.2	2.6	3.5	2.2	11.5	4.43	2.22	2.98	1.87	6.1	0.8	3.3	2.0
1941	18.3	6.4	3.3	4.1	4.5	13.2	4.61	2.38	2.95	3.24	5.2	0.6	2.3	9.9
1942	10.3	4.1	2.2	2.2	1.8	6.2	2.47	1.32	1.32	1.08	4.1	0.5	1.6	29.6
1943	6.3	3.7	1.8	1.4	-0.6	3.2	1.89	0.92	0.71	-0.31	3.4	0.5	0.8	40.6
1944	7.8	5.0	2.4	1.4	-1.0	3.7	2.34	1.12	0.66	-0.47	3.1	0.4	0.9	40.9
1945	11.3	7.3	3.3	1.7	-1.0	5.2	3.37	1.52	0.78	-0.46	3.4	0.4	0.5	33.9
1946	31.5	9.9	7.4	7.8	6.4	14.3	4.49	3.35	3.54	2.90	4.0	0.5	1.3	7.4
1947	35.0	15.3	8.1	12.1	-0.5	14.3	6.26	3.31	4.95	-0.20	4.5	0.7	1.5	4.1
1948	47.1	17.3	9.5	15.6	4.7	17.3	6.37	3.50	5.74	1.73	4.9	0.7	2.2	4.2

continued on p. 182

Table A24   continued

| | (a) | | | | | | | | | | (b) | | | |
| Year | 5.17A Total GPDI | 5.17B Prod. durable equip. | 5.17C Non-residential struct. | 5.17D Residential invest. | 5.17E Changes in business inventories | 5.17F Total GPDI | 5.17G Prod. durable equip. | 5.17H Non-residential struct. | 5.17I Residential invest. | 5.17J Changes in business inventories | 6.1A State & local govt purch. | 6.1B Federal govt purch. | 6.1C Federal non-defence purch. | 6.1D Defence purch. |
	(billions of dollars)					(per cent)					(per cent)			
1949	36.4	15.7	9.2	14.6	-3.1	13.2	5.68	3.33	5.28	-1.12	5.7	0.8	2.6	5.0
1950	55.1	17.8	10.0	20.5	6.8	18.1	5.85	3.29	6.74	2.24	5.7	0.8	1.5	4.7
1951	60.4	19.9	11.9	18.4	10.2	17.5	5.78	3.45	5.34	2.96	5.6	0.7	1.4	9.8
1952	53.6	19.7	12.2	18.6	3.1	14.8	5.44	3.37	5.14	0.86	5.7	0.7	1.8	12.7
1953	54.9	21.5	13.6	19.4	0.4	14.4	5.62	3.56	5.07	0.10	5.7	0.7	2.3	12.8
1954	54.2	20.8	13.9	21.1	-1.6	13.8	5.28	3.53	5.36	-0.41	6.3	0.7	1.7	10.6
1955	69.8	23.9	15.2	25.0	5.7	16.5	5.64	3.59	5.90	1.34	6.4	0.7	1.4	9.2
1956	72.6	26.3	18.2	23.5	4.6	16.3	5.90	4.08	5.27	1.03	6.7	0.7	1.3	9.1
1957	71.1	28.6	18.9	22.2	1.4	15.1	6.08	4.02	4.72	0.30	6.9	0.9	1.3	9.5
1958	63.6	24.9	17.5	22.7	-1.5	13.0	5.09	3.58	4.64	-0.31	7.2	1.1	1.7	9.4
1959	80.2	28.3	18.0	28.1	5.8	15.3	5.40	3.44	5.37	1.11	7.0	1.3	1.6	8.8
1960	78.3	29.7	19.2	26.3	3.1	14.4	5.45	3.53	4.83	0.57	7.3	1.2	1.7	8.3
1961	77.1	28.9	19.4	26.4	2.4	13.5	5.06	3.40	4.62	0.42	7.5	1.3	1.8	8.4
1962	87.7	32.1	20.5	29.0	6.1	14.4	5.29	3.38	4.78	1.00	7.5	1.3	2.1	8.6
1963	93.1	34.4	20.8	32.1	5.8	14.5	5.36	3.24	5.00	0.90	7.6	1.4	2.2	8.0
1964	99.6	38.7	22.7	32.8	5.4	14.6	5.66	3.32	4.79	0.79	7.7	1.5	2.3	7.4
1965	116.2	45.8	27.4	33.1	9.9	15.8	6.21	3.71	4.49	1.34	8.0	1.5	2.4	6.9
1966	128.6	53.0	30.5	30.9	14.2	16.0	6.61	3.80	3.85	1.77	8.0	1.8	2.3	7.7
1967	125.8	53.7	30.7	31.1	10.3	14.8	6.33	3.62	3.67	1.21	8.4	1.9	2.3	7.7
1968	137.3	58.8	32.9	37.7	7.9	14.8	6.36	3.56	4.08	0.85	8.5	2.0	2.3	8.6
1969	153.3	65.2	37.1	41.2	9.8	15.4	6.53	3.72	4.13	0.98	8.7	2.0	2.1	7.9

Year														
1970	148.9	66.1	39.2	40.5	3.1	14.0	6.20	3.67	3.80	0.29	8.9	2.3	2.1	7.2
1971	172.5	68.7	40.9	55.1	7.8	14.7	5.87	3.49	4.71	0.67	8.8	2.5	2.2	6.3
1972	202.1	78.5	44.5	68.6	10.5	15.7	6.12	3.47	5.35	0.82	8.3	2.9	2.2	6.0
1973	238.8	94.5	51.4	73.3	19.6	16.7	6.62	3.60	5.13	1.37	8.4	2.8	2.0	5.4
1974	240.8	103.6	57.0	64.8	15.4	15.4	6.65	3.66	4.16	0.99	8.9	2.8	2.2	5.3
1975	219.6	106.6	56.3	62.3	-5.6	12.6	6.12	3.23	3.57	-0.32	8.7	3.1	2.3	5.1
1976	277.7	119.9	60.1	81.7	16.0	14.4	6.22	3.12	4.24	0.83	8.3	3.2	2.2	4.8
1977	344.0	147.4	66.7	108.6	21.3	16.1	6.89	3.12	5.08	1.00	7.9	3.2	2.3	4.7
1978	416.8	178.0	81.0	129.2	28.6	17.4	7.44	3.39	5.40	1.20	7.8	3.2	2.2	4.5
1979	454.9	203.3	99.5	139.1	13.0	17.1	7.64	3.74	5.23	0.49	7.9	3.0	2.1	4.6
1980	437.0	208.9	113.9	122.5	-8.3	14.9	7.11	3.88	4.17	-0.28	7.9	3.0	2.2	4.9
1981	515.5	230.7	138.5	122.3	24.0	15.6	6.99	4.20	3.71	0.73	7.8	2.7	2.3	5.1
1982	447.3	223.4	143.3	105.1	-24.5	12.8	6.38	4.09	3.00	-0.70	8.1	2.4	2.3	5.5
1983	502.2	232.8	124.0	152.5	-7.1	13.4	6.19	3.30	4.05	-0.19	8.1	2.3	1.8	5.7
1984	664.8	274.9	141.1	181.1	67.7	16.3	6.75	3.46	4.45	1.66	8.1	2.3	1.9	5.7
1985	643.0	289.7	153.2	188.8	11.3	14.9	6.70	3.55	4.37	0.26	8.5	2.3	2.2	6.0
1986	659.4	296.2	139.0	217.3	6.9	14.5	6.52	3.06	4.78	0.15	8.8	2.3	1.9	6.1
1987	700.0	310.5	133.8	226.4	29.3	14.5	6.44	2.78	4.70	0.61	9.2	2.1	1.8	6.1
1988	750.1	346.8	140.3	232.4	30.6	14.5	6.72	2.72	4.50	0.59	9.2	2.2	1.6	5.8
1989	867.1	367.4	145.1	325.2	29.4	15.7	6.66	2.63	5.89	0.53	9.3	2.2	1.8	5.5

Table A25 Federal outlays by function, fiscal years 1940–91

Year	6.2A Natl defence	6.2B Education & train.	6.2C Health & medicare	6.2D Income & soc. sec.	6.2E Net interest	6.2F Other outlays	6.2G Total outlays	6.2H Natl defence	6.2I Education & train.	6.2J Health & medicare	6.2K Income & soc. sec.	6.2L Net interest	6.2M Other outlays
	(millions of dollars)							(per cent)					
1940	1 504	73	48	1 460	1 049	5 455	9 589	15.7	0.8	0.5	15.2	10.9	56.9
1941	6 062	142	53	1 628	1 116	4 979	13 980	43.4	1.0	0.4	11.6	8.0	35.6
1942	23 970	188	61	1 454	1 263	7 564	34 500	69.5	0.5	0.2	4.2	3.7	21.9
1943	63 212	198	73	1 136	1 786	12 504	78 909	80.1	0.3	0.1	1.4	2.3	15.8
1944	76 874	197	152	1 080	2 544	13 109	93 956	81.8	0.2	0.2	1.1	2.7	14.0
1945	81 585	234	186	1 173	3 549	8 457	95 184	85.7	0.2	0.2	1.2	3.7	8.9
1946	44 731	110	173	2 509	4 694	9 521	61 738	72.5	0.2	0.3	4.1	7.6	15.4
1947	13 059	97	146	2 762	4 903	15 964	36 931	35.4	0.3	0.4	7.5	13.3	43.2
1948	13 015	171	150	2 782	5 135	15 240	36 493	35.7	0.5	0.4	7.6	14.1	41.8
1949	13 097	165	183	3 580	5 414	18 131	40 570	32.3	0.4	0.5	8.8	13.3	44.7
1950	13 119	219	252	4 707	5 744	19 106	43 147	30.4	0.5	0.6	10.9	13.3	44.3
1951	22 544	227	307	4 442	5 628	12 649	45 797	49.2	0.5	0.7	9.7	12.3	27.6
1952	44 015	322	330	5 206	5 834	12 255	67 962	64.8	0.5	0.5	7.7	8.6	18.0
1953	50 413	425	318	6 128	6 450	13 035	76 769	65.7	0.6	0.4	8.0	8.4	17.0
1954	46 645	437	288	7 760	6 012	9 748	70 890	65.8	0.6	0.4	10.9	8.5	13.8
1955	40 245	573	271	9 122	6 030	12 268	68 509	58.7	0.8	0.4	13.3	8.8	17.9
1956	40 305	694	342	9 989	6 292	13 058	70 460	57.2	1.0	0.5	13.9	8.9	18.5
1957	42 760	672	461	11 522	6 679	14 647	76 741	55.7	0.9	0.6	15.0	8.7	19.1
1958	44 371	820	540	15 016	6 944	14 884	82 575	53.7	1.0	0.7	18.2	8.4	18.0
1959	46 617	870	654	17 247	7 070	19 646	92 104	50.6	0.9	0.7	18.7	7.7	21.3
1960	45 908	1 060	756	18 203	8 299	17 997	92 223	49.8	1.1	0.8	19.7	9.0	19.5
1961	47 381	1 227	873	21 227	8 108	18 979	97 795	48.4	1.3	0.9	21.7	8.3	19.4

Year													
1962	51 097	1 406	1 130	22 530	8 321	22 329	106 813	47.8	1.3	1.1	21.1	7.8	20.9
1963	52 257	1 502	1 379	24 084	9 215	22 874	111 311	46.9	1.3	1.2	21.6	8.3	20.5
1964	53 591	1 751	1 716	25 110	9 810	26 606	118 584	45.2	1.5	1.4	21.2	8.3	22.4
1965	49 578	2 284	1 704	25 702	10 357	28 805	118 430	41.9	1.9	1.4	21.7	8.7	24.3
1966	56 785	4 258	2 509	29 016	11 285	30 999	134 652	42.2	3.2	1.9	21.5	8.4	22.9
1967	70 081	5 853	6 669	31 164	12 588	25 901	152 254	46.0	3.8	4.4	20.5	8.3	17.0
1968	80 517	6 739	9 608	34 108	13 744	34 117	178 833	45.0	3.8	5.4	19.1	7.7	19.1
1969	81 232	6 525	11 611	37 699	15 791	31 690	184 548	44.0	3.5	6.3	20.4	8.6	17.2
1970	80 295	7 289	12 907	43 790	18 312	33 995	196 588	40.8	3.7	6.6	22.3	9.3	17.3
1971	75 808	9 839	14 716	55 426	19 602	36 034	211 425	35.9	4.7	7.0	26.2	9.3	17.0
1972	76 550	12 519	17 467	63 913	20 563	41 009	232 021	33.0	5.4	7.5	27.5	8.9	17.7
1973	71 541	12 735	18 832	72 965	22 782	48 219	249 074	29.0	5.2	7.6	29.5	9.2	19.5
1974	77 781	12 344	22 073	84 437	28 032	44 953	269 620	28.8	4.6	8.2	31.3	10.4	16.7
1975	85 552	15 870	27 648	108 610	30 911	57 594	326 185	26.2	4.9	8.5	33.3	9.5	17.7
1976	89 430	18 737	33 448	129 412	34 511	62 901	366 439	24.4	5.1	9.1	34.8	9.4	17.2
1977	97 501	20 985	38 785	137 915	38 009	69 530	402 725	24.2	5.2	9.6	34.2	9.4	17.3
1978	104 500	26 700	41 000	155 400	35 400	95 700	458 700	22.8	5.8	8.9	33.9	7.7	20.9
1979	116 300	30 200	47 000	170 500	42 600	96 900	503 500	23.1	6.0	9.3	33.9	8.5	19.2
1980	134 000	31 800	55 300	205 000	52 500	112 300	590 900	22.7	5.4	9.4	34.7	8.9	19.0
1981	157 513	33 709	66 015	239 307	68 734	112 931	678 209	23.2	5.0	9.7	35.3	10.1	16.7
1982	185 309	27 029	74 012	263 681	84 995	110 680	745 706	24.9	3.6	9.9	35.4	11.4	14.8
1983	209 903	26 606	81 229	293 322	89 774	107 493	808 327	26.0	3.3	10.0	36.3	11.1	13.3
1984	227 413	27 579	87 957	290 891	111 058	106 883	851 781	26.7	3.2	10.3	34.2	13.0	12.5
1985	252 748	29 342	99 364	316 823	129 430	118 609	946 316	26.7	3.1	10.5	33.5	13.7	12.5
1986	273 375	30 585	106 100	318 553	135 969	125 676	990 258	27.6	3.1	10.7	32.2	13.7	12.7
1987	281 999	29 724	115 088	330 603	138 570	107 846	1 003 830	28.1	3.0	11.5	32.9	13.8	10.7
1988	290 361	31 938	123 368	348 673	151 748	117 956	1 064 044	27.3	3.0	11.6	32.8	14.3	11.1
1989	303 559	36 684	133 354	368 573	169 137	131 336	1 142 643	26.6	3.2	11.7	32.3	14.8	11.5
1990	296 342	37 652	154 435	395 063	175 591	138 153	1 197 236	24.8	3.1	12.9	33.0	14.7	11.5
1991	303 251	41 005	162 313	418 549	172 979	135 234	1 233 331	24.6	3.3	13.2	33.9	14.0	11.0

Table A26 (a) Federal receipts by source, fiscal years 1940–91; (b) government budget surplus/deficit, 1929–89

	(a)									(b)				
	6.3A Indivi-dual income taxes	6.3B Cor-porate income taxes	6.3C Social insur-ance taxes	6.3D Other re-ceipts	6.3E Total re-ceipts	6.3F Indivi-dual income taxes	6.3G Cor-porate income taxes	6.3H Social insur-ance taxes	6.3I Other re-ceipts	6.4A Federal govt	6.4B State & local govt	6.5A GNP deflator (govt expd.) (1982=100)	6.5B Federal govt	6.5C State & local govt
Year	(millions of dollars)					(per cent)				(billions $) (nominal)			(blns of 1982 $) (real)	
1929	—	—	—	—	—	—	—	—	—	1.2	-0.2	9.4	12.8	-2.1
1930	—	—	—	—	—	—	—	—	—	0.3	-0.6	9.2	3.3	-6.5
1931	—	—	—	—	—	—	—	—	—	-2.1	-0.8	8.8	-23.8	-9.0
1932	—	—	—	—	—	—	—	—	—	-1.5	-0.3	8.1	-18.4	-3.7
1933	—	—	—	—	—	—	—	—	—	-1.3	-0.1	8.4	-15.5	-1.2
1934	—	—	—	—	—	—	—	—	—	-2.9	0.5	9.0	-32.4	5.6
1935	—	—	—	—	—	—	—	—	—	-2.6	0.6	9.0	-28.9	6.7
1936	—	—	—	—	—	—	—	—	—	-3.6	0.5	9.2	-39.3	5.5
1937	—	—	—	—	—	—	—	—	—	-0.4	0.7	9.4	-4.3	7.5
1938	—	—	—	—	—	—	—	—	—	-2.1	0.4	9.3	-22.5	4.3
1939	—	—	—	—	—	—	—	—	—	-2.2	0.0	9.4	-23.4	0.0
1940	1 110	978	1 715	3 076	6 879	16.1	14.2	24.9	44.7	-1.3	0.6	9.5	-13.7	6.3
1941	1 589	1 849	2 004	3 760	9 202	17.3	20.1	21.8	40.9	-5.1	1.3	10.6	-48.1	12.3
1942	3 238	4 740	2 429	4 697	15 104	21.4	31.4	16.1	31.1	-33.1	1.8	12.4	-266.9	14.5
1943	6 473	9 587	3 013	6 024	25 097	25.8	38.2	12.0	24.0	-46.6	2.5	12.5	-372.8	20.0
1944	20 179	15 255	3 428	8 956	47 818	42.2	31.9	7.2	18.7	-54.5	2.7	12.3	-443.1	22.0
1945	18 396	16 360	3 438	11 968	50 162	36.7	32.6	6.9	23.9	-42.1	2.6	11.8	-356.8	22.0
1946	16 132	12 235	3 078	12 092	43 537	37.1	28.1	7.1	27.8	3.5	1.9	12.3	28.5	15.4
1947	17 960	8 614	3 333	13 624	43 531	41.3	19.8	7.7	31.3	13.4	1.0	14.7	91.2	6.8
1948	19 310	9 678	3 966	12 403	45 357	42.6	21.3	8.7	27.3	8.4	0.1	16.3	51.5	0.6
1949	15 544	11 192	3 809	11 031	41 576	37.4	26.9	9.2	26.5	-2.4	-0.7	17.3	-13.9	-4.0
1950	15 747	10 449	4 386	10 358	40 940	38.5	25.5	10.7	25.3	9.1	-1.2	16.8	54.2	-7.1
1951	21 604	14 101	5 714	11 971	53 390	40.5	26.4	10.7	22.4	6.2	-0.4	18.3	33.9	-2.2
1952	27 918	21 226	6 496	12 371	68 011	41.0	31.2	9.6	18.2	-3.8	0.0	19.4	-19.6	0.0
1953	29 780	21 238	6 821	13 656	71 495	41.7	29.7	9.5	19.1	-7.0	0.1	19.8	-35.4	0.5
1954	29 542	21 101	7 210	11 866	69 719	42.4	30.3	10.3	17.0	-5.9	-1.1	20.1	-29.4	-5.5

Year														
1955	28 747	17 861	7 866	10 995	65 469	43.9	27.3	12.0	16.8	4.0	-1.3	20.8	19.2	-6.3
1956	32 188	20 880	9 323	12 156	74 547	43.2	28.0	12.5	16.3	5.7	-0.9	21.9	26.0	-4.1
1957	35 620	21 167	9 997	13 206	79 990	44.5	26.5	12.5	16.5	2.1	-1.4	22.9	9.2	-6.1
1958	34 724	20 074	11 239	13 599	79 636	43.6	25.2	14.1	17.1	-10.2	-2.3	24.1	-42.3	-9.5
1959	36 776	17 309	11 722	13 442	79 249	46.4	21.8	14.8	17.0	-1.2	-0.8	24.6	-4.9	-3.3
1960	40 741	21 494	14 684	15 573	92 492	44.0	23.2	15.9	16.8	3.0	0.1	24.9	12.0	0.4
1961	41 338	20 954	16 438	15 659	94 389	43.8	22.2	17.4	16.6	-3.9	-0.4	25.4	-15.4	-1.6
1962	45 571	20 523	17 046	16 536	99 676	45.7	20.6	17.1	16.6	-4.2	0.5	26.3	-16.0	1.9
1963	47 588	21 579	19 804	17 589	106 560	44.7	20.3	18.6	16.5	0.3	0.5	26.9	1.1	1.9
1964	48 697	23 493	22 012	18 460	112 662	43.2	20.9	19.5	16.4	-3.3	1.0	27.6	-12.0	3.6
1965	48 792	25 461	22 258	20 322	116 833	41.8	21.8	19.1	17.4	0.5	0.0	28.5	1.8	0.0
1966	55 446	30 073	25 567	19 770	130 856	42.4	23.0	19.5	15.1	-1.8	0.5	29.8	-6.0	1.7
1967	61 526	33 971	33 349	20 706	149 552	41.1	22.7	22.3	13.8	-13.2	-1.1	31.2	-42.3	-3.5
1968	68 726	28 665	39 918	21 658	153 671	44.7	18.7	22.5	14.1	-6.0	0.1	33.1	-18.1	0.3
1969	87 249	36 678	45 298	23 939	187 784	46.5	19.5	21.3	12.7	8.4	1.5	35.1	23.9	4.3
1970	90 412	32 829	48 578	25 204	193 743	46.7	16.9	23.4	13.0	-12.4	1.9	38.1	-32.5	5.0
1971	86 230	26 785	53 914	26 799	188 392	45.8	14.2	25.8	14.2	-22.0	2.6	41.0	-53.7	6.3
1972	94 737	32 166	64 542	27 832	208 649	45.4	15.4	25.8	13.3	-16.8	13.5	43.8	-38.4	30.8
1973	103 246	36 153	76 780	28 284	232 225	44.5	15.6	27.8	12.2	-5.6	13.4	47.1	-11.9	28.5
1974	118 952	38 620	86 441	30 580	264 932	44.9	14.6	29.0	11.5	-11.5	7.2	52.2	-22.0	13.8
1975	122 386	40 621	92 714	31 549	280 997	43.6	14.5	30.8	11.2	-69.3	4.5	57.7	-120.1	7.8
1976	131 603	41 409	108 688	34 279	300 005	43.9	13.8	30.9	11.4	-53.1	15.2	61.5	-86.3	24.7
1977	157 626	54 892	121 000	36 556	357 762	44.1	15.3	30.4	10.2	-45.9	26.9	65.8	-69.8	40.9
1978	181 000	60 000	138 900	37 700	399 700	45.3	15.0	30.3	9.4	-29.5	28.9	70.4	-41.9	41.1
1979	217 800	65 700	157 800	40 900	463 300	47.0	14.2	30.0	8.8	-16.1	27.6	76.8	-21.0	35.9
1980	244 100	64 600	182 720	50 600	517 100	47.2	12.5	30.5	9.8	-61.3	26.8	85.5	-71.7	31.3
1981	285 917	61 137	201 498	69 498	599 272	47.7	10.2	30.5	11.6	-63.8	34.1	93.4	-68.3	36.5
1982	297 744	49 207	208 994	69 317	617 766	48.2	8.0	32.6	11.2	-145.9	35.1	100.0	-145.9	35.1
1983	288 938	37 022	239 376	65 608	600 562	48.1	6.2	34.8	10.9	-176.0	47.5	104.0	-169.2	45.7
1984	298 415	56 893	265 163	71 773	666 457	44.8	8.5	35.9	10.8	-169.6	64.6	108.6	-156.2	59.5
1985	334 531	61 331	283 901	73 032	734 057	45.6	8.4	36.1	9.9	-196.9	65.1	112.3	-175.3	58.0
1986	348 959	63 143	303 318	73 088	769 091	45.4	8.2	36.9	9.5	-206.9	62.8	114.5	-180.7	54.8
1987	392 557	83 926	334 335	74 342	854 143	46.0	9.8	35.5	8.7	-161.4	51.3	118.5	-136.2	43.3
1988	401 181	94 508	359 416	78 930	908 954	44.1	10.4	36.8	8.7	-145.8	49.7	123.4	-118.2	40.3
1989	445 690	103 583	385 362	82 002	990 691	45.0	10.5	36.3	8.3	-149.9	45.0	128.7	-116.5	35.0
1990	489 444	112 030	421 449	86 615	1 073 451	45.6	10.4	35.9	8.1	–	–	–	–	–
1991	528 489	129 665		90 629	1 170 232	45.2	11.1	36.0	7.7	–	–	–	–	–

Table A27 State and local government revenue by source, selected fiscal years, 1927–88

Year	6.6A Property taxes	6.6B Sales & gross receipts taxes	6.6C Individual income taxes	6.6D Corporate net income taxes	6.6E Revenue from federal govt	6.6F All other rev.	6.6G Property taxes	6.6H Sales & gross receipts taxes	6.6I Individual income taxes	6.6J Corporate net income taxes	6.6K Revenue from federal govt	6.6L All other rev.
	(millions of dollars)						(per cent)					
1927	4 730	470	70	92	116	1 793	65.05	6.46	0.96	1.27	1.60	24.66
1928	–	–	–	–	–	–	–	–	–	–	–	–
1929	–	–	–	–	–	–	–	–	–	–	–	–
1930	–	–	–	–	–	–	–	–	–	–	–	–
1931	–	–	–	–	–	–	–	–	–	–	–	–
1932	4 487	752	74	79	232	1 643	61.74	10.35	1.02	1.09	3.19	22.61
1933	–	–	–	–	–	–	–	–	–	–	–	–
1934	4 076	1 008	80	49	1 016	1 449	53.09	13.13	1.04	0.64	13.23	18.87
1935	–	–	–	–	–	–	–	–	–	–	–	–
1936	4 093	1 484	153	113	948	1 604	48.76	17.68	1.82	1.35	11.29	19.11
1937	–	–	–	–	–	–	–	–	–	–	–	–
1938	4 440	1 794	218	165	800	1 811	48.11	19.44	2.36	1.79	8.67	19.63
1939	–	–	–	–	–	–	–	–	–	–	–	–
1940	4 430	1 982	224	156	945	1 872	46.10	20.63	2.33	1.62	9.83	19.48
1941	–	–	–	–	–	–	–	–	–	–	–	–
1942	4 537	2 351	276	272	858	2 123	43.55	22.57	2.65	2.61	8.24	20.38
1943	–	–	–	–	–	–	–	–	–	–	–	–
1944	4 604	2 289	342	451	954	2 269	42.20	20.98	3.14	4.13	8.75	20.80
1945	–	–	–	–	–	–	–	–	–	–	–	–

Year												
1946	4 986	2 986	422	447	855	2 661	40.35	24.16	3.42	3.62	6.92	21.53
1947	—	—	—	—	—	—	—	—	—	—	—	—
1948	6 126	4 442	543	592	1 861	3 685	35.52	25.75	3.15	3.43	10.79	21.36
1949	—	—	—	—	—	—	—	—	—	—	—	—
1950	7 349	5 154	788	593	2 486	4 541	35.14	24.65	3.77	2.84	11.89	21.72
1951	—	—	—	—	—	—	—	—	—	—	—	—
1952	8 652	6 357	998	846	2 566	5 763	34.36	25.24	3.96	3.36	10.19	22.89
1953	9 375	6 927	1 065	817	2 870	6 252	34.33	25.37	3.90	2.99	10.51	22.90
1954	9 967	7 276	1 127	778	2 966	6 897	34.36	25.08	3.88	2.68	10.22	23.77
1955	10 735	7 643	1 237	744	3 131	7 584	34.55	24.60	3.98	2.39	10.08	24.41
1956	11 749	8 691	1 538	890	3 335	8 465	33.89	25.07	4.44	2.57	9.62	24.42
1957	12 864	9 467	1 754	984	3 843	9 252	33.71	24.81	4.60	2.58	10.07	24.24
1958	14 047	9 829	1 759	1 018	4 865	9 699	34.08	23.85	4.27	2.47	11.80	23.53
1959	14 983	10 437	1 994	1 001	6 377	10 516	33.07	23.04	4.40	2.21	14.07	23.21
1960	16 405	11 849	2 463	1 180	6 974	11 634	32.48	23.46	4.88	2.34	13.81	23.04
1961	18 002	12 463	2 613	1 266	7 131	12 563	33.31	23.06	4.84	2.34	13.20	23.25
1962	19 054	13 494	3 037	1 308	7 871	13 489	32.71	23.16	5.21	2.25	13.51	23.16
1963	20 089	14 456	3 269	1 505	8 722	14 850	31.94	22.99	5.20	2.39	13.87	23.61
1964	21 241	15 762	3 791	1 695	10 002	15 951	31.04	23.03	5.54	2.48	14.61	23.31
1965	22 583	17 118	4 090	1 929	11 029	17 250	30.52	23.13	5.53	2.61	14.90	23.31
1966	24 670	19 085	4 760	2 038	13 214	19 269	29.71	22.98	5.73	2.45	15.91	23.21
1967	26 047	20 530	5 825	2 227	15 370	21 197	28.56	22.51	6.39	2.44	16.85	23.24
1968	27 747	22 911	7 308	2 518	17 181	23 598	27.40	22.63	7.22	2.49	16.97	23.30
1969	30 673	26 519	8 908	3 180	19 153	26 118	26.78	23.15	7.78	2.78	16.72	22.80
1970	34 054	30 322	10 812	3 738	21 857	29 971	26.04	23.19	8.27	2.86	16.72	22.92
1971	37 852	33 233	11 900	3 424	26 146	32 374	26.12	22.93	8.21	2.36	18.04	22.34
1972	42 877	37 518	15 227	4 416	31 342	36 162	25.59	22.39	9.09	2.64	18.71	21.58
1973	45 283	42 047	17 994	5 425	39 256	40 210	23.81	22.10	9.46	2.85	20.64	21.14

continued on p. 190

Table A27 continued

Year	6.6A Property taxes	6.6B Sales & gross receipts taxes	6.6C Individual income taxes	6.6D Corporate net income taxes	6.6E Revenue from federal govt	6.6F All other rev.	6.6G Property taxes	6.6H Sales & gross receipts taxes	6.6I Individual income taxes	6.6J Corporate net income taxes	6.6K Revenue from federal govt	6.6L All other rev.
	(millions of dollars)						(per cent)					
1974	47 705	46 098	19 491	6 015	41 820	46 541	22.97	22.20	9.39	2.90	20.14	22.41
1975	51 491	49 815	21 454	6 642	47 034	51 735	22.57	21.83	9.40	2.91	20.61	22.67
1976	57 001	54 547	24 575	7 273	55 589	57 191	22.25	21.29	9.59	2.84	21.70	22.32
1977	62 527	60 641	29 246	9 174	62 444	61 124	21.93	21.27	10.26	3.22	21.90	21.44
1978	66 422	67 596	33 176	10 738	69 592	68 436	21.02	21.39	10.50	3.40	22.03	21.66
1979	64 944	74 247	36 932	12 128	75 164	79 864	18.92	21.63	10.76	3.53	21.90	23.27
1980	68 499	79 927	42 080	13 321	83 029	95 466	17.92	20.91	11.01	3.48	21.72	24.97
1981	74 969	85 971	46 426	14 143	90 294	111 599	17.71	20.30	10.96	3.34	21.33	26.36
1982	82 067	93 613	50 738	15 028	87 282	128 926	17.93	20.45	11.09	3.28	19.07	28.17
1983	89 105	100 247	55 129	14 258	90 007	138 008	18.31	20.60	11.33	2.93	18.49	28.35
1984	96 457	114 097	64 529	17 141	96 935	153 570	17.77	21.02	11.89	3.16	17.86	28.30
1985	103 757	126 376	70 361	19 152	106 158	172 317	17.35	21.13	11.76	3.20	17.75	28.81
1986	111 709	135 005	74 365	19 994	113 099	187 314	17.42	21.05	11.59	3.12	17.63	29.20
1987	121 318	143 816	83 761	22 424	114 996	199 247	17.67	21.03	12.20	3.30	16.76	29.04
1988	132 204	156 257	88 349	23 741	117 602	208 956	18.19	21.49	12.15	3.26	16.17	28.74

Table A28   (a) State and local government expenditure by function, selected fiscal years, 1927–88; (b) tariff indexes, 1929–87

	(a)								(b)	
	6.7A	6.7B	6.7C	6.7D	6.7E	6.7F	6.7G	6.7H	6.8A	6.8B
			Public	All			Public	All	Average	Tariff
			welfare	others			welfare	others	tariff on	on dutiable
Year	Education	Highways			Education	Highways			all imports	imports
	(millions of dollars)				(per cent)				(per cent)	
1927	2 235	1 809	151	3 015	31.00	25.09	2.09	41.82	–	–
1928	–	–	–	–	–	–	–	–	–	–
1929	–	–	–	–	–	–	–	–	13.48	40.10
1930	–	–	–	–	–	–	–	–	14.83	44.71
1931	–	–	–	–	–	–	–	–	17.75	53.21
1932	2 311	1 741	444	3 269	29.76	22.42	5.72	42.10	19.59	59.06
1933	–	–	–	–	–	–	–	–	19.80	53.58
1934	1 831	1 509	889	2 952	25.50	21.01	12.38	41.11	18.41	46.70
1935	–	–	–	–	–	–	–	–	17.52	42.88
1936	2 177	1 425	827	3 215	28.48	18.64	10.82	42.06	16.84	39.28
1937	–	–	–	–	–	–	–	–	15.63	37.80
1938	2 491	1 650	1 069	3 547	28.45	18.84	12.21	40.50	15.46	39.30
1939	–	–	–	–	–	–	–	–	14.41	37.33
1940	2 638	1 573	1 156	3 862	28.58	17.04	12.53	41.85	12.51	35.64
1941	–	–	–	–	–	–	–	–	13.59	36.75
1942	2 586	1 490	1 225	3 889	28.14	16.21	13.33	42.32	11.51	31.96
1943	–	–	–	–	–	–	–	–	11.57	32.79
1944	2 793	1 200	1 133	3 737	31.51	13.54	12.78	42.16	9.45	31.41

continued on p. 192

Table A28 continued

	(a)								(b)	
	6.7A	6.7B	6.7C	6.7D	6.7E	6.7F	6.7G	6.7H	6.8A	6.8B
	Education	Highways	Public welfare	All others	Education	Highways	Public welfare	All others	Average tariff on all imports	Tariff on dutiable imports
Year	(millions of dollars)				(per cent)				(per cent)	
1945	–	–	–	–	–	–	–	–	9.29	28.24
1946	3 356	1 672	1 409	4 591	30.43	15.16	12.78	41.63	9.90	25.28
1947	–	–	–	–	–	–	–	–	7.55	19.34
1948	5 379	3 036	2 099	7 170	30.42	17.17	11.87	40.55	5.71	13.87
1949	–	–	–	–	–	–	–	–	5.53	13.46
1950	7 177	3 803	2 940	8 867	31.50	16.69	12.90	38.91	5.97	13.14
1951	–	–	–	–	–	–	–	–	5.47	12.26
1952	8 318	4 650	2 788	10 342	31.87	17.82	10.68	39.63	5.30	12.69
1953	9 390	4 987	2 914	10 619	33.64	17.87	10.44	38.05	5.42	12.02
1954	10 557	5 527	3 060	11 557	34.39	18.00	9.97	37.64	5.17	11.58
1955	11 907	6 452	3 168	12 197	35.31	19.13	9.39	36.17	5.59	11.95
1956	13 220	6 953	3 139	13 399	36.01	18.94	8.55	36.50	5.67	11.30
1957	14 134	7 816	3 485	14 940	35.01	19.36	8.63	37.00	5.76	10.79
1958	15 919	8 567	3 818	16 547	35.49	19.10	8.51	36.89	6.44	11.09
1959	17 283	9 592	4 136	17 876	35.35	19.62	8.46	36.57	7.02	11.53
1960	18 719	9 428	4 404	19 325	36.08	18.17	8.49	37.25	7.40	12.22
1961	20 574	9 844	4 720	21 063	36.61	17.52	8.40	37.48	7.21	12.10
1962	22 216	10 357	5 084	22 549	36.90	17.20	8.44	37.45	7.50	12.17

1963	23 776	11 136	5 481	24 423	36.68	17.18	8.46	37.68	7.29	11.54
1964	26 286	11 664	5 766	25 586	37.93	16.83	8.32	36.92	7.20	11.58
1965	28 563	12 221	6 315	27 579	38.25	16.36	8.46	36.93	7.72	11.86
1966	33 287	12 770	6 757	30 029	40.18	15.41	8.16	36.25	7.57	11.99
1967	37 919	13 932	8 218	33 281	40.62	14.92	8.80	35.65	7.54	12.20
1968	41 158	14 481	9 857	36 915	40.19	14.14	9.62	36.05	7.08	11.30
1969	47 238	15 417	12 110	41 963	40.47	13.21	10.37	35.95	7.11	11.19
1970	52 718	16 427	14 679	47 508	40.14	12.51	11.18	36.17	6.00	10.00
1971	59 413	18 095	18 226	54 940	39.43	12.01	12.10	36.46	6.00	9.00
1972	65 814	19 021	21 117	62 597	39.05	11.29	12.53	37.14	6.00	9.00
1973	69 714	18 615	23 582	69 446	38.44	10.26	13.00	38.29	5.00	8.00
1974	75 833	19 946	25 085	78 096	38.11	10.03	12.61	39.25	4.00	8.00
1975	87 858	22 528	28 155	92 180	38.08	9.76	12.20	39.95	4.00	6.00
1976	97 216	23 907	32 604	103 004	37.87	9.31	12.70	40.12	4.00	6.00
1977	102 780	23 058	35 906	112 472	37.48	8.41	13.09	41.02	4.00	5.00
1978	110 758	24 609	39 140	122 476	37.29	8.29	13.18	41.24	4.00	6.00
1979	119 448	28 440	41 898	137 731	36.47	8.68	12.79	42.05	3.00	7.00
1980	133 211	33 311	47 288	155 277	36.09	9.03	12.81	42.07	3.00	6.00
1981	145 784	34 603	54 121	172 941	35.78	8.49	13.28	42.44	3.00	5.00
1982	154 282	34 520	57 996	190 098	35.31	7.90	13.27	43.51	4.00	5.00
1983	163 876	36 655	60 906	205 079	35.13	7.86	13.06	43.96	4.00	5.00
1984	176 108	39 419	66 414	223 068	34.87	7.81	13.15	44.17	4.00	5.00
1985	192 676	44 989	71 479	244 745	34.79	8.12	12.90	44.19	4.00	5.00
1986	210 819	49 368	75 868	269 540	34.81	8.15	12.53	44.51	4.00	6.00
1987	226 658	52 199	82 520	294 687	34.55	7.96	12.58	44.92	4.00	5.00
1988	242 683	55 621	89 101	317 492	34.43	7.89	12.64	45.04	3.00	5.00
									–	–

Table A29   Trade per capita vs GNP per capita for 114 countries, 1985

No. Country	7.1A Population (millions)	7.1B GNP	7.1C Exports	7.1D Imports	7.1E Trade*
			(US dollars)		
1 United Arab Emirates	1.4	19 270	4890.00	11 120.71	8005.36
2 United States	239.3	16 690	1360.55	960.04	1160.29
3 Switzerland	6.5	16 370	4997.69	5 171.85	5084.77
4 Kuwait	1.7	14 480	3345.88	5 341.18	4343.53
5 Norway	4.2	14 370	3476.43	4 714.05	4095.24
6 Canada	25.4	13 680	2677.36	3 558.62	3117.99
7 Sweden	8.4	11 890	3201.90	3 723.45	3462.68
8 Japan	120.8	11 300	957.70	1 574.64	1266.17
9 Denmark	5.1	11 200	3429.41	3 328.24	3378.82
10 Germany, West	61.0	10 940	2365.21	2 976.23	2670.72
11 Finland	4.9	10 890	2487.55	3 116.33	2801.94
12 Australia	15.8	10 830	1516.58	1 656.33	1586.46
13 France	55.2	9 540	1899.29	1 841.21	1870.25
14 Netherlands	14.5	9 290	5262.97	4 949.52	5106.24
15 Austria	7.6	9 120	2709.87	2 340.53	2525.20
16 Saudi Arabia	11.5	8 850	2043.57	2 751.39	2397.48
17 United Kingdom	56.5	8 460	1785.93	1 797.17	1791.55
18 Belgium	9.9	8 280	5692.93	5 464.24	5578.59
19 Germany, East	16.7	8 000	246.47	316.59	281.53
20 Singapore	2.6	7 420	9820.00	7 153.08	8486.54
21 USSR	278.9	7 235	142.59	138.03	140.31
22 Libya	3.8	7 170	1269.21	3 144.74	2206.97
23 New Zealand	3.3	7 010	1576.36	1 952.12	1764.24
24 Oman	1.2	6 730	2513.33	3 829.17	3171.25
25 Italy	57.1	6 520	1379.37	1 366.92	1373.14
26 Hong Kong	5.4	6 230	5473.70	4 556.85	5015.28
27 Trinidad/Tobago	1.2	6 020	1251.67	1 714.17	1482.92
28 Czechoslovakia	15.5	5 429	310.06	366.13	338.10
29 Israel	4.2	4 990	1875.24	1 328.10	1601.67
30 Ireland	3.6	4 850	2677.78	2 768.61	2723.19
31 Spain	38.6	4 290	735.88	664.95	700.41
32 Greece	9.9	3 550	1144.44	595.15	869.80
33 Venezuela	17.3	3 080	397.86	800.92	599.39
34 Bulgaria	9.0	2 806	346.00	234.44	290.22
35 Algeria	21.9	2 550	378.08	608.63	493.36
36 Korea, Rep. of	41.1	2 150	583.65	634.48	609.06
37 Argentina	30.5	2 130	125.38	312.46	218.92
38 Panama	2.2	2 100	3314.09	897.73	2105.91
39 Mexico	78.8	2 080	233.93	364.49	299.21
40 Yugoslavia	23.1	2 070	520.39	539.70	530.04
41 Poland	37.2	2 050	283.90	318.31	301.10
42 Romania	22.7	2 020	338.02	461.54	399.78
43 South Africa	32.4	2 010	242.87	363.27	303.07

44	Malaysia	15.6	2 000	756.15	1 157.82	956.99
45	Portugal	10.2	1 970	707.65	589.12	648.38
46	Hungary	10.6	1 950	712.92	851.32	782.12
47	Uruguay	3.0	1 650	248.67	451.00	349.83
48	Brazil	135.6	1 640	102.63	213.71	158.17
49	Syrian Arab Rep.	10.5	1 570	329.62	165.90	247.76
50	Jordan	3.5	1 560	1090.00	278.29	684.14
51	Chile	12.1	1 430	219.42	345.45	282.44
52	Colombia	28.4	1 320	136.06	135.42	135.74
53	Costa Rica	2.6	1 300	407.31	466.54	436.92
54	Guatemala	8.0	1 250	135.25	155.38	145.31
55	Tunisia	7.1	1 190	374.65	233.24	303.94
56	Ecuador	9.4	1 160	188.30	369.26	278.78
57	Congo, PR	1.9	1 110	265.79	621.58	443.68
58	Mauritius	1.0	1 090	412.00	438.00	425.00
59	Turkey	50.2	1 080	224.02	158.61	191.31
60	Peru	18.6	1 010	86.56	173.33	129.95
61	Jamaica	2.2	940	468.18	325.45	396.82
62	Paraguay	3.7	860	188.11	124.86	156.49
63	Botswana	1.1	840	92.73	114.55	103.64
64	El Salvador	4.8	820	215.00	164.17	189.58
65	Cameroon	10.2	810	138.14	250.10	194.12
66	Nigeria	99.7	800	66.49	153.37	109.93
67	Thailand	51.7	800	160.97	151.62	156.30
68	Dominican Republic	6.4	790	244.53	190.47	217.50
69	Nicaragua	3.3	770	159.39	102.42	130.91
70	Honduras	4.4	720	178.41	200.23	189.32
71	Papua N. Guinea	3.5	680	231.14	289.14	260.14
72	Zimbabwe	8.4	680	51.07	100.83	75.95
73	Cote d'Ivoire	10.1	660	139.90	323.27	231.58
74	Egypt, Arab Rep.	48.5	610	248.12	122.70	185.41
75	Philippines	54.7	580	105.17	111.46	108.32
76	Morocco	21.9	560	177.49	125.39	151.44
77	Yemen Arab Republic	8.0	550	174.13	14.50	94.31
78	Indonesia	162.2	530	42.48	121.50	81.99
79	Yemen, PDR	2.1	530	325.24	163.53	244.29
80	Bolivia	6.4	470	85.78	103.13	94.45
81	Lesotho	1.5	470	16.67	4.00	10.33
82	Liberia	2.2	470	935.00	424.09	679.55
83	Mauritania	1.7	420	177.06	187.65	182.35
84	Zambia	6.7	390	80.30	124.78	102.54
85	Ghana	12.7	380	51.81	54.25	53.03
86	Pakistan	96.2	380	62.52	30.06	46.29
87	Sri Lanka	15.8	380	120.19	86.20	103.20
88	Senegal	6.6	370	128.18	66.06	97.12
89	Sierra Leone	3.7	350	40.54	40.27	40.41
90	Guinea	6.2	320	54.84	85.32	70.08

* Trade is the average of exports and imports. *continued on p. 196*

Table A29   continued

No. Country	7.1A Population (millions)	7.1B GNP	7.1C Exports	7.1D Imports	7.1E Trade*
				(US dollars)	
91 China	1040.3	310	36.87	29.67	33.27
92 Haiti	5.9	310	107.63	83.56	95.59
93 Sudan	21.9	300	65.25	28.31	46.78
94 Kenya	20.4	290	68.63	58.48	63.55
95 Tanzania	22.2	290	40.05	17.30	28.67
96 Rwanda	6.0	280	29.17	21.33	25.25
97 Somalia	5.4	280	64.07	23.52	43.80
98 India	765.1	270	21.10	14.40	17.75
99 Benin	4.0	260	108.00	41.50	74.75
100 C. African Rep.	2.6	260	36.15	46.54	41.35
101 Niger	6.4	250	41.41	32.97	37.19
102 Madagascar	10.2	240	32.65	29.31	30.98
103 Burundi	4.7	230	29.79	23.40	26.60
104 Togo	3.0	230	131.33	72.00	101.67
105 Burma	36.9	190	15.91	12.20	14.05
106 Malawi	7.0	170	16.43	41.29	28.86
107 Zaire	30.6	170	35.00	56.41	45.70
108 Bhutan	1.2	160	0.00	0.00	0.00
109 Mozambique	13.8	160	30.22	10.65	20.43
110 Nepal	16.5	160	16.12	8.67	12.39
111 Bangladesh	100.6	150	22.88	11.00	16.94
112 Burkina Faso	7.9	150	32.45	7.95	20.20
113 Mali	7.5	150	49.33	11.87	30.60
114 Ethiopia	42.3	110	26.43	9.46	17.94

* Trade is the average of exports and imports.

Table A30   Relative shares of world trade, average of exports and imports, 1960–86

Year	7.2A Western Europe	7.2B Japan	7.2C US & Canada	7.2D Eastern Europe	7.2E Asia	7.2F OPEC	7.2G Africa	7.2H Western Hemisph.	7.2I Australia & N. Zeal.
Millions of dollars									
1960	54 145	3 968	23 985	2 359	10 179	6 956	5 291	7 964	3 156
1961	57 818	4 555	24 550	3 033	9 691	6 956	5 395	8 377	2 997
1962	62 009	4 781	26 091	3 654	9 756	6 956	5 500	8 651	3 231
1963	68 029	5 630	27 713	3 857	10 147	6 956	6 111	8 739	3 641
1964	75 721	6 727	30 963	5 150	10 518	7 803	7 010	9 611	4 155
1965	79 325	7 128	32 378	5 512	10 387	8 409	7 125	9 755	4 039
1966	86 254	8 222	36 915	6 130	11 562	8 754	7 244	10 771	4 124
1967	90 191	9 677	39 422	6 432	11 807	9 245	7 537	10 796	4 316
1968	100 219	11 098	45 537	6 861	12 509	10 498	8 222	11 887	4 511

1969	123 397	14 001	51 880	9 642	16 450	11 644	9 300	13 473	5 227
1970	143 449	17 316	58 055	10 800	18 078	13 480	10 598	15 241	6 014
1971	160 769	19 799	64 204	11 807	19 859	16 885	10 828	16 033	6 457
1972	193 129	23 881	74 388	14 440	23 184	20 388	11 641	18 503	7 344
1973	267 898	35 470	97 141	19 712	34 536	30 932	15 599	19 430	10 715
1974	359 424	52 616	134 067	28 585	46 353	79 228	23 221	42 561	14 924
1975	373 867	52 283	135 465	33 711	46 725	82 794	23 971	42 082	14 149
1976	419 859	61 176	156 144	36 993	53 588	100 874	24 520	45 860	15 960
1977	478 529	70 455	176 694	40 645	64 202	118 333	28 878	52 922	16 680
1978	568 635	84 731	205 121	46 594	80 332	121 104	32 320	57 945	18 444
1979	726 513	102 057	251 587	57 024	110 995	158 207	38 834	76 122	22 998
1980	861 010	130 526	298 692	93 536	135 470	219 434	48 121	97 200	27 217
1981	780 342	139 659	315 747	91 068	142 649	219 654	45 698	101 424	29 100
1982	745 920	131 766	286 577	81 688	140 256	192 637	41 595	86 324	29 223
1983	726 369	132 866	299 919	80 679	145 666	163 220	37 398	80 564	26 426
1984	743 401	147 847	350 985	79 530	162 179	148 569	39 401	87 595	29 971
1985	779 723	152 953	356 856	80 541	168 445	130 057	37 938	84 966	30 268
1986	789 784	168 019	376 365	82 399	182 670	97 102	39 870	82 874	30 224

Per cent

1960	45.88	3.36	20.33	2.00	8.63	5.89	4.48	6.75	2.67
1961	46.86	3.69	19.90	2.46	7.85	5.64	4.37	6.79	2.43
1962	47.47	3.66	19.97	2.80	7.47	5.32	4.21	6.62	2.47
1963	48.31	4.00	19.68	2.74	7.21	4.94	4.34	6.21	2.59
1964	48.03	4.27	19.64	3.27	6.67	4.95	4.45	6.10	2.64
1965	48.35	4.34	19.74	3.36	6.33	5.13	4.34	5.95	2.46
1966	47.93	4.57	20.51	3.41	6.42	4.86	4.03	5.98	2.29
1967	47.61	5.11	20.81	3.40	6.23	4.88	3.98	5.70	2.28
1968	47.42	5.25	21.55	3.25	5.92	4.97	3.89	5.62	2.13
1969	48.39	5.49	20.34	3.78	6.45	4.57	3.65	5.28	2.05
1970	48.95	5.91	19.81	3.69	6.17	4.60	3.62	5.20	2.05
1971	49.22	6.06	19.66	3.61	6.08	5.17	3.31	4.91	1.98
1972	49.92	6.17	19.23	3.73	5.99	5.27	3.01	4.78	1.90
1973	50.41	6.67	18.28	3.71	6.50	5.82	2.94	3.66	2.02
1974	46.02	6.74	17.17	3.66	5.94	10.14	2.97	5.45	1.91
1975	46.44	6.49	16.83	4.19	5.80	10.28	2.98	5.23	1.76
1976	45.89	6.69	17.07	4.04	5.86	11.02	2.68	5.01	1.74
1977	45.69	6.73	16.87	3.88	6.13	11.30	2.76	5.05	1.59
1978	46.79	6.97	16.88	3.83	6.61	9.97	2.66	4.77	1.52
1979	47.04	6.61	16.29	3.69	7.19	10.24	2.51	4.93	1.49
1980	45.05	6.83	15.63	4.89	7.09	11.48	2.52	5.09	1.42
1981	41.83	7.49	16.93	4.88	7.65	11.78	2.45	5.44	1.56
1982	42.97	7.59	16.51	4.71	8.08	11.10	2.40	4.97	1.68
1983	42.90	7.85	17.71	4.77	8.60	9.64	2.21	4.76	1.56
1984	41.54	8.26	19.61	4.44	9.06	8.30	2.20	4.90	1.67
1985	42.80	8.40	19.59	4.42	9.25	7.14	2.08	4.66	1.66
1986	42.71	9.09	20.35	4.46	9.88	5.25	2.16	4.48	1.63

Appendix: Data Tables

Table A31   Relative shares of world trade, exports by major regions, 1960–86

Year	7.3A Western Europe	7.3B Japan	7.3C US & Canada	7.3D Eastern Europe	7.3E Asia	7.3F OPEC	7.3G Africa	7.3H Western Hemisph.	7.3I Australia & N. Zeal.
Millions of dollars									
1960	54 276	3 839	20 139	2 171	10 753	8 871	5 146	8 023	3 031
1961	58 024	4 876	19 927	2 841	10 352	8 871	5 312	8 570	2 612
1962	62 314	4 578	21 522	3 445	10 320	8 871	5 310	8 494	2 827
1963	69 313	5 676	22 661	3 618	10 544	8 871	6 017	8 192	3 128
1964	77 378	6 708	24 975	4 920	11 360	9 879	6 849	9 042	3 684
1965	80 953	6 479	28 596	5 345	11 464	10 242	7 241	9 336	4 027
1966	87 464	7 558	33 445	5 985	12 872	10 879	7 065	10 502	3 798
1967	91 085	9 201	35 456	6 204	13 307	11 388	7 573	10 593	4 091
1968	100 769	10 216	42 522	6 638	14 008	13 090	8 016	11 999	4 279
1969	123 867	12 609	47 670	9 435	18 260	14 359	8 881	13 461	4 550
1970	144 571	15 625	51 548	10 746	19 974	17 021	10 612	15 423	5 308
1971	160 673	16 139	60 487	11 730	21 702	22 221	11 582	16 821	5 554
1972	193 434	19 593	72 069	15 120	24 222	26 610	11 656	19 382	5 597
1973	268 608	34 327	89 244	20 983	35 568	41 506	15 445	14 879	8 422
1974	374 292	54 046	128 400	29 748	51 078	125 641	23 891	48 297	14 066
1975	376 580	50 118	123 436	37 622	51 825	113 507	25 710	48 197	12 249
1976	432 837	57 192	151 474	40 491	54 452	137 650	25 685	51 732	13 930
1977	485 455	61 837	180 182	42 191	65 547	151 276	29 015	55 842	15 064
1978	562 329	70 005	206 641	48 406	86 629	145 644	32 640	61 724	17 195
1979	740 522	96 129	249 775	57 171	123 084	217 492	38 063	81 165	20 584
1980	889 726	123 915	287 187	93 437	142 930	305 964	49 222	106 259	24 643
1981	792 609	124 130	309 157	90 755	155 623	282 667	50 392	109 801	28 585
1982	749 967	114 910	275 811	78 518	150 661	224 892	45 399	84 406	28 562
1983	725 624	113 540	310 718	77 546	156 122	182 079	39 536	69 574	26 019
1984	739 559	120 778	382 008	74 837	169 537	170 824	40 578	75 307	28 648
1985	766 377	115 690	393 584	77 903	178 226	154 545	37 162	72 555	29 164
1986	911 870	112 607	424 005	80 523	186 687	99 832	39 308	75 426	29 487
Per cent									
1960	46.69	3.30	17.32	1.87	9.25	7.63	4.43	6.90	2.61
1961	47.80	4.02	16.42	2.34	8.53	7.31	4.38	7.06	2.15
1962	48.80	3.58	16.85	2.70	8.08	6.95	4.16	6.65	2.22
1963	50.22	4.11	16.42	2.62	7.64	6.43	4.36	5.94	2.27
1964	49.99	4.33	16.13	3.18	7.34	6.38	4.42	5.84	2.38
1965	49.46	3.96	17.47	3.27	7.00	6.26	4.42	5.70	2.46
1966	48.71	4.21	18.63	3.33	7.17	6.06	3.93	5.85	2.12
1967	48.22	4.87	18.77	3.28	7.04	6.03	4.01	5.61	2.17
1968	47.64	4.83	20.10	3.14	6.62	6.19	3.79	5.67	2.02
1969	48.94	4.98	18.84	3.73	7.21	5.67	3.51	5.32	1.80
1970	49.71	5.37	17.72	3.69	6.87	5.85	3.65	5.30	1.83
1971	49.15	4.94	18.50	3.59	6.64	6.80	3.54	5.15	1.70
1972	49.89	5.05	18.59	3.90	6.25	6.86	3.01	5.00	1.44
1973	50.78	6.49	16.87	3.97	6.72	7.85	2.92	2.81	1.59
1974	44.06	6.36	15.12	3.50	6.01	14.79	2.81	5.69	1.66
1975	44.87	5.97	14.71	4.48	6.18	13.52	3.06	5.74	1.46
1976	44.83	5.92	15.69	4.19	5.64	14.26	2.66	5.36	1.44
1977	44.68	5.69	16.59	3.88	6.03	13.92	2.67	5.14	1.39
1978	45.67	5.69	16.78	3.93	7.04	11.83	2.65	5.01	1.40
1979	45.60	5.92	15.38	3.52	7.58	13.39	2.34	5.00	1.27
1980	43.97	6.12	14.19	4.62	7.06	15.12	2.43	5.25	1.22
1981	40.78	6.39	15.91	4.67	8.01	14.54	2.59	5.65	1.47
1982	42.78	6.55	15.73	4.48	8.59	12.83	2.59	4.81	1.63

1983	42.66	6.68	18.27	4.56	9.18	10.71	2.32	4.09	1.53
1984	41.04	6.70	21.20	4.15	9.41	9.48	2.25	4.18	1.59
1985	41.99	6.34	21.56	4.27	9.76	8.47	2.04	3.98	1.60
1986	46.53	5.75	21.64	4.11	9.53	5.09	2.01	3.85	1.50

Table A32   Relative shares of world trade, imports by major regions, 1960–86

Year	7.4A Western Europe	7.4B Japan	7.4C US & Canada	7.4D Eastern Europe	7.4E Asia	7.4F OPEC	7.4G Africa	7.4H Western Hemisph.	7.4I Australia & N. Zeal.
Millions of dollars									
1960	54 015	4 097	27 831	2 546	9 604	5 041	5 436	7 906	3 281
1961	57 612	4 235	29 174	3 225	9 030	5 041	5 479	8 184	3 382
1962	61 704	4 984	30 661	3 864	9 192	5 041	5 690	8 808	3 626
1963	66 744	5 585	32 765	4 095	9 751	5 041	6 205	9 287	4 155
1964	74 065	6 745	36 950	5 380	9 677	5 727	7 172	10 181	4 625
1965	77 697	7 777	36 160	5 680	9 310	6 575	7 009	10 174	4 050
1966	85 043	8 886	40 384	6 275	10 251	6 628	7 423	11 040	4 451
1967	89 297	10 154	43 389	6 661	10 308	7 101	7 502	10 999	4 541
1968	99 670	11 980	48 551	7 084	11 009	7 905	8 428	11 775	4 742
1969	122 926	15 393	56 090	9 848	14 640	8 929	9 719	13 485	5 904
1970	142 327	19 006	64 561	10 853	16 181	9 938	10 583	15 059	6 719
1971	160 864	23 459	67 920	11 883	18 015	11 549	10 074	15 244	7 360
1972	192 823	28 169	76 706	13 759	22 145	14 166	11 626	17 623	9 091
1973	267 187	36 613	105 038	18 441	33 503	20 358	15 752	23 981	13 007
1974	344 555	51 186	139 734	27 422	41 628	32 814	22 550	36 824	15 781
1975	371 154	54 447	147 494	29 799	41 624	52 081	22 232	35 966	16 048
1976	406 880	65 159	160 813	33 494	52 724	64 097	23 354	39 988	17 989
1977	471 603	79 073	173 205	39 098	62 856	85 389	28 741	50 002	18 296
1978	574 940	99 456	203 600	44 781	74 035	96 563	32 000	54 165	19 692
1979	712 503	107 984	253 399	56 877	98 905	98 922	39 605	71 079	25 411
1980	832 294	137 137	310 196	93 634	128 009	132 903	47 020	88 141	29 790
1981	768 074	155 187	322 337	91 381	129 674	156 640	41 003	93 046	29 615
1982	741 873	148 622	297 343	84 857	129 850	160 382	37 790	88 241	29 883
1983	727 113	152 191	289 120	83 812	135 209	144 360	35 260	91 553	26 833
1984	747 242	174 916	319 962	84 223	154 820	126 314	38 223	99 883	31 293
1985	793 069	190 216	320 127	83 179	158 663	105 569	38 713	97 377	31 372
1986	667 698	223 431	328 724	84 275	178 653	94 371	40 431	90 321	30 961
Per cent									
1960	45.10	3.42	23.24	2.13	8.02	4.21	4.54	6.60	2.74
1961	45.96	3.38	23.27	2.57	7.20	4.02	4.37	6.53	2.70
1962	46.20	3.73	22.95	2.89	6.88	3.77	4.26	6.59	2.71
1963	46.47	3.89	22.81	2.85	6.79	3.51	4.32	6.47	2.89
1964	46.14	4.20	23.02	3.35	6.03	3.57	4.47	6.34	2.88
1965	47.25	4.73	21.99	3.45	5.66	4.00	4.26	6.19	2.46
1966	47.15	4.93	22.39	3.48	5.68	3.67	4.12	6.12	2.47
1967	47.01	5.35	22.84	3.51	5.43	3.74	3.95	5.79	2.39
1968	47.20	5.67	22.99	3.36	5.21	3.74	3.99	5.58	2.25
1969	47.84	5.99	21.83	3.83	5.70	3.48	3.78	5.25	2.30
1970	48.21	6.44	21.87	3.68	5.48	3.37	3.58	5.10	2.28
1971	49.29	7.19	20.81	3.64	5.52	3.54	3.09	4.67	2.26
1972	49.94	7.30	19.87	3.56	5.74	3.67	3.01	4.56	2.35

continued on p. 200

Table A32   continued

Year	7.4A Western Europe %	7.4B Japan %	7.4C US & Canada %	7.4D Eastern Europe %	7.4E Asia %	7.4F OPEC %	7.4G Africa %	7.4H Western Hemisph. %	7.4I Australia & N. Zeal. %
1973	50.05	6.86	19.67	3.45	6.28	3.81	2.95	4.49	2.44
1974	48.36	7.18	19.61	3.85	5.84	4.61	3.16	5.17	2.21
1975	48.15	7.06	19.13	3.87	5.40	6.76	2.88	4.67	2.08
1976	47.07	7.54	18.60	3.87	6.10	7.41	2.70	4.63	2.08
1977	46.77	7.84	17.18	3.88	6.23	8.47	2.85	4.96	1.81
1978	47.94	8.29	16.98	3.73	6.17	8.05	2.67	4.52	1.64
1979	48.65	7.37	17.30	3.88	6.75	6.75	2.70	4.85	1.73
1980	46.26	7.62	17.24	5.20	7.12	7.39	2.61	4.90	1.66
1981	42.98	8.68	18.04	5.11	7.26	8.77	2.29	5.21	1.66
1982	43.16	8.65	17.30	4.94	7.55	9.33	2.20	5.13	1.74
1983	43.14	9.03	17.15	4.97	8.02	8.57	2.09	5.43	1.59
1984	42.05	9.84	18.01	4.74	8.71	7.11	2.15	5.62	1.76
1985	43.62	10.46	17.61	4.57	8.73	5.81	2.13	5.36	1.73
1986	38.40	12.85	18.90	4.85	10.27	5.43	2.33	5.19	1.78

Table A33 (a) World trade total, average of imports and exports, 1865–87; (b) exports and imports as percentage of GCP, 1929–89

(a)

Year	7.5A Trade total	Year	7.5A Trade total
	(bns of 1967 US $)		
1865	–	1927	66 207
1866	–	1928	67 370
1867	13 299	1929	69 878
1868	13 299	1930	62 287
1869	–	1931	52 806
1870	–	1932	39 964
1871	–	1933	35 544
1872	15 780	1934	30 181
1873	15 780	1935	28 814
1874	–	1936	30 815
1875	–	1937	34 944
1876	–	1938	34 198
1877	16 463	1939	–
1878	–	1940	–
1879	–	1941	–
1880	21 535	1942	–
1881	22 690	1943	–
1882	23 866	1944	–

(b)

Year	7.6A GCP	7.6B Exports	7.6C Imports	7.6D Exports	7.6E Imports	7.3F Net exports
	(billions of 1982 US dollars)				(per cent)	
1929	733.1	42.1	37.4	6.31	5.84	0.47
1930	704.1	–	–	5.21	4.68	0.53
1931	699.3	–	–	3.85	3.67	0.18
1932	666.5	–	–	3.05	2.95	0.09
1933	663.8	22.7	24.2	3.04	2.96	0.08
1934	685.4	–	–	3.40	3.30	0.11
1935	726.2	–	–	3.43	3.65	-0.22
1936	796.9	–	–	3.43	3.64	-0.22
1937	811.3	–	–	4.09	4.30	-0.21
1938	820.0	–	–	3.97	3.06	0.91
1939	865.5	36.2	30.1	4.17	3.08	1.08
1940	905.0	40.0	31.7	4.63	3.13	1.50
1941	1 009.3	42.0	38.2	4.40	3.37	1.03
1942	1 133.6	29.1	36.9	3.00	2.90	0.10
1943	1 300.9	25.1	48.0	2.36	3.32	-0.96
1944	1 397.0	27.3	51.1	2.61	3.37	-0.76
1945	1 381.0	35.2	54.1	3.41	3.63	-0.22
1946	1 141.4	69.0	42.0	6.87	3.31	3.56

continued on p. 202

Table A33 continued

(a)

Year	7.5A Trade total	Year	7.5A Trade total
	(bns of 1967 US $)		
1883	24 719	1945	–
1884	26 013	1946	–
1885	25 426	1947	64 248
1886	25 388	1948	67 150
1887	26 722	1949	71 283
1888	26 981	1950	69 438
1889	28 187	1951	85 401
1890	19 106	1952	85 553
1891	29 566	1953	95 423
1892	31 234	1954	–
1893	30 370	1955	–
1894	33 158	1956	–
1895	33 639	1957	110 000
1896	37 020	1958	117 300
1897	38 083	1959	–
1898	–	1960	139 100
1899	–	1961	–
1900	–	1962	154 000
1901	39 109	1963	167 200

(b)

Year	7.6A GCP	7.6B Exports	7.6C Imports	7.6D Exports	7.6E Imports	7.3F Net exports
	(billions of 1982 US dollars)			(per cent)		
1947	1 110.0	82.3	39.9	8.27	3.41	4.87
1948	1 152.5	66.2	47.1	6.45	3.88	2.57
1949	1 178.5	65.0	46.2	5.92	3.54	2.38
1950	1 271.1	59.2	54.6	4.75	4.04	0.71
1951	1 373.5	72.0	57.4	5.72	4.44	1.28
1952	1 422.7	70.1	63.3	5.30	4.42	0.88
1953	1 478.2	66.9	69.7	4.72	4.39	0.33
1954	1 498.6	70.0	67.5	4.78	4.13	0.65
1955	1 563.7	76.9	76.9	4.98	4.26	0.72
1956	1 590.8	87.9	83.6	5.63	4.46	1.17
1957	1 620.8	94.9	87.9	5.98	4.44	1.54
1958	1 651.5	82.4	92.8	4.98	4.30	0.68
1959	1 723.9	83.7	101.9	4.77	4.49	0.28
1960	1 762.2	98.4	102.4	5.49	4.39	1.09
1961	1 831.4	100.7	103.3	5.44	4.17	1.27
1962	1 904.1	106.9	114.4	5.45	4.31	1.14
1963	1 986.5	114.7	116.6	5.54	4.28	1.27
1964	2 081.5	128.8	122.8	5.90	4.32	1.58
1965	2 186.0	132.0	134.7	5.81	4.51	1.30

Year	
1902	37 921
1903	39 726
1904	40 584
1905	43 452
1906	46 412
1907	47 250
1908	45 710
1909	45 215
1910	48 049
1911	54 865
1912	56 584
1913	56 863
1914	–
1915	–
1916	–
1917	–
1918	–
1919	–
1920	41 332
1921	41 550
1922	45 391
1923	47 881
1924	56 267
1925	60 694
1926	60 116

Year	
1964	186 900
1965	198 800
1966	209 400
1967	221 000
1968	239 400
1969	262 000
1970	292 000
1971	283 200
1972	321 000
1973	392 800
1974	484 600
1975	508 835
1976	548 448
1977	588 488
1978	632 193
1979	706 842
1980	751 223
1981	683 150
1982	622 964
1983	606 814
1984	630 194
1985	636 330
1986	679 911
1987	773 805

Year						
1966	2 295.5	138.4	152.1	5.81	4.87	0.94
1967	2 361.1	143.6	160.5	5.84	4.96	0.88
1968	2 453.9	155.7	185.3	5.92	5.32	0.60
1969	2 511.2	165.0	199.9	6.05	5.48	0.56
1970	2 540.7	178.3	208.3	6.46	5.66	0.80
1971	2 640.6	179.2	218.9	6.18	5.64	0.54
1972	2 763.2	195.2	244.6	6.34	6.09	0.24
1973	2 885.5	242.3	273.8	7.98	6.80	1.18
1974	2 891.2	269.1	268.4	9.71	8.67	1.04
1975	2 945.4	259.7	240.8	9.23	7.46	1.77
1976	3 062.5	274.4	285.4	9.21	8.23	0.98
1977	3 184.7	281.6	317.1	8.94	8.85	0.09
1978	3 317.6	312.6	339.4	9.50	9.32	0.18
1979	3 389.0	356.8	353.2	10.93	10.23	0.71
1980	3 430.7	388.9	332.0	11.93	10.84	1.09
1981	3 516.0	392.7	343.4	11.59	10.56	1.03
1982	3 506.1	361.9	335.6	10.32	9.57	0.75
1983	3 627.3	348.1	368.1	9.36	9.52	-0.16
1984	3 785.3	371.8	455.8	9.54	11.00	-1.46
1985	3 899.5	367.2	471.4	8.58	10.38	-1.80
1986	3 997.7	397.1	526.9	8.72	10.86	-2.14
1987	4 108.4	450.5	566.6	9.31	11.64	-2.33
1988	4 258.6	530.1	605.0	10.61	12.04	-1.43
1989	4 374.4	587.6	643.9	11.32	12.24	-0.92

Table A34   (a) Foreign exchange rates of US dollars, 1967–89 (b) World
petroleum wholesale price, Libya (Es Sidra), 1960–87

	(a)				*(b)*
	Absolute		*Index*		
	7.7A	*7.7B*	*7.7C*	*7.7D*	*7.8A*
	Germany	*Japan*	*Germany*	*Japan*	*World petroleum*
Year	*(Mark)*	*(Yen)*	*(1973 = 100)*		*wholesale price*
			(currency units		*(US dollars/*
			per US dollars)		*barrel)*
1960	–	–	–	–	2.58
1961	–	–	–	–	2.58
1962	–	–	–	–	2.58
1963	–	–	–	–	2.58
1964	–	–	–	–	2.58
1965	–	–	–	–	2.58
1966	–	–	–	–	2.58
1967	3.9865	362.13	149.23	133.48	2.58
1968	3.9920	360.55	149.43	132.90	2.58
1969	3.9251	358.36	146.93	132.09	2.58
1970	3.6465	358.16	136.50	132.02	2.58
1971	3.4829	347.78	130.38	128.19	3.17
1972	3.1885	303.12	119.36	111.73	3.37
1973	2.6714	271.30	100.00	100.00	4.50
1974	2.5867	291.84	96.83	107.57	13.84
1975	2.4613	296.78	92.14	109.39	11.59
1976	2.5184	296.45	94.27	109.27	12.31
1977	2.3236	268.62	86.98	99.01	13.87
1978	2.0096	210.38	75.23	77.55	13.71
1979	1.8342	219.02	68.66	80.73	21.06
1980	1.8175	226.63	68.04	83.53	35.87
1981	2.2631	220.63	84.72	81.32	39.83
1982	2.4280	249.06	90.89	91.80	35.49
1983	2.5539	237.55	95.60	87.56	30.89
1984	2.8454	237.45	106.51	87.52	30.15
1985	2.9419	238.47	110.13	87.90	30.15
1986	2.1704	168.35	81.25	62.05	14.60
1987	1.7981	144.60	67.31	53.30	18.52
1988	1.7570	128.17	65.77	47.24	–
1989	1.8808	138.07	70.41	50.89	–

Table A35 Crude oil and petroleum product imports, 1973–89

Year	7.9A Total	7.9B Algeria	7.9C Libya	7.9D Saudi Arabia	7.9E Indonesia	7.9F Iran	7.9G Nigeria	7.9H Venezuela	7.9I Other OPEC	7.9J Canada	7.9K Mexico	7.9L Neth. Antilles	7.9M Virgin Islands	7.9N Other non-OPEC
Thousands of barrels per day														
1973	6256	136	164	486	213	223	459	1135	177	1325	16	585	329	1008
1974	6111	190	4	461	300	469	713	979	162	1070	8	511	391	853
1975	6055	282	232	715	390	280	762	702	239	846	71	332	406	798
1976	7312	432	453	1230	539	298	1025	700	388	599	87	275	422	864
1977	8807	559	723	1380	541	535	1143	690	622	517	179	211	466	1241
1978	8364	649	654	1144	573	555	919	645	611	467	318	229	429	1171
1979	8455	636	658	1356	420	304	1080	690	493	538	439	231	431	1179
1980	6910	488	554	1261	348	9	857	481	302	455	533	225	388	1009
1981	5993	311	319	1129	366	0	620	406	171	447	522	197	327	1178
1982	5114	170	26	552	248	35	514	412	189	482	685	175	316	1310
1983	5049	240	0	337	338	48	302	422	174	547	826	189	282	1344
1984	5437	323	1	325	343	10	216	548	283	630	748	188	294	1528
1985	5067	187	4	168	314	27	293	605	232	770	816	40	247	1364
1986	6223	271	0	685	318	19	440	793	309	807	699	25	244	1613
1987	6679	295	0	754	285	98	535	804	292	848	655	29	272	1812
1988	7402	300	0	1064	205	0	618	794	539	999	747	36	242	1858
1989	7978	265	0	1224	180	0	809	867	771	910	763	40	320	1829
Per cent														
1973	100.0	2.2	2.6	7.8	3.4	3.6	7.3	18.1	2.8	21.2	0.3	9.4	5.3	16.1
1974	100.0	3.1	0.1	7.5	4.9	7.7	11.7	16.0	2.7	17.5	0.1	8.4	6.4	14.0
1975	100.0	4.7	3.8	11.8	6.4	4.6	12.6	11.6	3.9	14.0	1.2	5.5	6.7	13.2

continued on p. 206

Table A35 continued

Year	7.9A Total %	7.9B Algeria %	7.9C Libya %	7.9D Saudi Arabia %	7.9E Indo-nesia %	7.9F Iran %	7.9G Nigeria %	7.9H Vene-zuela %	7.9I Other OPEC %	7.9J Canada %	7.9K Mexico %	7.9L Neth. Antilles %	7.9M Virgin Islands %	7.9N Other non-OPEC %
1976	100.0	5.9	6.2	16.8	7.4	4.1	14.0	9.6	5.3	8.2	1.2	3.8	5.8	11.8
1977	100.0	6.3	8.2	15.7	6.1	6.1	13.0	7.8	7.1	5.9	2.0	2.4	5.3	14.1
1978	100.0	7.8	7.8	13.7	6.9	6.6	11.0	7.7	7.3	5.6	3.8	2.7	5.1	14.0
1979	100.0	7.5	7.8	16.0	5.0	3.6	12.8	8.2	5.8	6.4	5.2	2.7	5.1	13.9
1980	100.0	7.1	8.0	18.2	5.0	0.1	12.4	7.0	4.4	6.6	7.7	3.3	5.6	14.6
1981	100.0	5.2	5.3	18.8	6.1	0.0	10.3	6.8	2.9	7.5	8.7	3.3	5.5	19.7
1982	100.0	3.3	0.5	10.8	4.8	0.7	10.1	8.1	3.7	9.4	13.4	3.4	6.2	25.6
1983	100.0	4.8	0.0	6.7	6.7	1.0	6.0	8.4	3.4	10.8	16.4	3.7	5.6	26.6
1984	100.0	5.9	0.0	6.0	6.3	0.2	4.0	10.1	5.2	11.6	13.8	3.5	5.4	28.1
1985	100.0	3.7	0.1	3.3	6.2	0.5	5.8	11.9	4.6	15.2	16.1	0.8	4.9	26.9
1986	100.0	4.4	0.0	11.0	5.1	0.3	7.1	12.7	5.0	13.0	11.2	0.4	3.9	25.9
1987	100.0	4.4	0.0	11.3	4.3	1.5	8.0	12.0	4.4	12.7	9.8	0.4	4.1	27.1
1988	100.0	4.1	0.0	14.4	2.8	0.0	8.3	10.7	7.3	13.5	10.1	0.5	3.3	25.1
1989	100.0	3.3	0.0	15.3	2.3	0.0	10.1	10.9	9.7	11.4	9.6	0.5	4.0	22.9

Table A36 (a) Federal Reserve discount rates vs prime rates, 1939–89; (b) corporate profit/(profit + interest) vs unemployment rate, 1929–87; (c) business inventories vs the unemployment rate, 1929–87

	(a)		(b)				(c)		
	8.1A Prime rate/ commercial banks	8.1B Fed. Res. discount rate	8.2–4A Corporate profit	8.2–4B Net interest	8.2–4C Unemployment rate	8.2–4D A/(A+B)	8.5–7A Chg. in business invent.	8.5–7B GCP	8.5–7C Invent. /GCP
Year	(per cent)		(per cent of national income)		(per cent)		(billions of dollars)		(per cent)
1929	–	–	11.33	5.55	3.14	67.12	1.7	107.3	1.58
1930	–	–	8.57	6.67	8.67	56.23	-0.4	99.8	-0.40
1931	–	–	2.74	8.40	15.82	24.60	-1.1	90.8	-1.21
1932	–	–	-3.81	10.95	23.53	-53.36	-2.5	76.6	-3.26
1933	–	–	-3.79	10.35	24.75	-57.77	-1.6	74.6	-2.14
1934	–	–	2.28	8.49	21.60	21.17	-0.7	83.8	-0.84
1935	–	–	4.81	7.31	19.97	39.69	1.1	91.1	1.21
1936	–	–	7.80	5.93	16.80	56.81	1.3	100.0	1.30
1937	–	–	8.03	5.12	14.18	61.06	2.5	106.5	2.35
1938	–	–	5.93	5.47	18.91	52.02	-0.9	105.4	-0.85
1939	1.50	1.00	7.70	5.04	17.05	60.44	0.4	110.3	0.36
1940	1.50	1.00	11.06	4.15	14.45	72.72	2.2	117.6	1.87
1941	1.50	1.00	13.91	3.21	9.66	81.25	4.5	139.3	3.23
1942	1.50	1.00	14.47	2.28	4.41	86.39	1.8	166.8	1.08
1943	1.50	1.00	14.14	1.59	1.66	89.89	-0.6	196.4	-0.31
1944	1.50	1.00	13.25	1.26	1.01	91.32	-1.0	214.0	-0.47

Note: For columns 8.2–4D, A = corporate profit, B = net interest.

continued on p. 208

Table A36 continued

	(a)		(b)				(c)		
	8.1A Prime rate/ commercial banks	8.1B Fed. Res. discount rate	8.2-4A Corporate profit	8.2-4B Net interest	8.2-4C Unemployment rate	8.2-4D A/(A+B)	8.5-7A Chg. in business invent.	8.5-7B GCP	8.5-7C Invent. /GCP
Year	(per cent)		(per cent of national income)		(per cent)		(billions of dollars)		(per cent)
1945	1.50	1.00	10.84	1.21	1.59	89.96	-1.0	217.5	-0.46
1946	1.50	1.00	9.52	1.00	3.72	90.49	6.4	221.0	2.90
1947	1.67	1.00	11.65	1.17	3.79	90.87	-0.5	244.7	-0.20
1948	1.93	1.34	13.67	1.08	3.67	92.68	4.7	271.9	1.73
1949	2.00	1.50	13.01	1.21	5.78	91.49	-3.1	276.7	-1.12
1950	2.07	1.59	14.55	1.25	5.19	92.09	6.8	304.4	2.23
1951	2.56	1.75	14.39	1.26	3.20	91.95	10.2	344.8	2.96
1952	3.00	1.75	12.86	1.34	2.92	90.56	3.1	362.5	0.86
1953	3.17	1.99	12.30	1.44	2.81	89.52	0.4	382.7	0.10
1954	3.05	1.60	11.95	1.70	5.37	87.55	-1.6	394.2	-0.41
1955	3.16	1.89	14.01	1.73	4.25	89.01	5.7	424.6	1.34
1956	3.77	2.77	12.83	1.82	4.01	87.58	4.6	446.5	1.03
1957	4.20	3.12	12.15	2.09	4.15	85.32	1.4	471.3	0.30
1958	3.83	2.15	10.74	2.53	6.62	80.93	-1.5	490.1	-0.31
1959	4.48	3.36	12.56	2.49	5.33	83.46	5.8	524.7	1.11
1960	4.82	3.53	11.65	2.66	5.39	81.41	3.1	545.3	0.57
1961	4.50	3.00	11.46	2.94	6.51	79.58	2.4	572.1	0.42
1962	4.50	3.00	12.32	3.08	5.38	80.00	6.1	608.0	1.00

Year									
1963	4.50	3.23	12.72	3.26	5.51	79.60	5.8	643.6	0.90
1964	4.50	3.55	13.15	3.38	5.04	79.55	5.4	685.4	0.79
1965	4.54	4.04	13.89	3.57	4.41	79.55	9.9	738.3	1.34
1966	5.63	4.50	13.49	3.79	3.69	78.07	14.2	802.5	1.77
1967	5.61	4.19	12.41	4.04	3.74	75.44	10.3	848.6	1.21
1968	6.30	5.16	12.27	4.03	3.48	75.28	7.9	926.0	0.85
1969	7.96	5.87	10.95	4.34	3.41	71.62	9.8	998.9	0.98
1970	7.91	5.95	8.97	4.95	4.82	64.44	3.1	1067.8	0.29
1971	5.72	4.88	9.70	5.15	5.81	65.32	7.8	1171.8	0.67
1972	5.25	4.50	10.13	5.13	5.49	66.38	10.5	1284.7	0.82
1973	8.03	6.44	10.09	5.31	4.79	65.52	19.6	1429.3	1.37
1974	10.81	7.83	8.45	6.27	5.50	57.40	15.4	1560.2	0.99
1975	7.86	6.25	9.12	6.50	8.31	58.39	-5.6	1746.9	-0.32
1976	6.84	5.50	10.07	6.16	7.57	62.05	16.0	1931.5	0.83
1977	6.83	5.46	10.80	6.51	6.94	62.39	21.3	2142.6	0.99
1978	9.06	7.46	10.73	6.87	5.97	60.97	28.6	2395.8	1.19
1979	12.67	10.28	9.77	7.73	5.76	55.83	13.0	2662.6	0.49
1980	15.27	11.77	8.04	9.12	7.04	46.85	-8.3	2940.8	-0.28
1981	18.87	13.42	7.69	10.15	7.50	43.11	24.0	3303.7	0.73
1982	14.86	11.02	5.96	10.81	9.54	35.54	-24.5	3506.1	-0.70
1983	10.79	8.50	7.86	10.33	9.47	43.21	-7.1	3761.8	-0.19
1984	12.04	8.80	8.81	10.06	7.41	46.69	67.7	4074.1	1.68
1985	9.93	7.69	8.59	9.76	7.09	46.81	10.0	4321.5	0.23
1986	8.33	6.33	8.31	9.53	6.89	46.58	15.7	4544.8	0.34
1987	8.21	5.66	8.40	9.26	6.11	47.57	45.7	4818.5	0.96
1988	9.32	6.20	—	—	—	—	—	—	—
1989	10.87	6.93	—	—	—	—	—	—	—

Note: For column 8.2–4D, A = corporate profit, B = net interest.

Index

210